Business Tax

(Finance Act 2019)

Tutorial

for assessments from January 2020

Aubrey Penning
Bob Thomas

Published by Osborne Books Limited
Tel 01905 748071
Email books@osbornebooks.co.uk
Website www.osbornebooks.co.uk

Design by Laura Ingham

Printed by CPI Group (UK) Limited, Croydon, CRO 4YY, on environmentally friendly, acid-free paper from managed forests.

British Library Cataloguing in Publication Data
A catalogue record for this book is available from the British Library

ISBN 978-1-911198-40-6

Contents

Please note that the eight chapters and subsequent sections of the book each have a self-contained numbering system, rather than the traditional form of pagination which runs through the book.

Also available from Osborne Books...

Workbooks

Practice questions and assessments
with answers

Student Zone

Login to access your free ebooks and
interactive revision crosswords

Download **Osborne Books App** free from the App Store or Google Play Store
to view your ebooks online or offline on your mobile or tablet.

www.osbornebooks.co.uk

Introduction

Qualifications covered

This book has been written specifically to cover the Unit 'Business Tax' which is an optional Unit for the following qualifications:

AAT Professional Diploma in Accounting – Level 4

AAT Professional Diploma in Accounting at SCQF – Level 8

The book contains a clear text with worked examples and case studies, chapter summaries and key terms to help with revision. Each chapter concludes with a wide range of activities, many in the style of AAT computer based assessments.

Osborne Study and Revision Materials

The materials featured on the previous page are tailored to the needs of students studying this unit and revising for the assessment. They include:

- ■ **Workbooks:** paperback books with practice activities and exams
- ■ **Student Zone:** access to Osborne Books online resources
- ■ **Osborne Books App:** Osborne Books ebooks for mobiles and tablets

Visit www.osbornebooks.co.uk for details of study and revision resources and access to online material.

Exams, Finance Acts and tax years

This book has been designed to include guidance and exercises based on Tax Year 2019/20 (Finance Act 2019). We understand that the AAT plan to assess this legislation from 1 January 2020 to 31 December 2020. Tutors and students are advised to check this with the AAT and ensure that they sit the correct computer based assessment.

Note that the pagination of each chapter is self-contained, eg Chapter 1 contains pages 1.2 to 1.24.

Tax data

NATIONAL INSURANCE

Tax Year 2019/20

Self-employed National Insurance contributions (sole traders and partners)

Class 2 contributions are payable at a flat rate of £3.00 per week (unless below the 'small profits threshold'), and in addition,

Class 4 contributions are payable on the profits as follows:

9% of profits for the year between £8,632 and £50,000, plus

2% of profits above £50,000

CORPORATION TAX

	Financial Year 2018 (ie 1/4/2018 – 31/3/2019)	**Financial Year 2019 (ie 1/4/2019 – 31/3/2020)**
All profits	Main Rate 19%	Main Rate 19%

INCOME TAX

Personal Allowance for tax year 2019/20: £12,500

Tax bands 2019/20
(General Income)

	£
Basic rate 20%	0 – 37,500
Higher rate 40%	37,501 to 150,000
Additional rate 45%	over 150,000

CAPITAL GAINS TAX – FOR INDIVIDUALS

2019/20

Annual Exempt Amount £12,000

Rates

Gains	10% and/or 20%
	(10% where entrepreneurs' relief is claimed)

RETAIL PRICE INDEX (for indexation allowance for companies only)

	Jan	Feb	Mar	Apr	May	Jun	Jul	Aug	Sept	Oct	Nov	Dec
2017	265.5	268.4	269.3	270.6	271.7	272.3	272.9	274.7	275.1	275.3	275.8	278.1
2016	258.8	260.0	261.1	261.4	262.1	263.1	263.4	264.4	264.9	264.8	265.5	267.1
2015	255.4	256.7	257.1	258.0	258.5	258.9	258.6	259.8	259.6	259.5	259.8	260.6
2014	252.6	254.2	254.8	255.7	255.9	256.3	256.0	257.0	257.6	257.7	257.1	257.5
2013	245.8	247.6	248.7	249.5	250.0	249.7	249.7	251.0	251.9	251.9	252.1	253.4
2012	238.0	239.9	240.8	242.5	242.4	241.8	242.1	243.0	244.2	245.6	245.6	246.8
2011	229.0	231.3	232.5	234.4	235.2	235.2	234.7	236.1	237.9	238.0	238.5	239.4
2010	218.0	219.2	220.7	222.8	223.6	224.1	223.6	224.5	225.3	225.8	226.8	228.4
2009	210.1	211.4	211.3	211.5	212.8	213.4	213.4	214.4	215.3	216.0	216.6	218.0
2008	209.8	211.4	212.2	214.0	215.1	216.8	216.5	217.2	218.4	217.7	216.0	212.9
2007	201.6	203.1	204.4	205.4	206.2	207.3	206.1	207.3	208.0	208.9	209.7	210.9
2006	193.4	194.2	195.0	196.5	197.7	198.5	198.5	199.2	200.1	200.4	201.8	202.7
2005	188.9	189.6	190.5	191.6	192.0	192.0	192.2	192.6	193.1	193.3	193.6	194.1
2004	183.1	183.8	184.6	185.7	186.5	186.8	186.8	187.4	188.1	188.6	189.0	189.9
2003	178.4	179.3	179.9	181.2	181.5	181.3	181.3	181.6	182.5	182.6	182.7	183.5
2002	173.3	173.8	174.5	175.7	176.2	176.2	175.9	176.4	177.6	177.9	178.2	178.5
2001	171.1	172.0	172.2	173.1	174.2	174.4	173.3	174.0	174.6	174.3	173.6	173.4
2000	166.6	167.5	168.4	170.1	170.7	171.1	170.5	170.5	171.7	171.6	172.1	172.2
1999	163.4	163.7	164.1	165.2	165.6	165.6	165.1	165.5	166.2	166.5	166.7	167.3
1998	159.5	160.3	160.8	162.6	163.5	163.4	163.0	163.7	164.4	164.5	164.4	164.4
1997	154.4	155.0	155.4	156.3	156.9	157.5	157.5	158.5	159.3	159.5	159.6	160.0
1996	150.2	150.9	151.5	152.6	152.9	153.0	152.4	153.1	153.8	153.8	153.9	154.4
1995	146.0	146.9	147.5	149.0	149.6	149.8	149.1	149.9	150.6	149.8	149.8	150.7
1994	141.3	142.1	142.5	144.2	144.7	144.7	144.0	144.7	145.0	145.2	145.3	146.0
1993	137.9	138.8	139.3	140.6	141.1	141.0	140.7	141.3	141.9	141.8	141.6	141.9
1992	135.6	136.3	136.7	138.8	139.3	139.3	138.8	138.9	139.4	139.9	139.7	139.2
1991	130.2	130.9	131.4	133.1	133.5	134.1	133.8	134.1	134.6	135.1	135.6	135.7

	Jan	Feb	Mar	Apr	May	Jun	Jul	Aug	Sept	Oct	Nov	Dec
1990	119.50	120.20	121.40	125.10	126.20	126.70	126.80	128.10	129.30	130.30	130.00	129.90
1989	111.00	111.80	112.30	114.30	115.00	115.40	115.50	115.80	116.60	117.50	118.50	118.80
1988	103.30	103.70	104.10	105.80	106.20	106.60	106.70	107.90	108.40	109.50	110.00	110.30
1987	100.00	100.40	100.60	101.80	101.90	101.90	101.80	102.10	102.40	102.90	103.40	103.30
1986	96.25	96.60	96.73	97.67	97.85	97.79	97.52	97.82	98.30	98.45	99.29	99.62
1985	91.20	91.94	92.80	94.78	95.21	95.41	95.23	95.49	95.44	95.59	95.92	96.05
1984	86.84	87.20	87.48	88.64	88.97	89.20	89.10	89.94	90.11	90.67	90.95	90.87
1983	82.61	82.97	83.12	84.28	84.64	84.84	85.30	85.68	86.06	86.36	86.67	86.89
1982	-	-	79.44	81.04	81.62	81.85	81.88	81.90	81.85	82.26	82.66	82.51

1 Introduction to business taxation

this chapter covers...

In this chapter we provide a brief review of the various types of UK tax that apply to businesses and are studied in this book. Corporation Tax is payable by limited companies, while sole traders and partnerships are subject to Income Tax. We will also look at the role of HM Revenue & Customs, and see how sources of law relate to tax.

We will briefly look at how tax computations for both Corporation Tax and Income Tax work, before examining how income is divided up into categories for these taxes.

We need to understand how income and profits are taxed under these two taxes, and we will examine the impact of financial years and tax years on the calculation and reporting of tax. This includes a study of the way that tax returns work and when they need to be submitted by and the payment dates of tax.

Next we will learn how National Insurance is calculated for the self-employed and those in partnership.

Finally we will examine the responsibilities of the tax practitioner, including those relating to confidentiality and record keeping.

WHAT IS 'BUSINESS TAX'?

The 'business tax' that we are going to study in this book is not a single tax, but instead is a number of UK taxes that have an impact on businesses.

The specific taxes that affect any business in the UK will depend primarily on the legal structure of the business. You will probably be aware from your accounting studies of the three main ways (listed below) that businesses can be formed. We are going to examine the tax situation for:

■ limited companies

■ sole traders, and

■ partnerships

Limited companies (whether public or private) are incorporated bodies and therefore have their own legal existence that is quite separate from that of the owners. The profits that limited companies generate are subject to **Corporation Tax**.

Sole traders and **partnerships** are both unincorporated businesses, which means that there is no legal separation between the owner(s) of the business and the business itself. For this reason the profits from these businesses are dealt with under **Income Tax**, where they are assessed directly in relation to the business owners – the sole trader or partners. This is the same Income Tax that most of us pay on our income from employment or savings. If you have studied the learning area 'personal tax', you will have seen how Income Tax works in some detail. To succeed in the 'Business Tax' Unit you only have to understand the impact of Income Tax on business profits.

In the first part of this book we will be examining how Corporation Tax works, and how we can calculate how much Corporation Tax limited companies should pay. To do this we will need to work out the amount of trading profits that are subject to Corporation Tax. We will also need to work out the chargeable gains that result from the disposal of certain assets, and incorporate this along with other company profits in the Corporation Tax computation. The tax return for a limited company will also be studied so that we can complete it.

In the second part of the book we will be looking at how the profits of sole traders and partnerships are assessed under Income Tax. We will also see how Capital Gains Tax can affect these business owners if they dispose of certain business assets. We will also learn how to complete the parts of the Income Tax return that deal with self-employment, and partnerships.

We will also look at the impact of National Insurance on the self-employed and those in partnerships, and learn how to calculate the amounts that need to be paid.

The table on the opposite page shows the topics we will study in this Unit. The content of the Unit 'Personal Tax' is also shown for comparison. There are other taxes, such as Value Added Tax and Inheritance Tax, which affect businesses, but they are beyond the requirements of your studies here and so are not covered in this book.

THE TAX SYSTEM

We will first look at the background to the way that the tax system works. We will then outline the way in which numerical tax calculations are carried out.

HM Revenue & Customs

Income Tax, Corporation Tax and Capital Gains Tax are all administered by HM Revenue & Customs, which also collects National Insurance Contributions and VAT. This is a government organisation that has an administrative structure containing the following three parts:

- taxpayer service offices are the main offices that individual taxpayers deal with, and handle much of the basic Income Tax assessment and collection functions
- taxpayer district offices deal with Corporation Tax and more complex Income Tax issues
- tax enquiry centres deal with enquiries and provide forms and leaflets to taxpayers

These three functions are located in offices throughout the UK. In smaller centres some functions may be combined into one office, while in larger towns and cities they may be located separately.

the law governing tax – statute law

The authority to levy taxes comes from two sources. The first is legislation passed by Parliament, known as **statute law**. You may have heard of the Finance Acts. These are generally published each year and give details of any changes to taxes. These changes will have been proposed by the Chancellor of the Exchequer (usually in the budget) and passed by Parliament. In this book we will be using information from the Finance Act 2019, which relates to the financial year 2019 for companies and the tax year 2019/20 for individuals.

We will see exactly what is meant by financial years and tax years later in this chapter. There are also other relevant statute laws that were designed to create frameworks for the way that certain taxes work.

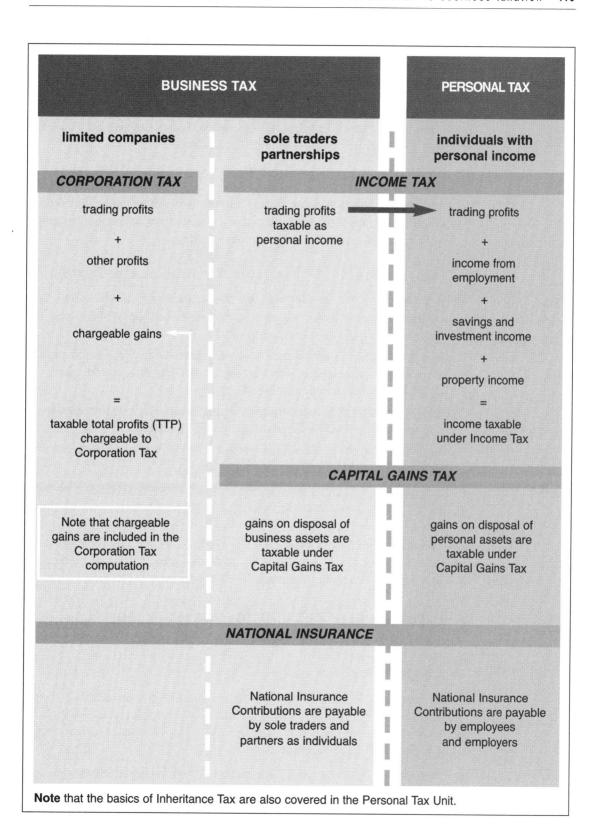

BUSINESS TAX		PERSONAL TAX
limited companies	**sole traders partnerships**	**individuals with personal income**
CORPORATION TAX	*INCOME TAX*	
trading profits	trading profits taxable as personal income	trading profits
+		+
other profits		income from employment
+		+
chargeable gains		savings and investment income
		+
		property income
=		=
taxable total profits (TTP) chargeable to Corporation Tax		income taxable under Income Tax
	CAPITAL GAINS TAX	
Note that chargeable gains are included in the Corporation Tax computation	gains on disposal of business assets are taxable under Capital Gains Tax	gains on disposal of personal assets are taxable under Capital Gains Tax
	NATIONAL INSURANCE	
	National Insurance Contributions are payable by sole traders and partners as individuals	National Insurance Contributions are payable by employees and employers

Note that the basics of Inheritance Tax are also covered in the Personal Tax Unit.

the law governing tax – case law

The second source of tax law is called **'case law'**, and draws its authority from decisions taken in court cases. Taxation can be very complicated, and sometimes disagreements between HM Revenue & Customs and taxpayers result in court cases. The final outcome of such cases can then become 'case law' and influences future interpretation of statute law.

Although there is a substantial amount of statute law and case law that is relevant to the taxation of businesses in the UK, this book will try to keep references to specific law to a minimum. While it will be important to know the rules that apply to certain situations, you will not be required to quote from the legislation or cases in your examination.

information available from HM Revenue & Customs

In addition to the tax law outlined above, there are interpretations and explanations of various issues that are published by HM Revenue & Customs. The main ones are as follows:

- extra-statutory concessions issued when HM Revenue & Customs agree to impose a less strict interpretation of the law than would otherwise apply in particular circumstances
- HM Revenue & Customs statements of practice are public announcements of how HM Revenue & Customs interpret specific rules
- Guides and Help Sheets are issued to help taxpayers complete the necessary return forms and calculate their tax

A large array of publications and forms can be downloaded from the HM Revenue & Customs website at www.gov.uk. This website also provides data on Corporation Tax and Income Tax rates for a range of tax years. You will find it useful to have a look at what is available on this site when you have an opportunity. It will also mean that you can obtain copies of tax returns to practice on when you reach that part of your business tax studies.

CALCULATION OF CORPORATION TAX AND INCOME TAX

Corporation Tax

In Chapters 2 to 5 in this book we will be looking in some detail about the way in which Corporation Tax is calculated. At this point we will just show how the system works in outline, by using a simple format for a **Corporation Tax computation**.

We will then use a numerical example that reflects a straightforward situation for a company.

```
            an outline Corporation Tax computation

                                                           £

            Trading Profits                                X

      +     Income from Investments                        X

      +     Chargeable Gains                               X

      =     Taxable Total Profits (TTP)                    X

            Corporation Tax on TTP                         X
```

A simple Corporation Tax computation would look like this if we assume the following figures:

```
        Corporation Tax Computation for AB Company Limited
                     for year ended 31/3/2020

                                                         £


        Trading Profits                            1,300,000

        Income from Investments                      400,000

        Chargeable Gains                             300,000

        Taxable Total Profits (TTP)                2,000,000


        Corporation Tax on TTP (£2,000,000 x 19%)    380,000
```

Income Tax

In the later chapters in this book we will be looking at how trading profits are assessed under Income Tax. Although we will not need to use a full Income Tax computation in this learning area, we will now just briefly see how it will appear. This is so that you can envisage how the trading profit figures would be used to work out Income Tax.

<table>
<tr><td colspan="2">**an outline Income Tax computation**</td></tr>
<tr><td></td><td>£</td></tr>
<tr><td>Income – earnings and other income</td><td>X</td></tr>
<tr><td>*Less* personal allowance</td><td>(X)</td></tr>
<tr><td>= Taxable income</td><td>X</td></tr>
<tr><td>Tax payable on taxable income</td><td>X</td></tr>
</table>

A simple Income Tax computation for a sole trader might appear as follows:

Income Tax Computation

	£
Trading Profits	15,000
Other General Income	1,000
	16,000
Less Personal Allowance	12,500
Taxable income	3,500
Tax payable at 20%*	700

*Other rates of Income Tax can also apply.

HOW INCOME IS CATEGORISED FOR TAX PURPOSES

The income that a company or an individual receives is divided into categories, depending on what sort of income it is and where it comes from. These categories apply to both Corporation Tax and Income Tax, and are based on descriptions of income. This is done so that:

■ the correct rules on how to work out the income are used (since these vary with the categories), and

■ the correct rates of tax are used (since they can also depend on the type of income when applying income tax)

When studying this learning area we will only need to know the outline detail of most of these categories, because we will be mainly concentrating on trading income. The list and descriptions shown below have been simplified to include only the categories that you need to know about in this learning area. It does not include, for example, the categories that relate to overseas income.

'Property Income' – Rental income from land and property

'Trading Income' – Profits of trades and professions

'Savings & Investment Income' – UK Interest

FINANCIAL YEARS AND TAX YEARS

Corporation Tax – financial years

The rates of Corporation Tax are changed from time-to-time (normally in the Chancellor's budget) and relate to specific **financial years.** These years run from 1 April in one calendar year to 31 March in the following year. The year that runs from 1 April 2019 to 31 March 2020 is known as the financial year 2019 – in other words, the financial year is named after the calendar year that most of it falls into.

Income Tax – tax years

For Income Tax purposes time is divided into **tax years** (sometimes called **fiscal years**). Individuals' income and Income Tax is worked out separately for each tax year. The tax year runs from 6 April in one calendar year to 5 April in the next calendar year. The tax year running from 6 April 2019 to 5 April 2020 would be described as the 2019/20 tax year.

HOW TAX RETURNS WORK

A **Tax Return** is a document issued by HM Revenue & Customs and used to collect information about a company's or an individual's income and gains. The Company Tax Return (the CT600 form) is used to collect information for Corporation Tax purposes, whereas the tax return for individuals provides data relating to Income Tax and Capital Gains Tax. Both companies and individuals are subject to the **self-assessment** system of tax. This means that they declare their profits and other taxable income on the tax return, and can then pay their own tax without HM Revenue & Customs sending them a bill. Individuals who submit a paper-based return within a certain deadline can ask HM Revenue & Customs to work the tax out for them, but otherwise the taxpayer (company or individual) or their agent must calculate the tax. Where the Income Tax return is submitted online, the tax is calculated automatically.

The tax forms relevant to your studies for this learning area are reproduced in the Appendix to this book. The forms are also available for download from the HM Revenue & Customs website: www.gov.uk or the Resources Sections of www.osbornebooks.co.uk. As we progress through this book we will examine how the various relevant parts of the returns should be completed.

tax returns for limited companies

A company must submit a CT600 form for every **chargeable accounting period** (CAP). Provided the accounts are produced for a period of twelve months or less, the company's normal accounting period will be the same as the CAP. Longer accounting periods are divided into two CAPs, one based on the first twelve months of the accounting period, and the other based on the remainder of the period. We will look at the practicalities of dividing up the figures for a long accounting period later in the book.

Note that the company tax return relates to the company's chargeable accounting period, not a particular financial year. The form sets out the information that is needed by HM Revenue & Customs, and provides a standard format for calculations. It must be submitted within twelve months after the end of the company's accounting period from which the CAP was derived. All companies must file returns online. The CT600 Version 3 shown in the Appendix to this book is the one that we will show how to complete in part.

Note that the term **'accounting period' (AP)** can also be used to describe a chargeable accounting period (CAP). The AAT reference material (which is reproduced in the appendix to this book) takes this approach.

tax returns for individuals

Individuals with complex tax affairs (including all those in business as sole traders or partners) need to complete a separate tax return for each tax year. Note that individuals' tax returns relate to tax years, not accounting periods. The normal way that accounting periods are linked to tax years under Income Tax is that the assessable profits for a particular tax year are derived from the accounting period that ends in that tax year. This is known as a basis period for the tax year. For example a sole trader who makes accounts up to 31 December each year would use the accounts for the year ended 31/12/2019 as the basis period for the tax year 2019/20.

Later on in this book we will look at the rules that link accounting periods to tax years in various special situations.

structure of the income tax return

Because different individuals have different circumstances, the tax return is divided into two parts.

The first part is used by every person that needs to complete a tax return, and is therefore common to all returns. It requests general information, as well as details of certain personal income.

The second part of the tax return consists of a series of supplementary pages that are only used by relevant taxpayers. In this text we will only be looking at these business-related supplementary pages, since other parts of the return are not required for this Unit.

There are supplementary pages for income from **self-employment** (ie for sole traders) and income from **partnerships**. For those in partnership, the supplementary page is completed for the individual's share of partnership profits. The partnership as a whole will also need to submit a form that summarises the total profits of the partnership.

scheduling of the income tax return

Individuals and partnerships can submit their tax returns either in the traditional paper format, or online. HMRC are encouraging the use of online submissions, and have introduced the following different deadlines for each method of tax return submission:

- submission of paper-based tax returns must be made by the 31 October following the end of the tax year. This means that the 2019/20 return would need to be submitted by 31 October 2020. If required, HMRC will calculate the tax relating to a properly completed return if it meets this deadline

- submission of an online return can be made at any time up to 31 January following the end of the tax year. The amount of tax is automatically calculated by the computer program once the online form has been completed, and the taxpayer can print out a copy for their records. An online return for the tax year 2019/20 would therefore need to be submitted by 31 January 2021

WHEN TO PAY TAX

The payment dates for companies and individuals differ, so we will examine them separately.

companies – Corporation Tax

We saw in the last section that company tax returns are completed for each chargeable accounting period (CAP). Unless instalment payments are necessary, the Corporation Tax that has been calculated is normally payable nine months and one day after the end of the chargeable accounting period that it relates to. For example, the Corporation Tax relating to the chargeable accounting period 1/1/2019 to 31/12/2019 will normally be payable on 1/10/2020. If the period falls into more than one financial year this will be taken account of in the tax calculation, if necessary, but it does not affect the payment date. The payment date relates only to the period, not to the financial year.

If a company is 'large', then it will pay most of its Corporation Tax earlier in instalments, with only the final amount falling due on the date referred to above. We will look at this situation in more detail after we have seen how Corporation Tax is calculated.

Notice that for companies the payment of tax is due before the final filing date for the tax return. This means that the tax calculation will have to have been carried out by the payment date (so that the payment amount is known), even though the actual form need not be submitted until nearly three months later! The return can always be submitted early if desired.

individuals – Income Tax

For income from trading profits there is no system set up to automatically deduct Income Tax as there is for employees. The outstanding balance of Income Tax that relates to business profits and other income from which tax has not been deducted will need to be paid to HM Revenue & Customs according to the following rules.

The *final* date for payment of the Income Tax that relates to a tax year is the 31 January *following the end of that tax year*.

For some taxpayers there may also be payments on account that must be made before the final date. These are due as follows:

- first payment on account is due on 31 January within the tax year
- second payment on account is due on 31 July following the end of the tax year

For the tax year 2019/20 the payment dates would be:

> 31 January 2020 for the first payment on account,
>
> 31 July 2020 for the second payment on account, and
>
> 31 January 2021 for the final payment

Notice that when payments on account are required, two payments will be due on each 31 January. For example, on 31 January 2020 there would be due both:

> the final payment for the tax year 2018/19, and
>
> the first payment on account for the tax year 2019/20

Later in the book we will see how the payments on account are calculated, and which taxpayers need to make these early payments.

We saw earlier that 31 January following the tax year was also the final date for submitting an online tax return, so for Income Tax these two dates coincide.

The table below illustrates the main points relating to tax returns and payment dates.

Companies	Individuals (Sole Traders and Partnerships)
Corporation Tax	**Income Tax**
Company Tax Return (CT600) includes calculation of Corporation Tax for chargeable accounting period (CAP).	Tax return includes supplementary pages for sole traders and partners, and relates to tax year.
Return submitted online by 12 months after end of period that accounts are based on.	Paper return submitted by 31 Oct following tax year, or online return submitted by 31 Jan following tax year.
Final payment by nine months and one day after end of CAP.	Final payment by 31 Jan following tax year.
Large companies also make earlier instalment payments.	Many taxpayers also make two payments on account.

Case Study

DIVERSE ACCOUNTING PRACTICE: TAX RETURNS

It is August 2019. You are a trainee employed by the Diverse Accounting Practice, working in their Tax Department. The practice uses online submission for all tax returns. You are currently scheduling work related to two clients as follows:

The Mammoth Company Limited produces annual accounts to the 31 January. The accounts for the year ended 31/1/2019 have been completed and are awaiting the necessary tax work.

Jo Small is a sole trader who has been trading for many years. The practice has produced accounts for her for the year ended 30/6/2019.

required

State the type of tax return that will need to be completed for each of the clients. Explain how each return is related to the client's accounting period, and the latest submission dates for the returns. State the final date for the payment of outstanding tax after any instalments or payments on account have been made.

solution

The Mammoth Company Limited will require a company tax return (form CT600). This will relate to the chargeable accounting period (CAP) 1/2/2018 to 31/1/2019. The form must be submitted online by 12 months after the end of the accounting period – 31/1/2020. The final Corporation Tax payment must be made by 1/11/2019 (nine months and one day after the end of the CAP).

Jo Small will need a tax return for the tax year 2019/20. The accounting period of 1/7/2018 to 30/6/2019 will form the basis period for this tax year. The main part of the form will need to be completed, along with the supplementary pages relating to self-employment. The online tax return must be submitted by 31/1/2021. The final Income Tax payment relating to 2019/20 will also have to be made by 31/1/2021.

NATIONAL INSURANCE

If you are an employee, you are probably familiar with employee National Insurance Contributions (NIC), which are deducted through Pay-As-You-Earn, along with Income Tax. In our study of business tax we will be looking at National Insurance Contributions, payable by self-employed individuals (sole traders and partners) in respect of their own profits.

self-employed National Insurance contributions

There are two classes of NIC that apply to both sole traders and partners.

■ **Class 2 contributions** are payable at a flat rate of £3.00 per week (unless the profits are below the 'small profits threshold' [see below]), and, in addition,

■ **Class 4 contributions** are payable on profits above £8,632 per year

The profits for self-employed NIC purposes are the same ones that are used for Income Tax purposes – the assessable trading profits. Where profits are less than £6,365 (2019/20) then the small profits threshold means that Class 2 contributions need not be paid.

Neither Class 2 nor Class 4 NIC is payable by those either under 16 years of age or over pensionable age at the start of the tax year.

The rates for Class 4 contributions for 2019/20 are:

■ 9% of profits for the year between £8,632 and £50,000, plus

■ 2% of profits above £50,000

If profits are below £8,632 then there are no Class 4 contributions.

example – NI for the self-employed

Sonita is a sole trader with trading profits of £60,000 in 2019/20.

Her NIC liability for the year would be:

		£	£
Class 2 contributions:	£3.00 x 52 =		156.00
Class 4 contributions:	(£50,000 – £8,632) x 9% =	3,723.12	
	plus		
	(£60,000 – £50,000) x 2% =	200.00	
		3,923.12	
			4,079.12

Both Class 2 and Class 4 contributions are calculated at the same time as Income Tax under the self-assessment system, and entered on the tax return and paid along with the Income Tax for the year.

TAX PLANNING, TAX AVOIDANCE AND TAX EVASION

Tax planning involves looking at an individual's or a company's financial planning from a tax perspective. The purpose of tax planning is to see how to accomplish all the other elements of the financial plan in the most tax-efficient manner, and so minimise tax. Tax planning should only involve legal and ethical methods of minimising the tax liability.

It is important to distinguish between the legal practice of **tax avoidance**, and **tax evasion**, which is illegal. Tax avoidance involves using legitimate tax rules and allowances to minimise the amount of tax that is due. This could include an individual investing in ISAs so that any interest received is tax free.

Tax evasion involves using illegal methods to escape paying the correct amount of tax. Examples would include entering false information in a tax return, or failing to notify HMRC about a taxable source of income on which tax has not been paid. Those who carry out tax evasion risk criminal prosecution.

While tax avoidance and tax evasion may appear to be easily distinguishable at each end of the scale, there will always be situations that may not be so clear cut. In particular, some 'tax avoidance schemes' have been developed that may not be legal.

HMRC has stated that where a scheme relies **on concealment**, **pretence**, **non-disclosure** or **misrepresentation** of the true facts then this is **illegal tax evasion**.

The government has developed various ways that they hope to prevent so-called 'aggressive' tax avoidance schemes. Tax avoidance schemes need to be disclosed to HMRC, who will then investigate the schemes to ensure that they are legal. HMRC has stated that using a tax avoidance scheme marks the individual out as a high-risk taxpayer, and that this will lead to close scrutiny of all their tax affairs, not just those involving the tax avoidance scheme.

In 2013 legislation was introduced to outlaw some schemes that were deemed to be 'abusive'. This legislation is known as the 'General Anti-Abuse Rule' (GAAR). It is based on the rejection of the old approach taken by the Courts that taxpayers are free to use their ingenuity to reduce their tax bills by any lawful means, however contrived those means might be.

In broad terms, the GAAR outlaws action taken by a taxpayer to achieve a favourable tax result that Parliament **did not anticipate** when it introduced the tax rules in question, where that course of action cannot '**reasonably be regarded as reasonable**'.

This 'double reasonableness test' sets a high threshold for HMRC to prove that an arrangement is abusive and therefore illegal.

Aggressive tax avoidance schemes are certainly unethical and rely on taxpayers not paying their fair share of tax.

The key to using legal tax avoidance measures is to only use tax rules in the way that they were originally intended by Parliament. So the use of ISAs to avoid paying tax on savings interest is entirely proper, since it is in line with the original intention of the legislation.

In general, anyone who suspects that tax evasion is being carried out is advised to report this to HMRC. This can be done anonymously. HMRC advise the person reporting not to attempt to discover any more information about the suspected tax evasion, and not to tell anyone else.

In the next section we will see how the AAT code of professional ethics deals with situations where a **client is suspected of tax evasion**. It is important that the code is followed in these circumstances.

THE DUTIES AND RESPONSIBILITIES OF A TAX PRACTITIONER

A person who acts as a professional by helping clients (either companies or individuals) with their tax affairs has responsibilities:

■ to the client, and
■ to HM Revenue & Customs

The AAT has published a revised **Code of Professional Ethics** that deals with these and other issues. This applies to both AAT students and members and the document can be downloaded from the website www.aat.org.uk

A summary of the duties and responsibilities outlined by the AAT is as follows:

- maintain client confidentiality
- adopt an ethical approach and maintain an objective outlook
- give timely and constructive advice to clients
- conduct themselves honestly and professionally with HMRC

A tax advisor is liable to a penalty if they assist in making an incorrect return.

confidentiality

Keeping a client's or customer's dealings confidential is an essential element of professional ethics. As far as confidentiality for a tax practitioner is concerned, the Code referred to above states that confidentiality should always be observed, unless either:

- authority has been given to disclose the information (by the client), or
- there is a legal or professional right or duty to disclose

The Code also says that:

> *'Information about a past, present, or prospective client's or employer's affairs, or the affairs of clients of employers, acquired in a work context is likely to be confidential if it is not a matter of public knowledge.'*

The rules of confidentiality apply in a social environment as well as a business one, and care should be taken to not inadvertently disclose confidential information. The need to comply also extends after a business relationship has ended – for example if there was a change of employment.

One important **exception to the normal rules of confidentiality** is where **'money laundering'** is known or suspected. 'Money laundering' includes any process of concealing or disguising the proceeds of any criminal offence, including tax evasion.

Where a practitioner has knowledge or suspicion that his client is money laundering, then he has a duty to inform the relevant person or authority. For those in a group practice this would be the Money Laundering Reporting Officer (MLRO), and for a sole practitioner the National Crime Agency (NCA).

It is an offence to warn the client that a report of this type is going to be made about him. Money laundering therefore is not a situation where authority would be sought from the client to disclose information!

taxation services

The Code states the following regarding taxation services:

'A member providing professional tax services has a duty to put forward the best position in favour of a client or an employee. However the service must be carried out with professional competence, must not in any way impair integrity or objectivity, and must be consistent with the law.'

The Code also states that:

'A member shall only undertake taxation work on the basis of full disclosure by the client or employer. The member, in dealing with the tax authorities, must act in good faith and exercise care in relation to facts and information presented on behalf of the client or employer. It will normally be assumed that facts and information on which business tax computations are based were provided by the client or employer as the taxpayer, and the latter bears ultimate responsibility for the accuracy of the facts, information and tax computations. The member shall avoid assuming responsibility for the accuracy of facts, etc. outside his or her knowledge.

'When a member learns of a material error or omission in a tax return of a prior year, or of a failure to file a required tax return, the member has a responsibility to advise promptly the client or employer of the error or omission and recommend that disclosure be made to HMRC. If the client or employer, after having had a reasonable time to reflect, does not correct the error, the member shall inform the client or employer in writing that it is not possible for the member to act for them in connection with that return or other related information submitted to the authorities.'

dealing with professional ethics problems

Dealing with professional ethics can be a difficult and complex area, and we have only outlined some main points. If you find yourself in a position where you are uncertain how you should proceed because of an ethical problem then you should first approach your supervisor or manager. If you are still unable to resolve the problem then further professional or legal advice may need to be obtained.

tax records

It is also important to know what records will need to be kept regarding the client's income and tax affairs, and to ensure that such records are kept secure. The records must be sufficient to substantiate the information provided to HM Revenue & Customs. This would include documentation such as invoices, receipts, and working papers.

These records must be kept as follows:

- **companies** must keep records relating to the information in their tax returns until at least six years after the end of the accounting period. For example, records relating to the chargeable accounting period (CAP) from 1/4/2019 until 31/3/2020 must be kept until 31/3/2026

- **individuals** in business (sole traders and partners) must keep records for approximately five years plus 10 months from the end of the tax year to which they relate. For example documents relating to 2019/20 must be retained until 31 January 2026

For both types of organisation this date for record keeping is five years after the latest filing date for the return (assuming the Income Tax return is submitted online). If there is a formal HM Revenue & Customs enquiry into a taxpayer's affairs then the records need to be kept at least until the end of the enquiry.

There can be a penalty for not keeping the required records of up to £3,000 for each tax year (for individuals) or £3,000 per accounting period (for companies).

compliance checks

HMRC can carry out 'compliance checks' relating to a range of taxes including Corporation Tax, Income Tax and Capital Gains Tax to ensure that the correct amount of tax is paid and that proper records are kept. HMRC have powers to:

- visit businesses to inspect premises, assets and records

- ask taxpayers and third parties (for example tax practitioners) for more information and documents

In most situations at least seven days prior notice would be given of a visit. HMRC are required by law to 'act reasonably' with regard to compliance checks.

- The taxes that UK businesses are subject to will depend on the type of organisation.

- The profits and gains of limited companies are subject to Corporation Tax, while sole traders and partners' trading profits are subject to Income Tax, along with any other personal income. The self-employed are also subject to Capital Gains Tax on the disposal of certain business assets. National Insurance contributions are applied to the self-employed and partners on their profits.

- Income Tax and Corporation Tax are administered by HM Revenue & Customs, which collects tax and National Insurance Contributions. It is also responsible for publishing documents and forms to gather information about how much tax is owed and is governed by statute law and case law.

- Under both Corporation Tax and Income Tax, the assessable amount is divided into categories so that appropriate rules can be applied to calculate the amount of each different form of income.

- Corporation Tax rates relate to financial years that run from 1 April. The tax is calculated separately for each Chargeable Accounting Period (CAP) that is linked to the period for which the accounts are produced.

- The Company Tax Return (CT600) is based on the CAP. Corporation tax is payable within nine months and one day after the end of the CAP. Large companies must also make instalment payments.

- Income Tax, which applies to individuals (sole traders and partners), is calculated separately for each tax year (6 April to the following 5 April). An Income Tax computation is used to calculate the tax by totalling the income from various sources, and subtracting the personal allowance. Each tax year has a separate tax return, which is used to collect information about the income and tax of individuals. It consists of a common section plus supplementary pages relating to self-employment. Income Tax must be paid to HM Revenue & Customs by the 31 January following the end of the tax year. For some taxpayers there is also a requirement to make payments on account before this date.

- National Insurance is applied to the self-employed and partners in respect of their profits. They must pay a flat rate (Class 2), plus an amount calculated as percentages of their profits (Class 4).

- Tax practitioners have responsibilities to their clients (including confidentiality) and to HM Revenue & Customs. They must also ensure that all necessary records are kept for the required period of time.

Key Terms		
	limited company	a limited company is a separate legal entity from its owners (the shareholders). Its profits are subject to Corporation Tax
	sole trader	an individual who is self-employed on his or her own. There is no legal distinction between the business entity and the individual, and the sole trader is subject to Income Tax on the profits of the business
	partnership	an organisation made up of several individuals who share the responsibilities and profits of the partnership. Since there is no legal separation between the partnership and the individuals who are partners, they are individually subject to Income Tax on their share of the profits. Effectively, a partnership is a collection of sole traders
	Corporation Tax	a tax that applies to the trading and other profits of limited companies, including any chargeable gains
	Income Tax	the tax that individuals (including sole traders and partners) pay on their income, including business profits
	Capital Gains Tax	the tax that applies to certain disposals that individuals make on business and private assets
	National Insurance	effectively a tax that is applied to the self-employed and partners
	statute law	legislation that is passed by Parliament, for example the annual Finance Act
	case law	the result of decisions taken in court cases that have an impact on the interpretation of law
	financial year (Corporation Tax)	each financial year runs from 1 April to 31 March Corporation Tax rates are based on financial years
	tax year (Income Tax)	each tax year runs from 6 April to the following 5 April. Tax years are also known as fiscal years
	company tax return	this document (the CT600) is filed online for each Chargeable Accounting Period, normally the period for which the company prepares accounts
	tax return (individuals)	the self-assessment tax return is issued for each tax year to certain taxpayers and relates to Income Tax and Capital Gains Tax. It is divided into a common section, plus supplementary pages including pages relating to sole traders and partners. It can be submitted in paper form, or online

tax planning	carrying out financial planning in the most tax-efficient way in order to minimise tax
tax avoidance	minimising tax by legal means (unless avoidance is 'abusive')
tax evasion	illegally relying on concealment, pretence, non-disclosure or misrepresentation to pay less tax

Activities

1.1 The following statements are made by a trainee in the Tax Department of Jenner & Co.

Indicate whether each statement is true or false.

		True	False
(a)	One of the reasons that income is divided into categories is so that the correct rules can be applied to each type of income.		
(b)	The only law that is relevant to tax matters is the current Finance Act.		
(c)	Companies must complete a separate CT600 tax return for every financial year in which they operate.		
(d)	A Corporation Tax Computation is the name given to the calculation of Corporation Tax, based on the taxable total profits chargeable to Corporation Tax for the chargeable accounting period.		
(e)	A sole trader with profits assessable in 2019/20 of £21,500, and no other taxable income, would pay Income Tax of £1,800.		
(f)	It is the job of a tax practitioner to ensure that his client pays the least amount of tax. This may involve bending the rules, or omitting certain items from a tax computation.		
(g)	Most self-employed people pay tax under PAYE and so don't have to worry about completing tax returns.		

1.2   DonCom plc has the following assessable income agreed for the chargeable accounting period from 1/4/2019 to 31/3/2020:

Trading Profits	£1,300,000
Chargeable Gains	£500,000
Profits from renting property	£100,000

Required:

(a)   Assuming a Corporation Tax rate of 19%, use a Corporation Tax computation to calculate the tax liability for DonCom plc.

(b)   State the filing date of the CT600 form, and the date by which the final Corporation Tax payment must be made.

1.3   Parmajit is trading in partnership. Her share of the partnership profits for the accounting period 1/6/2018 to 31/5/2019 was £16,000. In addition she had other general taxable income in the tax year 2019/20 of £2,000. She uses paper-based tax returns.

Required:

(a)   Assuming that Parmajit is entitled to a personal allowance of £12,500 for the tax year, and pays Income Tax at 20% for that year, calculate her Income Tax liability.

(b)   State the date that her tax return must be submitted if HM Revenue & Customs were to calculate her tax, and the date by which the balance of Income Tax must be paid for the tax year.

1.4   John is self-employed, and has assessable trading profits for the tax year 2019/20 of £25,000.

Required:

Calculate the National Insurance Contribution liability under each class for John.

State how payment would be made.

1.5 You are a trainee employed by Osborne Accounting Practice, working in their Tax Department. The practice uses online return submission for Income Tax. You are currently scheduling work related to two clients as follows:

The Walvern Water Company Limited produces annual accounts to 31 July. The accounts for the year ended 31/7/2019 have been completed and are awaiting the necessary tax work.

Wally Weaver is a sole trader who has been trading for many years. The practice has produced accounts for him for the year ended 31/7/2019.

Required:

- State the type of tax return that will need to be completed for each of the clients.

- Explain how each tax return is related to the client's accounting period, and state the latest submission dates for the returns.

- State in each case the final date for the payment of outstanding tax after any instalments or payments on account have been made.

1.6 **(1)** Which of the following statements is correct?

(a)	Every self employed taxpayer must pay Class 2 NIC, irrespective of the level of profits	
(b)	Self employed taxpayers pay either Class 2 or Class 4, but not both	
(c)	Class 4 NIC is based on the amount of money taken out of the business by the taxpayer	
(d)	An individual failing to keep appropriate records for the correct length of time is subject to a penalty of up to £3,000 for each tax year	

(2) A taxpayer has self employed income of £70,000 for 2019/20.

The amount chargeable to NIC at 2% would be £ _____

(3) A taxpayer has self employed income of £35,000 for 2019/20.

The amount of total Class 4 NIC payable would be £ _____

2 Corporation tax – trading profits

this chapter covers...

In this chapter we provide a brief review of the Corporation Tax computation, and examine the step by step procedures for compiling the computation, before concentrating on the calculation of adjusted trading profits.

We examine in detail how to adjust the data provided in an income statement so that it is valid for tax purposes. This involves adjusting income and expenditure. We will note the main types of expenditure that cannot be set against trading income, as well as specific examples of expenditure that is allowable.

There will be opportunities to practice adjusting accounts that have been prepared for internal purposes, as well as using published accounts.

We will then see how to deal with the situation when accounts have been prepared for a long period and need to be split into two Chargeable Accounting Periods.

Finally, we will learn the rather complex rules about the options that are available to companies to offset any trade losses that they incur.

THE CORPORATION TAX COMPUTATION

We saw in the last chapter that the Corporation Tax computation comprises a summary of profits from various sources that are chargeable to Corporation Tax. The computation then goes on to calculate the amount of Corporation Tax that is payable. A simple version of this computation is repeated here:

	Trading Income	X
+	Profits from Investments	X
+	Chargeable Gains	X
=	Taxable Total Profits (TTP)	X
	Corporation Tax on taxable total profits	X

Note that 'taxable total profits' were previously known as 'profits chargeable to Corporation Tax' (PCTCT).

You will notice that 'Trading Income' is listed as the first item in the computation, and is often the most important one. We will be looking in detail in this chapter at why and how the trading profits from the financial accounts are adjusted for tax purposes.

Before we do that, we will examine briefly the main steps that need to be undertaken to complete the full Corporation Tax computation. We can then refer to this procedure as we look at the components in detail over the next chapters. The following diagram shows in summary how it all fits together.

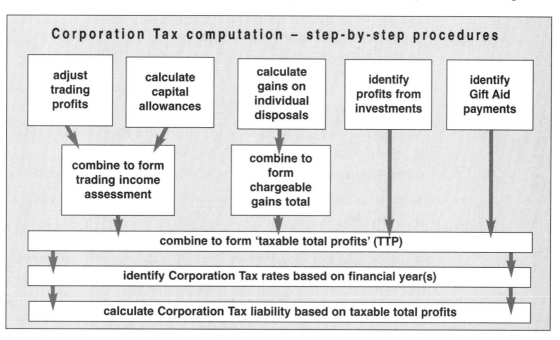

In this chapter we are going to learn how to adjust the trading profit (the top left-hand box in the diagram). We will also see how trade losses can be set against profits to reduce total taxable profits.

In Chapter Three we will see how to calculate capital allowances so that we can incorporate the result into the trading income assessment.

In Chapter Four we will examine chargeable gains and then we will see how it all fits together.

In Chapter Five we will explain how to calculate the Corporation Tax liability.

ADJUSTMENT OF PROFITS

The starting point for the calculation of trading profits is the statement of profit or loss (income statement) that has been prepared by the company. Whether you are asked to work from a set of accounts prepared for internal use, or in published format, the process is the same.

The 'basis of assessment' for trading profits is the **tax-adjusted trading profits** of the **chargeable accounting period**, prepared on an accruals basis. In this section of the book we will start by using accounts that have been prepared for the chargeable accounting period (ie no more than 12 months). We will see later how we deal with accounts that have been prepared for a longer period. Since the financial accounts that will be our starting point will always have been prepared on an accruals basis, that aspect should not cause us any problems.

The reason that accounts need to be adjusted for tax purposes is not because they are wrong, but because Corporation Tax does not use exactly the same rules as financial accounting. We need to arrive at a profit figure that is based on the tax rules! For example, there are some costs that although quite legitimate from an accounting point of view are not allowable as a deduction in arriving at the profit figure for tax purposes.

The object of adjusting the financial accounts is to make sure that:

■ the only **income** that is credited is **trading income**

■ the only **expenditure** that is deducted is **allowable trading expenditure**

When we adjust profits, we will start with the profit from the financial accounts, and

■ deduct any income that is not trading income, and

■ add back any expenditure that has already been deducted but is not allowable

This approach is much more convenient than re-writing the whole profit and loss account based on tax rules. It is quite logical, because it effectively cancels out income and expenditure that is not relevant for tax purposes.

example – adjusting the profits

Suppose that we wish to adjust a set of financial accounts (shown here in summary form):

	£000
Sales	500
less cost of sales	200
Gross trading profit	300
Non-trading income	150
	450
less expenditure	120
Net profit	330

Analysis of the accounts has shown that the cost of sales is entirely allowable, but £40,000 of the £120,000 expenditure is not allowable for tax purposes.
To adjust the profits we would carry out the following computation:

	£000
Net profit per accounts	330
Less non-trading income	(150)
Add expenditure that is not allowable	40
Adjusted trading profit	220

This provides us with the same answer that we could get by writing out the accounts in full, using only the trading income and allowable expenditure. If we did that it would look as follows. This is shown just for comparison – we won't actually need to rewrite the accounts in this way.

	£000
Sales	500
Less allowable cost of sales	200
Gross trading profit	300
Less allowable expenditure	80
Net profit	220

We will now look in more detail at adjustments for income, followed by expenditure.

adjusting income

Provided the 'sales', 'turnover' or 'revenue' figure relates entirely to trading, this figure will not need adjusting. Other income may or may not be taxable, but if it is not trading income, then it will need to be adjusted for in the trading profit calculation.

The following are examples of income that are **not assessable as trading income**, and should therefore be adjusted for by **deducting** from the net profit shown in the financial accounts:

■ non-trading interest receivable

- rent receivable (property income)
- gains on the disposal of non-current assets (fixed assets)
- dividends received

All these examples should be adjusted by simply deducting the amount that was credited to the financial accounts. There is no need to worry about exactly how the figure was originally calculated. We will then have arrived at what the profit would have been if these items had not been included originally. Items that originate from the trade (eg discounts received) are taxable as part of trading income, and therefore need no adjustment.

Non-trading interest and **rent received** will reappear in the taxable total profits (TTP) computation as investment income and property income respectively. Throughout the examples in this book you can assume that any interest received is non-trading and is therefore dealt with as outlined here unless stated otherwise.

Gains on the disposal of non-current assets could result in chargeable gains. These gains need to be calculated according to special rules before being incorporated into the taxable total profits as we will see in Chapter 4. **Dividends received** from UK companies are not assessable under Corporation Tax at all (since they have been paid out of another company's taxed income).

adjusting expenditure

We will only need to adjust for any expenditure accounted for in the financial accounts profit if it is **not allowable**. We do this by **adding it back** to the financial accounts profit. Expenditure that is allowable can be left unadjusted in the accounts. Although this may seem obvious, it is easy to get confused.

The general rule for expenditure to be allowable in a trading income computation is that it must be:

- revenue rather than capital in nature, and
- 'wholly and exclusively' for the purpose of the trade

Although we will look at how to deal with various specific types of expenditure shortly, these rules are fundamental, and should always be used to guide you in the absence of more precise information. This part of the unit will require a good deal of study, since it is quite complex, and the rules and examples that follow will need to be remembered. The best way to approach this is to continually revise the topic and practise lots of examples.

expenditure that is not allowable

The following are examples of expenditure that is not allowable, and therefore require adjustment. Some clearly follow the rules outlined above, while others may have arisen from specific regulations, or court cases forming precedents (case law).

■ **any capital expenditure**
This follows the normal financial accounting use of the term, to mean expenditure on assets that will have a value to the business over several accounting periods. Capital expenditure includes expenditure to improve non-current assets, and installation costs and legal expenses in connection with acquiring non-current assets.

■ **depreciation of non-current assets**
This is because capital allowances are allowable instead, as HM Revenue & Customs alternative to depreciation, as we will see in the next chapter. Even where there are no capital allowances available, depreciation is still not allowed. Other items which are similar to depreciation (eg amortisation of certain assets, and losses on disposal of non-current assets) are also not allowable.

■ **part of lease rental payments for high emission cars**
When a car with an emission level of more than 110g/km of CO_2 is leased for over 45 days through an operating lease, 15% of the lease rental payment is disallowed, leaving an allowable expenditure of 85% of the payment. If the car has emission levels lower than this then all of the lease rental payment is allowable.

■ **entertaining expenditure**
This relates to business entertaining of customers or suppliers. Entertaining of the businesses' own staff is however allowable (see page 2.9).

■ **gifts to customers**
Virtually all gifts made to customers are not allowable. There is an exception for some low-value items, as we will see shortly.

■ **increases in general bad debt provisions**
Any such increase (that is debited to the income statement) must be added back in the computation, and decreases in general provisions adjusted for by deducting from profits. A general provision could be based on a lump sum, or a percentage of total trade receivables (debtors). Increases in specific provisions and the actual write-off of bad debts are however allowable. Where accounts have been prepared using 'impairment' as a means of calculating the bad debt provision, the provision will be treated in the same way as a specific bad debt provision. This applies as long as objective evidence was used to calculate the amount of impairment. This situation could arise if, for example, the accounts are prepared under International Accounting Standards. See also the additional note on page 2.9.

■ **charitable payments**
These items can be deducted from the total profits of the company in the taxable total profits (TTP) calculation as Gift Aid payments, or

'Qualifying Charitable Donations'. Where this occurs the expenditure cannot also be deducted in the calculation of trading profits. We will look a little more closely at these payments in Chapter 5.

■ **fines for law breaking**

Fines imposed on the company itself for lawbreaking (eg for breaches of health & safety legislation) are not allowable, nor are the associated legal costs. The costs of tax appeals are also not allowable. Fines for minor motoring offences incurred by employees whilst on business are allowable, but not if the employee is a Director of the company.

■ **certain legal expenses**

Legal expenses incurred on forming a company or acquiring new leases (both long and short leases).

■ **illegal payments**

For example bribes, or payments made in response to threats.

■ **donations to political parties**

These are not for the purpose of 'the trade' and so are not allowable.

■ **writing off non-trade loans**

For example, loans to employees or directors (unless they were incurred in the normal course of trade).

■ **dividends payable**

The payment of dividends is not an allowable expense. However if these occur in the accounts after the net profit that we have used as the starting point for our calculation, there will be no need for an adjustment.

■ **Corporation Tax**

Logically, the tax payment itself is not tax deductible!

expenditure that is allowable

As already stated, revenue expenditure that is 'wholly and exclusively' for the purpose of the trade is allowable. We will now list some illustrative examples, a few of which were referred to above.

■ normal **cost of sales**

■ normal **business expenditure**, for example:

- distribution costs
- administration
- salaries and wages, and employers' NIC
- rent, rates and insurance
- repairs
- advertising
- business travel and subsistence
- accountancy services
- research & development expenditure

■   **specifically allowable expenditure**:
  – operating lease rental payments for cars with emission levels of 110g/km or less
  – legal expenses on renewing (but not acquiring) a short (ie 50 years or shorter) lease
  – interest payable on trade loans
  – staff entertaining (eg staff Christmas parties)
  – trade bad debts written off (note, however, that writing off of a loan to an employee is not allowable, since it is not a trade item)
  – increases in specific provisions for trade bad debts and impairment provisions based on objective evidence (see note below). Specific provisions are those based on named debtors
  – gifts to customers that contain a conspicuous advertisement, costing up to £50 per recipient per year – this however does not apply to food, drink, tobacco or gift vouchers, gifts of which can never be allowable – allowable examples would include calendars and diaries
  – gifts of trading stock to educational establishments, charities or registered amateur sports clubs
  – employees' parking fines incurred while on business, but not those of directors

■   **capital allowances**
  We will see how to calculate capital allowances in the next chapter. In the exercises in this chapter we will use capital allowance figures that have already been calculated. Because capital allowances will not be recorded in the financial accounts, they will be deducted as a separate item in the adjustment to the accounts.

note regarding trade bad debts and provisions

Whereas a sum written off a trade debt or an increase in a specific provision is allowable, any recovery of amounts previously written off and any decrease in specific provisions is taxable, and no adjustment is needed. This can be a confusing area. The following table summarises the position:

Expenditure	Treatment	Action
Trade Bad Debts Written Off	Allowable	No adjustment
Increases in Specific Bad Debt Provisions	Allowable	No adjustment
Increases in General Bad Debt Provisions	Not allowable	Add back
Income	**Treatment**	**Action**
Trade Bad Debts Recovered	Taxable	No adjustment
Decreases in Specific Bad Debt Provisions	Taxable	No adjustment
Decreases in General Bad Debt Provisions	Not taxable	Deduct

special rules for research and development expenditure

If a company incurs revenue expenditure on qualifying research and development (R & D) the allowable expenditure will be greater than the actual amount spent.

■ for small and medium sized companies (SMEs) the allowable cost is 230% of the actual R & D expenditure

Broadly, SMEs are those with fewer than 500 employees, with a turnover of not more than 100 million euros, and assets of not more than 86 million euros.

To qualify for the additional tax relief, the research and development project must seek to achieve an advance in overall knowledge or capability in a field of science or technology through **the resolution of scientific or technological uncertainty**. It is not sufficient that the project will just advance the company's own state of knowledge or capability. The project must also relate to the company's existing or intended trade.

Qualifying expenditure can include costs such as employees, materials, payments to clinical trials volunteers, utilities and software.

For small and medium sized companies with qualifying R & D expenditure there is an additional option available if losses are incurred. This will be explained a little later when we examine the set off of company losses.

Case Study

TRADING ALOUD LIMITED: ADJUSTING THE PROFIT

Trading Aloud Limited is a company that specialises in selling acoustic equipment. The unadjusted income statement for the year ended 31/3/2020 is as follows:

	Notes	£	£
Sales			900,000
less cost of sales			530,000
Gross profit			370,000
Rental income			120,000
Dividends received			140,000
			630,000
less expenses:			
Salaries and wages	(1)	95,400	
Depreciation		51,000	
Directors' fees		45,000	
Administration expenses		17,600	

Advertising	(2)	12,600
Travel and entertaining	(3)	19,500
Bad debts and provisions	(4)	21,650
		262,750
Net Profit		367,250

Notes:

(1) Salaries and wages includes £4,350 employers' NIC.

(2) Advertising includes:
   (a) gifts of food hampers to 70 customers £3,250
   (b) gifts of 100 mouse-mats with company logos £500

(3) Travel and entertaining is made up as follows:

	£
Employees' travel expenses	7,400
Employees' subsistence allowances	5,450
Entertaining customers	6,650
	19,500

(4) Bad debts and provisions is made up of:

	£
Trade bad debts written off	13,400
Increase in general bad debt provision	5,000
Increase in specific bad debt provision	3,250
	21,650

Capital allowances for the period have been calculated at £15,000.

required

Adjust the net profit shown to arrive at the trading income assessment for Corporation Tax purposes.

solution

The computation is shown here with notes that explain the rationale behind each adjustment and allowed item. Items that are to be deducted are shown in the left-hand column, and those to be added kept in the main (right-hand) column for clarity.

	£
Net Profit per accounts	367,250

Add Back:

Expenditure that is shown in the accounts but is not allowable

Depreciation	51,000
Food Hampers	3,250
Entertaining Customers	6,650
Increase in General Bad Debt Provision	5,000
	433,150

Deduct:

	£	£
Income not taxable as trading income		
Rental Income	120,000	
Dividends Received	140,000	
Capital Allowances	15,000	
		(275,000)
Trading Income Assessment		158,150

Notes:

- The sales and cost of sales appear to be normal trading items.

- The rental income will be brought into the main Corporation Tax computation as property income.

- The dividends received are not subject to Corporation Tax.

- Salaries and Wages (including employers' NIC) are allowable.

- Depreciation is never allowable.

- Director's fees are treated in the same way as other staff salaries.

- Administration expenses appear to be wholly and exclusively for the trade.

- The advertising costs are allowable, including the mouse-mats that fall under the provision regarding items under £50 per person. The hampers cannot be covered by this rule as they contain food.

- Employees' travel and subsistence costs are allowable, but entertaining customers is never allowable.

- Changes in general provisions for bad debts must always be adjusted for, but specific provision increases and bad debts written off are allowable.

- The capital allowance figure is shown here as a final deduction in arriving at the assessable trading income.

working from published accounts

The principle of adjusting profits for tax purposes is the same when using a published version of financial accounts. The only issue that requires extra care is the choice of profit figure as a starting point from the range of figures available. It makes sense to use the profit figure that will require the least number of adjustments. The best profit figure to use will therefore be profit before tax so that this item will not need further adjustment. We will now use a Case Study to illustrate this procedure. Since you will probably be familiar with the International Accounting Standards (IAS) format, we will use it here.

Case Study

FORMAT COMPANY LIMITED: ADJUSTING PUBLISHED ACCOUNTS

The published accounts of Format Company Limited under IAS for the year ended 31 March 2020 are shown below, together with notes that provide some analysis of the summarised data.

Capital allowances have already been calculated, and amount to £86,400.

	£000
Revenue	963
Cost of Sales	(541)
Gross Profit	422
Other Income	390
Distribution Costs	(56)
Administrative Expenses	(123)
Finance Costs	(24)
Profit before Tax	609
Tax	(150)
Profit for the Year	459

Notes:

- Cost of Sales includes depreciation of £140,000
- Administrative Expenses include the following:
  - Increase in Bad Debt Provision due to impairment calculation based on objective evidence   £7,700
  - Entertaining Customers   £9,600
- Other Income consists of:
  - Rental Income   £220,000
  - Interest Received from Investments   £60,000
  - Profit on Sale of Non-current Assets   £95,000
  - Dividends Received   £15,000
- Finance Costs relates to bank overdraft interest.

required

Calculate the trading income as adjusted for tax purposes.

solution

We will start our computation with the 'Profit before Tax' since the item that follows that figure is not allowable, whereas the items that precede it could be a mixture of allowable and non-allowable.

	£	£
Profit before Tax		609,000
Add Back:		
Expenditure that is shown in the accounts but is not allowable		
Depreciation		140,000
Entertaining Customers		9,600
		758,600
Deduct:		
Income that is not taxable as trading income		
Rental Income	220,000	
Interest Received from Investments	60,000	
Profit on Sale of Non-current Assets	95,000	
Dividends Received	15,000	
Capital Allowances	86,400	(476,400)
Trading Income Assessment		282,200

DEALING WITH ACCOUNTS FOR LONG PERIODS

In Chapter One we saw that a **chargeable accounting period** (CAP – the period that we must use for Corporation Tax purposes) is the same as the period that the accounts have been prepared for, but only if that period is for 12 months or less. Where the company produces its financial accounts for a period exceeding 12 months, this will be divided into two CAPs (and require two Corporation Tax computations):

■ one CAP for the first 12 months of the financial accounting period and
■ one CAP for the balance of the financial accounting period

For example, if a company produces financial accounts for the 18 month period 1/7/2018 to 31/12/2019, there will be two CAPs:

■ a 12 month CAP: 1/7/2018 to 30/6/2019, and
■ a 6 month CAP: 1/7/2019 to 31/12/2019

The mechanism for dealing with the two Corporation Tax computations for these periods is:

- the financial accounts for the long period are adjusted in one operation, with the exception of the capital allowances deduction
- the adjusted profits (before the deduction of any capital allowance) are then time-apportioned into the two CAPs
- capital allowances are calculated separately for each CAP (as we will see in the next chapter)
- each CAP's adjusted trading profit is then finalised by deducting the capital allowances that have been calculated for the specific period

We will now use a Case Study to illustrate this principle.

Case Study

THYME LIMITED: ACCOUNTS FOR A LONG PERIOD

Thyme Limited is changing its accounting dates, and to accommodate this has produced one long set of financial accounts, from 1/10/2018 to 31/3/2020.

Capital allowances have already been calculated for each of the two CAPs as follows:

CAP 1/10/2018 to 30/9/2019 £15,000

CAP 1/10/2019 to 31/3/2020 £6,000

The financial accounts for the 18 months to 31/3/2020 are as follows:

	£	£
Sales		237,000
less cost of sales		103,000
Gross profit		134,000
less expenses:		
Salaries and wages	43,500	
Rent, rates, and insurance	8,700	
Depreciation etc	11,000	
Selling expenses	15,780	
General expenses	15,630	
Bad Debts	19,400	
		114,010
Net Profit		19,990

The following information is also provided:

- salaries and wages relate to the two directors, who are the only employees

- depreciation etc is made up as follows:

– Depreciation	£35,000
– Loss on sale of motors	£9,500
– Profit on sale of building	(£33,500)

- selling expenses include:

– Entertaining customers	£4,700
– Gifts of wine to customers	£1,900
– Gifts of calendars to customers (£10 each, with company advert)	£500

- general expenses include accountancy fees of £2,800

- bad debts are made up of:

– Increase in specific provision	£8,000
– Bad debts written off	£23,600
– Bad debts recovered	(£12,200)

required

1   Adjust the financial accounts for the 18-month period, before deduction of capital allowances.

2   Time-apportion the adjusted profit figure into CAPs.

3   Calculate the trading income assessment for each CAP.

solution

1

	£	£
Net Profit for 18-month period per accounts		19,990
Add back non-allowable expenditure:		
Depreciation		35,000
Loss on sale of motors		9,500
Entertaining customers		4,700
Gifts of wine		1,900
		71,090
Deduct income that is not taxable as trading income		
Profit on sale of building	33,500	
		(33,500)
Adjusted profit before capital allowances		37,590

Notes:

- The profit on the sale of the building is not taxable as trading income, and

is therefore deducted. An alternative approach would be to add back the net £11,000 that relates to the three items under the heading of 'depreciation'.

- The calendars are allowable under the gift rules.

- All the items under the bad debts heading are allowable/taxable, and therefore do not require adjustment.

2   The adjusted profit for the 18-month period is time-apportioned as follows:

CAP 1/10/2018 to 30/9/2019 £37,590 x 12/18 = £25,060

CAP 1/10/2019 to 31/3/2020 £37,590 x 6/18 = £12,530

3   Capital allowances are then deducted from the adjusted profit for each CAP:

	1/10/18 – 30/9/19	1/10/19 – 31/3/20
	£	£
Adjusted profit	25,060	12,530
Capital allowances	15,000	6,000
Trading Income	10,060	6,530

DEALING WITH TRADE LOSSES

If, once profits have been tax-adjusted and any capital allowances deducted, the result is a minus figure, a 'trading loss' will have arisen. This will have two implications:

■ the **trading income assessment** for the chargeable accounting period will be **zero** (not the negative profit figure)

■ the amount of the **negative profit figure** will form the **trading loss**, and the company can choose how to deal with it

How does one deal with this situation? The options are as follows:

1 A trading loss that occurred **from 1/4/2017** can be carried forward to set against the **total profits** (TTP before Gift Aid deduction) of future CAPs,

within certain limits. The limits are outside the scope of your studies. The company may choose which future CAP(s) to offset the loss against.

A trading loss that occurred **up to 31/3/2017** can be carried forward to set against the **future profits from the same trade**.

2   The trading loss can be used to reduce (or eliminate) all of the taxable total profits (TTP before Gift Aid deduction) in the same CAP that the loss arose. This set off would be against all taxable investment income and chargeable gains for the period, before deducting Gift Aid payments.

3   Only if option (2) above is chosen, the loss can then be carried back against the taxable total profits (TTP before Gift Aid deduction) of the CAP in the 12 months immediately before the one in which the loss occurred. If there were two CAPs partly falling into that 12-month period, then both could be used.

The diagram on the next page illustrates these options, using as an example a company making up accounts to the 31 December each year. A loss arises in the year ended 31/12/2019.

We will discuss Gift Aid in more detail in Chapter 5.

Where a small or medium sized company has qualifying research and development expenditure and incurs a loss it has a further option available. Instead of claiming the loss and offsetting it as described above, it can exchange **the lower of:**

■   the research and development tax relief (ie 230% of the R & D expenditure) and

■   the loss for the CAP

for tax credits equal to 14.5% of the surrendered amount.

The tax credits can then be repaid to the company by HMRC.

There is no equivalent tax credit scheme for large companies.

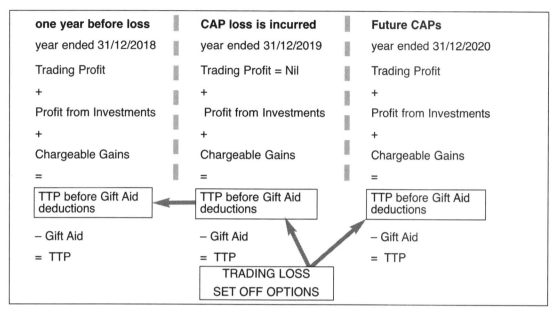

Where option (2) has been used, or option (2) followed by option (3), and the whole loss has still not been offset, any balance will follow option (1).

We can now revise our diagram (see page 2.3) illustrating the Corporation Tax Computation procedures to incorporate possible trading loss set off. The dark box is an addition to the diagram.

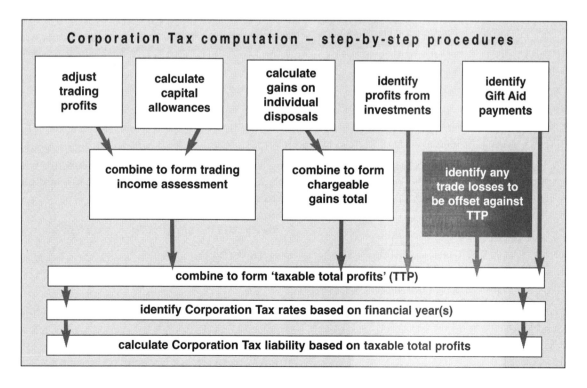

We will now use a Case Study to illustrate these options. We will also return to this topic in later chapters when we have studied the build-up of the taxable total profits (TTP) in more detail.

DOWNSEA PANS LIMITED: TRADING LOSS OPTIONS

Downsea Pans Limited has the following tax-adjusted results for the three chargeable accounting periods to 31/12/2020.

CAP	year ended 31/12/18	year ended 31/12/19	year ended 31/12/20
	£000	£000	£000
Trading Profit/(Loss)	120	(150)	160
Profits from investments	40	50	55
Chargeable gains	75	15	80

The company did not make any Gift Aid payments.

required

State the options available for offsetting the £150,000 trading loss incurred in the CAP year ended 31/12/2019.

Demonstrate the effects on the relevant taxable total profits (TTP) figures by showing Corporation Tax computation extracts.

solution

We will show the options one by one, but with all the three years' details shown in columnar form for reference.

Option One

The trading loss could be carried forward and set against the TTP of y/e 31/12/2020, (or a later CAP). Since this profit is larger than the loss, the whole loss could be offset in this way. The Corporation Tax computation extract for y/e 31/12/2020 would be affected, and the three years would look as follows:

	y/e 31/12/18	y/e 31/12/19	y/e 31/12/20
	£000	£000	£000
Trading Income	120	0	160
Profits from Investments	40	50	55
Chargeable Gains	75	15	80
less loss relief			(150)
TTP	235	65	145

Option Two

The trading loss could be set against the other profits and chargeable gains of the CAP y/e 31/12/2019 (the CAP in which the loss was incurred). Due to the size of the loss this will not be sufficient to offset the whole loss. The balance of the loss could then be carried back to the CAP y/e 31/12/2018 and set against the TTP in that period as well. This would give the following Corporation Tax computation extracts:

	y/e 31/12/18	y/e 31/12/19	y/e 31/12/20
	£000	£000	£000
Trading Income	120	0	160
Profits from Investments	40	50	55
Chargeable Gains	75	15	80
	235	65	295
less loss relief			
first set off		(65)	
second set off	(85)		
TTP	150	0	295

Note that the loss can only be carried back after the current year set off has been carried out to its full extent.

Option Three

Following the current year set off as in option two, the previous year TTP need not be utilised. In that case the balance of the loss could be carried forward against the TTP of y/e 31/12/2020, (or a later CAP). This would give the following figures for the three years.

	y/e 31/12/18	y/e 31/12/19	y/e 31/12/20
	£000	£000	£000
Trading Income	120	0	160
Profits from Investments	40	50	55
Chargeable Gains	75	15	80
	235	65	295
less loss relief (first set off)		(65)	
less loss relief (second set off)			(85)
TTP	235	0	210

The actual choice of option would depend on factors such as cash flow and the tax rates that would apply to the levels of TTP in each year. We will examine this issue in Chapter 5.

Chapter Summary

- The 'taxable total profits' (TTP) include trading income, profits from investments, and chargeable gains. To arrive at the trading income, the profits based on the financial accounts must be adjusted, and capital allowances calculated and deducted from the adjusted profit figure.

- To adjust the profit based on the financial accounts, any income shown in the accounts that is not taxable as trading income is deducted, and any expenditure that is not allowable is added. The capital allowances that will have been calculated separately are then deducted to arrive at the assessable trading income.

- To be allowable, expenditure must be revenue (not capital), and wholly and exclusively for the purpose of the trade. There are also detailed rules about whether certain items of expenditure are allowable.

- Where the financial accounts are prepared for a period exceeding twelve months, the period will form two chargeable accounting periods. One CAP will be for the first twelve months, and the other for the balance of the financial accounting period. To deal with this situation, the financial accounts are adjusted as a whole, apart from the capital allowances. The adjusted profit is then time-apportioned into the two CAPs, and separate capital allowance figures deducted from each to form two trading income assessments.

- Where the adjusted trading profits (after capital allowances) result in a negative figure, the trading income assessment is zero, and a trading loss is formed that can be relieved in several ways. It may be carried forward and set off against the taxable total profits before Gift Aid deductions of future CAPs. It may alternatively be set against the taxable total profits (TTP before any Gift Aid deductions) of the CAP in which the loss was incurred. Where this happens and not all the loss is used up, the balance can be carried back against the taxable total profits (TTP before any Gift Aid deductions) arising in the preceding twelve months.

Key Terms	

taxable total profits (TTP)

the figure used as the basis for calculation of Corporation Tax for a limited company. It includes trading profits, profits from investments, and chargeable gains. It is calculated for each chargeable accounting period (CAP) that the company operates in

chargeable accounting period (CAP)

the period for which the taxable total profit (TTP) must be calculated. It is the same as the period for which the company produces financial accounts, unless that period is for more than twelve months. In that case the financial accounting period is divided into two CAPs

adjusted trading profits

the trading profits that have been adjusted for tax purposes by excluding income not taxable as trading income, and non-allowable expenditure

trading income assessment

the taxable trading profits for the CAP. It is made up of adjusted trading profits, after deducting any capital allowances

trading loss

this occurs when the adjusted trading profits after deducting capital allowances produces a negative figure. the negative figure is the trading loss, whilst the trading income assessment is zero.

loss relief

the offsetting of the trading loss against taxable total profits (TTP)

Activities

2.1 The numbered items listed below appear in an income statement (before the net profit figure).

If you are adjusting the trading profit for tax purposes, state whether each item should be:

- added to the net profit
- deducted from the net profit
- ignored for adjustment purposes

1   accountancy fees payable

2   amortisation of lease

3   non–trade interest received

4   dividends received

5   employees' travel expenses payable

6   gain on sale of non-current asset

7   decrease in specific provision for bad debts

8   gifts of cigars (with company adverts) to customers, costing £40 per recipient.

9   increase in general bad debt provision

10   donation to political party

11   employers' National Insurance contributions

12   charitable donation under the Gift Aid scheme

2.2 Ahoy Trading Limited is a company that specialises in selling yachting equipment.

The unadjusted income statement for the accounting year is as follows:

	£
Sales	500,000
less cost of sales	220,000
Gross profit	280,000
Interest received	20,000
Dividends received	70,000
	370,000

less expenses:	£	£
Salaries and wages	99,000	
Depreciation	42,000	
Loss on sale of non-current assets	5,000	
Administration expenses	19,600	
Advertising	18,000	
Interest payable	22,000	
Travel and entertaining	19,100	
Bad debts and provisions	15,000	
		239,700
Net Profit		130,300

Notes:

- Administration includes £350 employees' parking fines incurred while on company business.

- Advertising includes:
  - gifts of chocolates with company logos to 100 top customers £4,900
  - gifts of sailing books with company logos to 200 other customers £5,000

- Travel and entertaining is made up as follows:

	£
– Employees' travel expenses	3,400
– Employees' subsistence allowances	5,600
– Entertaining customers	6,000
– Entertaining staff at Christmas	4,100
	19,100

- Bad debts and provisions is made up of:

	£
– Trade bad debts written off	18,400
– Decrease in general bad debt provision	(5,000)
– Increase in specific bad debt provision	1,600
	15,000

Capital allowances for the period have been calculated at £23,000.

Required:

Adjust the net profit shown to arrive at the trading income assessment for Corporation Tax purposes.

2.3   All I Need Trading Limited has an unadjusted income statement for the accounting year as follows:

	£	£
Sales		770,000
less cost of sales		420,000
Gross profit		350,000
Interest received		40,000
Gains on disposal of non-current assets		50,000
Rental income received		60,000
		500,000
less expenses:		
Discounts allowed	10,000	
Salaries and wages	80,500	
Depreciation	51,000	
Bad debts written off	12,000	
Rates and insurance	12,500	
Postage and stationery	11,050	
Administration expenses	12,600	
Advertising	14,000	
Travel and entertaining	19,750	
		223,400
Net Profit		276,600

Notes:

- Administration includes £2,000 directors' speeding fines incurred while on company business.
- Advertising consists of:
  - gifts of CDs with company logos to 1000 customers £9,000
  - gifts vouchers with company logos to 200 other customers £5,000
- Travel and entertaining is made up as follows:

	£
Employees' travel expenses	6,400
Employees' subsistence allowances	5,600
Entertaining customers	4,000
Entertaining staff on company trip to races	3,750
	19,750

Capital allowances for the period have been calculated at £31,500.

Required:

Adjust the net profit shown to arrive at the trading income assessment for Corporation Tax purposes.

2.4 Mint Limited is changing its accounting dates, and to accommodate this has produced a set of financial accounts over an extended period, from 1/12/2018 to 31/3/2020.

Capital allowances have already been calculated for each of the two CAPs as follows:

CAP 1/12/2018 to 30/11/2019	£8,000
CAP 1/12/2019 to 31/3/2020	£2,500

The financial accounts for the 16 months to 31/3/2020 are as follows:

	£	£
Sales		293,000
less cost of sales		155,000
Gross profit		138,000
add:		
Bad debts recovered		3,100
Discounts received		2,000
		143,100
less expenses:		
Salaries and wages	68,500	
Rent, rates, and insurance	9,200	
Depreciation etc	10,000	
General expenses	15,630	
Interest payable	8,300	
Bad debts written off	12,400	
Selling expenses	15,000	
		139,030
Net Profit		4,070

The following information is also provided:
- depreciation etc is made up as follows:

Depreciation	£45,000
Loss on sale of computer	£19,500
Profit on sale of Building	£54,500

- general expenses include debt recovery fees of £800
- selling expenses include:

Entertaining customers	£1,930
Gifts of diaries to customers	£600
(£6 each, with company advert)	

Required:
- Adjust the financial accounts for the 16-month period, before deduction of capital allowances.
- Time-apportion the adjusted profit figure into CAPs.
- Calculate the trading income assessment for each CAP.

2.5   The published accounts of Doormat Company Limited for the year ended 31 March 2020 are shown below, together with notes that provide some analysis of the summarised data. Capital allowances have already been calculated, and amount to £153,000.

	£000
Revenue	743
Cost of Sales	(302)
Gross Profit	441
Other Income	290
Distribution Costs	(144)
Administrative Expenses	(243)
Finance Costs	(50)
Profit before Tax	294
Tax	(71)
Profit for the Year	223

Notes:

- Cost of Sales includes depreciation of £20,000

- Administrative Expenses include the following:

Loan to employee written off	£8,000
Increase in Specific Bad Debt Provision	£2,800
Increase In General Bad Debt Provision	£7,700
Entertaining Customers	£9,100

- Other Income consists of:

Rental Income	£200,000
Discounts received from trade suppliers	£12,000
Interest Received from Investments	£30,000
Profit on Sale of Non-current Assets	£33,000
Dividends Received	£15,000

- Finance Costs relates to bank overdraft interest.

Required:

- Calculate the trading income assessable figure as adjusted for tax purposes, and the amount of any trading loss.

- State how the trading loss could be relieved without carrying it forward to future periods.

2.6 State whether the following statements are true or false:

		True	False
(a)	Expenditure on purchasing a second hand van is an example of revenue expenditure		
(b)	Expenditure on purchasing a new van is an example of capital expenditure		
(c)	If a company wishes to carry a loss incurred after 1/4/2017 forward, then it can only set it off against trading profits from the same trade		
(d)	A company can opt to set a trade loss against the taxable total profits (TTP) of the year before the loss whether or not it has first set the loss against the taxable total profits (TTP) relating to the year of the loss		

3 Corporation tax – capital allowances

this chapter covers...

In this chapter we examine in detail the capital allowances that are available on 'plant and machinery' for companies. These allowances are used instead of depreciation on certain non-current assets for Corporation Tax purposes.

We start by examining what is classed as 'plant and machinery' for capital allowances purposes, and then go on to see what type of allowances are available.

We will learn about the 'Annual Investment Allowance' and then examine the other (more complicated) capital allowances that can be claimed. We will see how capital allowance computations involve pooling certain assets together while keeping others separate.

The final section is devoted to calculating capital allowances for short chargeable accounting periods, and how the length of period affects some (but not all) allowances.

INTRODUCTION TO CAPITAL ALLOWANCES

As we saw in the last chapter, depreciation of non-current (fixed) assets is not an allowable expense for Corporation Tax purposes, but **capital allowances** are often provided instead.

A **capital allowance** reduces the taxable profit for a chargeable accounting period. It results from the acquisition and use of certain non-current assets.

Capital allowances are not, however, automatically available for any non-current asset owned and depreciated by a company. Although many categories of non-current asset do attract capital allowances, there are some that do not. The company's own depreciation policy is also irrelevant when calculating the amount of capital allowance that can be claimed – the same HM Revenue & Customs rules apply for all companies.

To be eligible for capital allowances, the expenditure on the non-current assets must firstly be defined as **capital expenditure**, rather than revenue. Here the definition of capital is generally the same as in financial accounting – expenditure on assets that will benefit the business over several accounting periods.

Secondly, the expenditure must be on assets that attract specific capital allowances. There are several categories of capital allowances, but in this learning area we will be examining the main rules relating to **Plant and Machinery**.

Capital allowances are claimable for each Chargeable Accounting Period (CAP) separately, based on expenditure incurred in that period and any balances of expenditure brought forward. We will see exactly how this works shortly.

For all expenditure on non-current assets that attract capital allowances, it does not matter how the funding is obtained, whether from:

■ cash reserves and money in the bank

■ a loan

■ hire purchase

■ finance leases of at least five years

In all these cases capital allowances are available on the full capital cost as soon as the expenditure is incurred – not when all payments have finally been made. Any interest on loans or hire purchase agreements etc is not capital expenditure, but forms allowable revenue expenditure.

If however an asset is leased on an **operating lease** then no capital allowances are available as the expenditure is treated as **revenue** as we saw in Chapter 2.

WHAT IS 'PLANT AND MACHINERY'?

Plant and machinery capital allowances form a major area of study in this learning area, and a large number of assets come under this category. As we will see, 'plant and machinery' covers not only items that most of us would expect to be classified in this way, but also a number of unexpected types of asset.

The exact definition of 'plant and machinery' has been subject to debate and modification through statute and case law over the years. One idea that may be useful as a starting point is that plant and machinery covers 'apparatus with which' the business operates, rather than assets 'in which' the business operates. This excludes assets which are simply part of 'the setting' of the business (eg buildings) from being plant and machinery. Examples of plant and machinery that we will deal with are listed below. Both new and second-hand items qualify.

- **plant or machinery** in the normal use of the phrase. This includes moveable and fixed items and their installation costs, and ranges from factory conveyor equipment to cement mixers
- **vans, lorries, and other commercial vehicles**. This category also includes tractors, trailers and other specialist vehicles
- **cars** owned by a limited company and used by the employees (including for private use) are included as plant and machinery
- **furniture, carpets and other moveable items**. Equipment such as specialist lighting used for shop displays or to create atmosphere have been classed as plant and machinery
- **computers and other electronic equipment**. This includes 'information and communications technology'. Software is also eligible expenditure where it is a capital purchase

CAPITAL ALLOWANCES FOR PLANT & MACHINERY

Capital allowances for plant and machinery are currently provided in two ways:
- the Annual Investment Allowance (AIA), and
- through other capital allowances, such as First Year Allowances (FYAs) and Writing Down Allowances (WDAs)

Note that capital allowances are not scaled down according to when in the chargeable accounting period (CAP) an asset is bought. If (for example) an asset is eligible for an 18% allowance, the full 18% is claimable whether the asset is bought in the first month of the CAP or the last month.

We will look at each of these two procedures in turn, and see how they work.

Annual Investment Allowance (AIA)

This provides a very simple system for companies to claim capital allowances. The Annual Investment Allowance applies to virtually all plant and machinery **except cars**, and provides an allowance of the whole amount spent on this plant and machinery, up to a total amount of £200,000 for CAPs ending on or before 31/12/2018. The limit is £1,000,000 for CAPs starting on or after 1/1/2019. For CAPs that straddle 31/12/2018 there are special rules that we will examine shortly.

Any acquisitions in a year that exceed the relevant limit are dealt with through the pooled system that we will look at shortly, and will then be eligible for other capital allowances.

The key features of the scheme are:

■ it applies to the acquisition in the chargeable accounting period of virtually all plant and machinery except cars

■ it is available for the first £200,000/£1,000,000 of qualifying expenditure per 12 month CAP

■ the relevant limit is reduced proportionally if the CAP is less than 12 months (eg the limit is £750,000 for a nine month CAP starting on or after 1/1/2019)

■ it gives a capital allowance equal to the whole of such expenditure, and this allowance can then be deducted in the calculation of adjusted trading profits

example

Suppose A Limited had adjusted trading profits (before capital allowances) of £1,900,000 for the CAP 1/1/2019 to 31/12/2019.

If during the CAP it spent £120,000 on plant and machinery, it could set the whole £120,000 against trading profits, giving a trading income assessment of £1,780,000.

or

If during the CAP it spent £1,045,000 on plant and machinery it could set £1,000,000 (the maximum) against trading profits, giving a trading income assessment of £900,000 before other capital allowances. The remaining £45,000 expenditure would be subject to capital allowance claims through the pooling system.

We will shortly look at how this works and what allowances can be claimed.

In some cases groups of companies may not be entitled to the normal annual limit for each company in the group, but may be required to share the limit between the companies. This could occur if the companies shared premises or had similar activities.

AIA in CAPs straddling 31 December 2018

As noted already, the AIA annual limit changed on 31 December 2018 from £200,000 per year to £1,000,000 per year. Where a CAP straddles 31 December 2018, the maximum AIA for the whole CAP will be based on calculating proportions of each limit based on the length of time of each part of the CAP and adding them together.

For example, the maximum AIA for a CAP for the 12 month period from 1 October 2018 to 30 September 2019 would be calculated as follows:

Period 1/10/2018 – 31/12/2018	£200,000 x 3/12	£50,000
Period 1/1/2019 – 30/9/2019	£1,000,000 x 9/12	£750,000
Maximum AIA for whole CAP		£800,000

Where some eligible expenditure takes place in the part of the CAP that is before 31/12/2018, there is a further restriction of £200,000. This means that expenditure before the date that the limit changed can never be entitled to more AIA than it would if the limit was unchanged.

There is no equivalent further restriction for expenditure incurred on or after 1/1/2019.

pooled expenditure calculations

There are some situations that fall outside of the AIA. These are:
- balances of unrelieved capital expenditure brought forward from earlier periods
- expenditure during the period on cars
- expenditure on plant and machinery during an accounting period in excess of the AIA limit
- disposals during the period of plant and machinery

These situations require a working involving one or more expenditure 'pools'. Each pool requires a separate calculation (shown in a separate column) in the capital allowance computation that will be used to calculate any capital allowances that are claimable. Separate pools are used for:
- each piece of plant deemed to have a 'short life' – one 'single asset pool' each
- a 'special rate pool' that is used for cars that have high emissions levels

(over 110g/km) and is also used for certain long-life assets and 'integral features'

■ the general (or 'main') pool for everything else, including cars of 110g/km emissions or less all merged together

The pool workings will carry forward from one period to the next, and keep running totals of unrelieved expenditure.

The capital allowances that can be calculated and claimed through this system are as follows:

■ **100% First Year Allowances (FYAs).** These are **only** available for **new low emission cars, new zero emission goods vehicles** and certain **'energy efficient' and 'water efficient' plant**. 'Low emission' cars (also known as 'ultra low emission' cars) are defined as those with emissions not exceeding 50 grams per kilometre of CO_2. This includes electric cars. This means that the whole cost of a new low emission car can be claimed as a capital allowance. This is separate to, and in addition to any Annual Investment Allowance claimed for other plant. Other cars (that aren't new and / or don't meet the definition of low-emission) are not entitled to 100% First Year Allowances.

■ **18% Writing Down Allowance (WDA)** is available on **pool balances, except** single asset pools where the asset has been disposed of before the end of the period, and the special rate pool.

■ **8% or 6% Writing Down Allowance (WDA)** is available for the pool balance on the special rate pool.

The rate changed from 8% to 6% on 1 April 2019. For CAPs that straddle this date, a hybrid rate is calculated based on the proportion of CAP falling before and after 1 April 2019. For example, a 12 month CAP from 1 January 2019 to 31 December 2019 would use a rate of (3/12 x 8%) + (9/12 x 6%) = 6.5%.

■ **Balancing Allowances** (or the opposite – a **balancing charge**) are calculated when a single asset pool is closed because the asset has been disposed of. It can also occur in the general pool if the business ceases.

carrying out a computation using pools

In order to follow logically through the process, it is best to deal with the elements in the following order, using as many pools as necessary:

■ **start** with the written down values brought forward from the previous period

■ **add** the eligible expenditure on any acquisitions that do not qualify for first year allowances or annual investment allowance. This will be expenditure on 'normal' cars (ie not new low-emission) and will need to be analysed into:

– those over 110g/km (these go into the special rate pool), and

– those between 50g/km and 110g/km (that go into the general pool)

– second hand low-emission cars also go into the general pool

■ **calculate** 100% first year allowances on any new low-emission cars or other qualifying plant

■ **calculate** the annual investment allowance on qualifying expenditure. Where the expenditure exceeds the available AIA, add any remaining balance of expenditure into the relevant pool

■ **deduct** the proceeds of disposals (limited to the original cost)

■ **calculate** the writing down allowances (WDAs) on the pool balances after the above transactions

■ **calculate** any balancing allowances or balancing charges

■ **calculate** the written down values of each pool to be carried forward to the next chargeable accounting period

■ **calculate** the total capital allowances that can be claimed

This is quite complicated, but once a few examples have been looked at it should become clearer. Let us first look at a fairly basic example so that we can get the idea of the way that it works.

example

The Simple Company Limited has a chargeable accounting period running from 1 January 2019 to 31 December 2019. At the start of the period there was a brought forward balance of £26,000 in the general (main) pool from the previous year:

During the chargeable accounting period y/e 31/12/2019, the Simple Company Ltd had the following transactions in plant and machinery:

Purchases (cost)

Plant & Machinery	£1,015,000
Car (emissions 100g/km)	£18,000

Disposals (proceeds)

Plant (main pool)	£5,000

The Simple Company Limited had adjusted trading profits (before capital allowances) for the CAP y/e 31/12/2019 of £1,750,000.

Required

(a) Calculate the total capital allowances claimable for the CAP.

(b) Calculate the assessable trading profits after deducting capital allowances.

Solution

(a) The capital allowance computation using the pool is built up as follows. The column on the right hand side is to collect and total the allowances. Note that allowances are deducted from the pool balances, but appear as positive figures in the capital allowances column.

		Main Pool	Capital Allowances
		£	£
WDV bf		26,000	
add			
Acquisitions without FYA or AIA:			
Car (100g/km)		18,000	
Acquisitions qualifying for AIA:			
Plant & Machinery	1,015,000		
AIA Claimed	(1,000,000)		1,000,000
Balance into main pool		15,000	
less			
Proceeds of Disposals		(5,000)	
		54,000	
18% WDA		(9,720)	9,720
WDV cf		44,280	
Total Capital Allowances			1,009,720

Note the following important points:

The cost of the car enters the main pool. This is because it has an emission rating of 110g/km or less.

The plant and machinery is entitled to annual investment allowance (AIA) of £1,000,000. This calculation is carried out next, and the excess of £15,000 is added to the main pool. This £15,000 will form part of the balance of £54,000 that is entitled to 18% writing down allowance (WDA).

The proceeds on disposal are deducted from the pool before the writing down allowance (WDA) is calculated.

The total capital allowance is made up of the AIA and the WDA in this example.

(b) The assessable trading profit can now be calculated:

	£
Adjusted trading profits (before capital allowances)	1,750,000
Less capital allowances	(1,009,720)
Assessable trading profit	740,280

'Short-Life' Assets

Short-life assets are those that the company believes it will dispose of within eight years of the end of the current CAP. Any assets (except cars) that the company choses to categorise in this way are dealt with by entering each asset into a separate short-life asset pool. This will enable balancing allowances to be claimed if the asset is disposed of for a small amount.

Under the annual investment allowance scheme the full value of all plant (including short-life assets) up to £200,000 or £1,000,000, or a hybrid figure per year can be claimed in full, so this arrangement could be useful for assets in excess of the AIA limit. If the asset is not sold within eight years of the end of the CAP in which it was acquired the balance of expenditure brought forward is transferred to the main pool and the short-life asset pool is closed.

small pools allowance

Where the sub total in either the main pool or the special rate pool at the end of a CAP is £1,000 or less, the whole amount can be claimed as a 'small pools allowance' instead of the normal writing down allowance. The £1,000 limit relates to the pool balance that the writing down allowance would normally be calculated on.

After the small pools allowance has been claimed there will be no balance in the relevant pool to carry forward to the next CAP.

The small pools allowance does not apply to single asset pools (for example short life assets).

We will now use a slightly more complex Case Study to see how the capital allowance computation works in more detail.

Case Study

SPENDER PLC:
PLANT AND MACHINERY CAPITAL ALLOWANCES

Spender plc has a chargeable accounting period running from 1 October 2018 to 30 September 2019. At the start of the period, the following balances were brought forward in its capital allowances computation from the previous year:

General (main) pool	£48,000
Single asset pools:	
Short-life asset	£20,000

During the chargeable accounting period y/e 30/9/2019, Spender plc had the following transactions in plant and machinery:

Purchases (cost) (All purchased after 1/1/2019)

Equipment	£32,000
Van	£17,000
Lorries	£850,000
New 'Low Emission' Car	£28,000
Car with emissions of 200g/km	£19,000

Disposals (proceeds)

Short-life asset	£13,000
Plant (main pool)	£10,000

Spender plc had adjusted trading profits (before capital allowances) for the CAP y/e 30/9/2019 of £1,500,000.

required

(a) Calculate the total capital allowances claimable for the CAP.

(b) Calculate the assessable trading profits after deducting capital allowances.

solution

(a) Of the expenditure during the CAP, the following items are eligible for AIA, but their total exceeds the annual limit of £800,000 (calculated as [3/12 x £200,000] + [9/12 x £1,000,000]).

	£
Equipment	32,000
Van	17,000
Lorries	850,000
	899,000

Note that the expenditure on the cars is not eligible for this allowance.

The expenditure in excess of the AIA allowance will be added to the main pool and be eligible for writing down allowances (WDA) at 18%.

The capital allowance computation using the pools can now be built up (*see table on the next page*). We will use one column for each pool, plus a further column on the right hand side to collect and total the allowances.

(b) Following the capital allowances computation shown on the next page, the assessable trading profit can now be calculated:

	£
Adjusted trading profits (before capital allowances)	1,500,000
Less capital allowances	(860,990)
Assessable trading profit	639,010

The notes below explain some of the more complex issues in the capital allowances computation. Make sure that you can understand all the points so that you could build up a similar solution without any template.

(1) The new low-emission car had a 100% first year allowance (FYA). The balance after deducting the allowance from the cost (in this case zero) is notionally added to the main pool. When the car is ultimately sold the proceeds will be deducted from the main pool.

(2) The acquisitions qualifying for AIA exceed the £800,000 limit. The excess is added to the main pool.

(3) The writing down allowances are calculated as:
  (a) main pool £137,000 x 18% = £24,660
  (b) short-life asset – no WDA since asset has been disposed of
  (c) special rate pool £19,000 x 7% = £1,330. The car was entered into this pool as it has emissions over 110g/km. The hybrid rate of 7% is calculated as [6/12 x 8%] + [6/12 x 6%]

(4) The balancing allowance on the short-life asset pool is claimed to close the pool with a zero balance.

(5) The written down values carried forward on the two remaining pools will be used to start the computation for the next period.

	Main pool £	Short-life asset £	Special rate pool £	Capital allowances £
WDV bf	48,000	20,000		
add				
Acquisitions				
without FYA or AIA:				
Car (200g/km)			19,000	
Acquisitions				
with 100% FYA:				
Low-emission				
car (1) £28,000				
100% FYA £(28,000)	0			28,000
Acquisitions				
qualifying for AIA (2)				
Equipment £32,000				
Van £17,000				
Lorries £850,000				
£899,000				
AIA £(800,000)				800,000
Excess	99,000			
less				
Proceeds of disposals:	(10,000)	(13,000)		
	137,000	7,000	19,000	
18% WDA (3)	(24,660)			24,660
7% WDA (3)			(1,330)	1,330
Balancing Allowance (4)		(7,000)		7,000
WDV cf (5)	112,340	0	17,670	
Total Capital Allowances				860,990

The reference numbers shown above are linked to the explanation shown on the previous page.

CAPITAL ALLOWANCES FOR SHORT CAPS

So far in this chapter we have examined the way that capital allowances for plant and machinery are calculated for chargeable accounting periods of twelve months.

It is, however, possible to have CAPs for less than twelve months, and this can arise either:

- if the accounts are prepared for a period of less than twelve months, or
- where accounts are prepared for a period exceeding twelve months, and are divided into two CAPs, one for the first twelve months, and another for the balance, which will be for less than twelve months

In each of these situations, the impact on capital allowances for plant and machinery in the short CAP is as follows:

- First Year Allowances, Balancing Allowances and Balancing Charges are unaffected and are calculated as normal.
- Writing Down Allowances are time-apportioned based on the short CAP (taking account of the change in special pool rate on 1 April 2019 if applicable).
- the Annual Investment Allowance maximum limit is time-apportioned based on the short CAP. This is also based on the limits that apply to the periods before and/or after 31 December 2018. .

DEALING WITH THE ACCOUNTS FOR A LONG PERIOD

As we saw in the last chapter, where we have accounts that are prepared for a long period, the procedure is:

- the accounting profits for the long period are adjusted in one computation, before deducting capital allowances
- this adjusted profits figure is then time-apportioned into the two CAPs
- capital allowances are calculated separately for each CAP
- each CAP's adjusted profit is then finalised by deducting the capital allowances that have been calculated for that CAP

We can now examine the issues involved in creating two capital allowance computations, one for each CAP within a long period for which accounts were prepared. The points to note are:

- each acquisition and disposal of assets needs to be allocated to the correct CAP, and incorporated in the appropriate computation

■ the written-down values at the end of the first CAP will become the brought forward amounts at the start of the second CAP

■ the rules regarding time apportionment of WDAs for short CAPs as described above need to be used in the second CAP

Now that we have seen all the principles explained, we can use a Case Study to illustrate the way they work.

<table>
<tr><td>**Case Study**</td><td>

CHOPPITT PLC:
DEALING WITH ACCOUNTS FOR A LONG PERIOD

Choppitt plc has produced a set of accounts for the period 1/9/2018 to 31/12/2019. The adjusted trading profit for the 16-month period has already been produced from the accounts, and provides a profit of £1,600,000, before any capital allowances are taken account of.

The plant and machinery capital allowance computation for the CAP y/e 31/8/2018 provided carried forward written down values as follows:

- general pool   £50,000

Analysis of the accounts reveals that the following assets were acquired or disposed of during the 16-month period:

1/4/2019	disposal of plant for £2,000 (original cost £20,000)
1/10/2019	acquisition of second-hand BMW car for £17,500 (95g/km)
1/11/2019	acquisition of plant costing £370,000

required

1   State the periods for the two CAPs.

2   Calculate the Plant & Machinery capital allowances for each of the two CAPs.

3   Calculate the trading income assessments for each of the two CAPs.

solution

1   The CAPs will be:

1/9/2018 - 31/8/2019	(12 months)
1/9/2019 - 31/12/2019	(4 months)

2   To calculate the Plant and Machinery capital allowances we will need to prepare two computations, one for each CAP.

Each one will incorporate the acquisitions and disposals that occur in that CAP.

Within the CAP for the 12 months ending 31/8/2019 is disposal of plant.

There are no acquisitions of plant and machinery in this period that can be used to claim annual investment allowance (AIA). The maximum AIA would have been calculated as [4/12 x £200,000] + [8/12 x £1,000,000] = £733,333

</td></tr>
</table>

The capital allowance computation is as follows:

CAP FOR THE 12 MONTHS ENDING 31/8/2019		
	Main pool	**Capital allowances**
	£	£
WDV bf	50,000	
Disposals:		
Plant	(2,000)	
Sub Total	48,000	
WDA 18%	(8,640)	8,640
WDV cf	39,360	
Total Capital Allowances		8,640

Within the four-month CAP ending 31/12/2019 are the acquisition of plant, and the BMW car.

The limit for annual investment allowance for this four-month period is £1,000,000 x 4/12 = £333,333. The amount spent on plant is £370,000, so the maximum of £333,333 AIA is claimed, and the remaining £36,667 joins the main pool.

Note that the annual WDA % for the main pool is 18%. The 18% is reduced to 4/12 since is a short CAP.

CAP FOR THE 4 MONTHS TO 31/12/2019		
	Main pool	**Capital allowances**
	£	£
WDV bf	39,360	
add		
Acquisitions without FYA or AIA:		
Car (95g/km)	17,500	
Acquisitions qualifying for AIA:		
Plant £370,000		
AIA claimed £(333,333)		333,333
Excess	36,667	
	93,527	
WDA 18% x 4/12	(5,612)	5,612
WDV cf	87,915	
Total Capital Allowances		338,945

3 Calculation of trading income assessments.

Firstly the adjusted trade profits are time-apportioned:

CAP 1/9/2018 to 31/8/2019   £1,600,000 x 12/16   = £1,200,000

CAP 1/9/2019 to 31/12/2019 £1,600,000 x 4/16   = £400,000

Capital allowances are then deducted from the adjusted profit for each CAP:

	1/9/18 - 31/8/19	1/9/19 - 31/12/19
	£	£
Adjusted profit	1,200,000	400,000
Capital allowances:		
P & M	(8,640)	(338,945)
Trading Income	1,191,360	61,055

CAPITAL ALLOWANCES WHEN COMPANIES CEASE TRADING

When a company ceases trading the capital allowances in the final CAP are subject to a special approach, as follows:

■ there can be **no** WDA, FYA or AIA in this final CAP

■ all remaining assets will have been disposed of by the company, with any proceeds brought into the computation as normal

■ there can be no written down values to carry forward in **any** pools, so the pools must be closed by using balancing allowances or balancing charges to bring all the pool balances to zero

As the only capital allowances will be balancing allowances or charges the length of the final CAP will not cause any complications. This is because balancing allowances and balancing charges are unaffected by short CAPs as we discussed a little earlier.

Chapter Summary

- Capital allowances are available on certain non-current (fixed) assets, and act for tax computation purposes as an alternative to depreciation, which is never allowable as tax-deductible (set off against tax).

- The main type of capital allowances is for 'plant and machinery'.

- Plant and machinery includes vehicles, computers, and various other assets.

- An annual investment allowance is available for the whole cost of virtually all plant and machinery, except cars, up to a maximum of £200,000 for 12-month periods ending before 1/1/2019, and £1,000,000 for 12-month periods starting on or after 1/1/2019.

- Allowances include 100% first year allowances for new low emission cars, zero emission goods vehicles, and energy-saving and water-saving plant. There are also writing down allowances at various rates depending on the circumstances.

- Most assets are merged together or 'pooled' in the capital allowance computation, but some need to be kept separately in 'single asset pools'. Single asset pools are used for short-life assets. Balancing allowances and charges occur in single asset pools when the asset has been disposed of, and also in the general pool and special rate pool when the business ceases.

- When capital allowances are calculated for a chargeable accounting period of less than twelve months any writing down allowances are time-apportioned. The AIA limit is also time-apportioned.

- First year allowances and balancing allowances and charges are unaffected by short CAPs. Where the accounts for a company have been prepared for a period of over 12 months, the two CAPs that result will each require a separate capital allowance computation. Non-current asset acquisitions and disposals will need to be allocated to the correct CAP before these capital allowance computations are carried out.

Key Terms

capital allowance

the term used for allowances that reduce taxable profit for a chargeable accounting period, resulting from the acquisition and use of certain non-current assets

chargeable accounting period (CAP)

the period for which the profits chargeable to Corporation Tax must be calculated. It is the same as the period for which the company produces financial accounts, unless that period is for more than twelve months. In that case the financial accounting period is divided into two CAPs

plant and machinery

one of the major non-current asset categories for capital allowance purposes. It includes vehicles and computers

annual investment allowance (AIA)

this is an allowance that can be claimed against the whole cost of most plant and machinery, with the exception of cars. The maximum that can be claimed depends on the dates of the CAP

first year allowances

first year allowances are available at 100% for new low-emission cars, zero emission goods vehicles, and energy-saving and water-saving plant

writing down allowances

these allowances (WDA) are available at a percentage of the pool value for plant and machinery. This percentage is time-apportioned for short CAPs

written down value

this term relates to the balance at the end of a CAP that remains in a plant and machinery pool. It represents the part of the pool value that has not yet been claimed as allowances, and is carried forward to the next CAP

balancing allowance

this allowance can be claimed when an asset is sold for less than the written-down value (unrelieved expenditure) in a single asset pool. A balancing allowance or balancing charge will also occur in all pools when a company ceases trading

balancing charge

this charge is the opposite of an allowance, and occurs when the disposal proceeds of an asset in a single asset pool are more than the written-down value (unrelieved expenditure). It is in effect a reclaiming of excess allowances previously obtained

Activities

3.1 A company has a 12-month CAP from 1/1/2019 to 31/12/2019. At the start of the period the written down value in the main pool was £21,000. There were no single asset pools.

During the CAP the company had the following transactions in plant and machinery:

Acquisitions (Costs)

Car (emissions 100g/km)	£16,000
Plant	£993,000
Van	£10,000

Disposals (Proceeds – less than original cost)

Machinery	£2,000

Required:

Calculate the total capital allowances for the CAP.

3.2 The Capital Company Limited has a twelve month chargeable accounting period running from 1/4/2019 to 31/3/2020. The adjusted trading profit for this CAP has already been calculated at £154,000 before deduction of capital allowances for plant & machinery.

The capital allowance computation for the last CAP closed with written down values is as follows:

Main pool	£60,000
Short-life single asset pool (machine bought in 2017 to use for temporary contract)	£10,000

During the CAP the following assets were acquired and disposed of:

30/4/2019	a new fork-lift truck was bought for £30,000
31/7/2019	a new BMW car was bought for £24,000 (emissions 95g/km)
31/7/2019	a computer system was bought for £5,000 (not a short-life asset)
31/10/2019	the machine in the short-life pool was sold for £4,000
31/12/2019	a machine in the main pool was sold for £3,000

All disposal proceeds were less than original cost.

Required:

- Using a plant and machinery capital allowance computation, calculate the total allowances for the CAP year ended 31/3/2020.

- Calculate the assessable trading income for the CAP year ended 31/3/2020.

3.3   The Middle Company Limited has a 12-month CAP from 1/10/2018 to 30/9/2019. At the start of the period the written down value in the main pool was £10,000, and there was also a special rate pool with a balance of £2,800.

During the CAP the company had the following transactions in plant and machinery:

Acquisitions (Costs)

Plant	£996,750
Machinery	£12,000

Disposals (Proceeds – less than cost)

Machinery in main pool	£3,500

Required:

Calculate the total capital allowances, assuming the maximum is claimed.

3.4   Solvitt plc has produced a set of accounts for the period 1/4/2018 to 30/6/2019. The adjusted trading profit for the 15-month period has already been computed as £480,000, before any capital allowances are taken account of.

The plant and machinery capital allowance computation for the CAP y/e 31/3/2018 provided carried forward written-down values as follows:

General pool	£60,000
Special rate pool	£14,000

Analysis of the accounts reveals that the following assets were acquired or disposed of during the 15-month period.

1/12/2018	Disposal of plant for £4,000 (original cost £30,000)
1/2/2019	Acquisition of second-hand Ford car for £16,000 (emissions 103g/km)
1/5/2019	Acquisition of plant costing £45,000

Required:

•   State the periods for the two CAPs that need to be formed.

•   Calculate the Plant and Machinery capital allowances for each of the two CAPs.

•   Calculate the trading income assessments for each of the two CAPs.

3.5 Tuffwun Limited has produced a set of accounts for the period 1/4/2019 to 31/1/2020. The adjusted trading profit for the 10-month period has already been produced from the accounts, and provides a profit of £1,510,000, before any capital allowances are taken account of.

Tuffwun Limited's plant and machinery capital allowance computation for the CAP y/e 31/3/2019 provided carried forward written down values as follows:

| General pool | £90,000 |
| Special rate pool | £13,000 |

Analysis of the accounts reveals that the following assets were acquired or disposed of during the ten month period:

Acquisition of new 'low emission' car for £20,000

Acquisition of a BMW car for £27,000 (emissions 189g/km)

Disposal of plant for £1,000 (original cost £10,000)

Acquisition of plant costing £857,500

Required:

- Calculate the Plant and Machinery capital allowances for Tuffwun Limited for the CAP to 31/1/2020.

- Calculate the trading income assessment for Tuffwun Limited for the CAP to 31/1/2020.

4 Corporation tax – chargeable gains

this chapter covers...

In this chapter we learn about how chargeable gains (and the opposite – capital losses) are calculated. These gains then form part of the taxable total profits (TTP) for a limited company.

We start by examining the basis of assessment, including what constitutes the disposal of an asset, and list the main exempt assets. We then learn how to calculate gains using the basic format, before going on to look at some special situations.

The situations that we examine further are:

■ part disposals

■ improvement expenditure

■ special rules for chattels

■ matching rules for shares

■ bonus and rights share issues

Finally we examine a deferral relief that can be opted for when a company buys assets in certain categories within a defined time of disposing of an asset. This 'rollover relief' has the effect of postponing the impact of the gain on the first asset.

INTRODUCTION TO CHARGEABLE GAINS

A chargeable gain (or its opposite – a capital loss) occurs when a company disposes of certain assets that it has previously acquired. The gain is then brought into the Corporation Tax computation. It does not apply to a trading situation, where items are regularly bought and sold to make a profit. Such profits would be assessed as trading income, as we have already seen. The assets that can form chargeable gains will often be non-current (fixed) assets or investments that the company has acquired outside of its trading activities. A chargeable gain often applies to the sale of an asset that may have been owned for quite some time.

In addition to applying to the business assets of companies, chargeable gains can also arise for individuals who are subject to capital gains tax on the disposal of both personal assets and business assets. In this book, however, we are only going to examine how disposals of business assets are taxed. In this chapter we will examine the way that companies' chargeable gains are subject to Corporation Tax, and later in this book we will look at how Capital Gains Tax applies to the disposal of business assets by individuals.

Gains on the disposal of personal assets are dealt with in Osborne Books' *Personal Tax*.

a note for those familiar with Capital Gains Tax for individuals

Although there are similarities between Capital Gains Tax for individuals and the treatment of chargeable gains for companies under Corporation Tax, there are also **significant differences**. If you have already studied personal taxation you should be very careful to study the way in which the gains of companies are taxed. Do not be lulled into a false sense of security by the similarities to the system that you have already studied.

The following main differences between Capital Gains Tax for individuals and chargeable gains for companies will now be highlighted in advance so that you can appreciate their impact. In calculating the chargeable gains of companies:

- there is no annual exempt amount
- there is an indexation allowance, claimed up to the earlier of the date of disposal or December 2017
- the matching rules for shares are different from those for individuals

These are important differences, and can cause confusion.

basis of assessment

Chargeable gains are calculated according to the same Chargeable Accounting Periods (CAPs) as are used for the rest of the Corporation Tax computation. The basis of assessment is the chargeable gains less capital losses arising from disposals that occur during the CAP. We will look at how losses are dealt with a little later in this chapter. The main issue to understand at this point is that the chargeable gain that is brought into the Corporation Tax computation is based on the total (or aggregate) of gains that have occurred during the CAP, and that a gain can only arise when a disposal has taken place.

disposals

A disposal arises when an asset is:

- sold (or part of it is sold), or
- given away, or
- lost, or
- destroyed

Most of the situations that we will deal with will be based on the sale of an asset.

CHARGEABLE AND EXEMPT ASSETS

For a chargeable gain or capital loss to arise, the asset that has been disposed of must be a 'chargeable' asset. Disposals of exempt assets cannot form chargeable gains or capital losses. Instead of there being a long list of the assets that are chargeable, there is a fairly short list of assets that are exempt. The simple rule is that if an asset is not exempt, then it must be chargeable!

Chargeable business assets that are popular in tasks include:

- land and buildings
- shares

You must remember that these are only examples – all assets are chargeable unless they are exempt.

exempt assets

The following is a list of the main **exempt assets** that relate to companies:

- trading inventory (as discussed earlier, this is part of the trading profit)
- cars

- chattels bought and sold for £6,000 or less (chattels are tangible moveable property)
- Government Securities (also known as 'Gilts', these are a form of investment)
- animals (for example racehorses)

CHARGEABLE GAINS AND CORPORATION TAX

Where, during a CAP, there are several disposals that result in chargeable gains, these are aggregated and the result brought into the Corporation Tax computation. This total chargeable gain then forms part of the 'taxable total profits' (TTP) along with trading profits as Trading Income and any income from investments. The Corporation Tax is then calculated on the total profits, as we will see in the next chapter.

If any disposals result in capital losses, then these are set against any chargeable gains relating to the same CAP. Provided the net result is a chargeable gain, this amount is brought into the Corporation Tax computation as described above. If the losses exceed the chargeable gains of the same CAP, then the result is that:

- no chargeable gains are brought into the TTP computation, and
- the net capital loss is carried forward to be set against the chargeable gain that arises in the next CAP (and so on if necessary until all the loss is utilised)

Note that **capital losses cannot be set against any other profits** (eg from trading or investment) in the Corporation Tax computation, but must be carried forward against future chargeable gains.

We must now turn our attention to how to calculate the chargeable gain or loss on each separate disposal.

THE COMPUTATION OF EACH GAIN

Each disposal of a chargeable asset requires a calculation to determine the amount of any gain or loss. This computation follows a standard format that is in effect a 'mini' statement of profit or loss (income statement) for the item disposed of.

There are some minor variations to this format in particular circumstances, as we will see later. The basic format is shown on the next page:

computation of a chargeable gain	
	£
Proceeds on disposal	X
less	
Incidental costs of disposal	(x)
Net proceeds	X
less:	
Original cost	(x)
Incidental costs of acquisition	(x)
Unindexed gain	X
less	
Indexation allowance	(x)
Chargeable Gain	X

We will now look at the components of the individual gain computation in more detail.

proceeds on disposal

This normally refers to the amount that the asset was sold for, ie the selling price. However, there are some special situations where the figure used is different:

- if the asset is given away, or sold to a connected company or person at less than the market value, the market value is used in the computation instead of the actual amount received. Companies under the same control are connected with each other and with the person(s) controlling them

- if the asset is lost or destroyed then the asset will have been disposed of for zero proceeds, and zero will be used in the computation. The exception to this would be if an insurance claim had been made, in which case the claim proceeds would be used

incidental costs of disposal

These are the costs incurred by the company in selling the asset. Examples include advertising expenses, auction costs, or estate agent's fees for selling a property.

original cost, and incidental costs of acquisition

These relate to the amount paid to acquire the asset in the first place, plus any other costs incurred to buy it. Examples of these costs include legal fees and auction costs. We will examine later on in this chapter how to deal with expenditure that is incurred after purchase to improve the asset.

indexation allowance

This is a deduction that is used to compensate for the impact of inflation on the value of the asset. It works by using figures from the Retail Price Index (RPI) to calculate an inflation factor to multiply by the original cost and any other acquisition costs. This allows for general inflation of the **cost** between the date of acquisition and the earlier of the date of disposal and December 2017.

If acquisition was before December 2017, the indexation factor is calculated as:

$$\frac{\text{(RPI at the date of disposal or December 2017 – RPI at the date of acquisition)}}{\text{RPI at the date of acquisition}}$$

Notice that indexation only takes account of inflation up to December 2017. If an asset is disposed of after this date, the RPI at December 2017 will be used instead of the RPI at the date of disposal. This is sometimes known as 'freezing' the indexation allowance.

If an asset was **acquired after December 2017** there will be no indexation allowance.

The result of this fraction is rounded to three decimal places before being multiplied by the **historical cost figure.**

A common error is to multiply the indexation factor by the unindexed gain instead of the cost. This is illogical.

If the fraction calculation produces a negative figure, because the RPI at disposal is lower than the RPI at acquisition, then no indexation is applied. This would occur if there was deflation occurring between the two dates. This means that indexation can never increase a gain.

Note also that the indexation allowance cannot either:

■ turn an unindexed gain into a loss, or

■ increase the amount of an unindexed loss

This means that the indexation allowance cannot be a larger amount than the unindexed gain that it follows in the computation. If the figure before indexation is applied is a loss, then there can be no indexation allowance at all.

We will now use a Case Study to show how the computation is carried out.

Note that the RPI figures are shown in the Tax Data section at the beginning of this book. The figures that we need in this Case Study are, however, repeated here for convenience. **You will normally be provided with the indexation factor itself** in an assessment.

THE SIMPLE COMPANY LIMITED: CALCULATING A CHARGEABLE GAIN

The Simple Company Limited bought a retail shop in August 1990. The company paid £59,000 for the shop, and also paid legal fees of £1,000 at the same time to arrange the purchase. The shop was sold in April 2019. The company prepares its accounts annually to 31 December, and the sale of the shop was the only chargeable disposal that the company made in 2019. It had no capital losses brought forward.

We will assume three different selling prices for the sale of the shop. In each case the estate agent's fees for the sale were £3,000, and the company incurred further legal fees of £2,000.

1   Assume that the company sold the shop for £240,000

2   Assume that the company sold the shop for £75,000

3   Assume that the company sold the shop for £58,000

required

Using the RPI figures of 128.1 for August 1990 and 278.1 for December 2017, calculate the chargeable gain or capital loss resulting from the disposal of the shop (to the nearest £) for each of the situations 1, 2 and 3. Notice that because the disposal was after December 2017, the December 2017 RPI will be used, not the April 2019 RPI.

Also state the amount of chargeable gain to be brought into the TTP for the CAP year ended 31/12/2019 for each situation, and explain how any capital loss should be dealt with.

solution

Option 1   £

Proceeds on disposal   240,000

less:

Incidental costs of disposal   (5,000)

Net proceeds   235,000

less:

Original cost   (59,000)

Incidental costs of acquisition   (1,000)

Unindexed gain   175,000

less:

Indexation allowance*   (70,260)

Chargeable Gain   **104,740**

*the indexation factor is calculated as:

$$\frac{(278.1 - 128.1)}{128.1} = 1.171 \text{ (rounded to three decimal places)}$$

The indexation factor is multiplied by the costs incurred in August 1990 of £59,000 + £1,000 = £60,000:

1.171 x £60,000 = £70,260

The chargeable gain of £104,740 would form part of the TTP for the CAP for the year ended 31/12/2019.

Option 2

	£
Proceeds on disposal	75,000
less:	
Incidental costs of disposal	(5,000)
Net proceeds	70,000
less:	
Original cost	(59,000)
Incidental costs of acquisition	(1,000)
Unindexed gain	10,000
less:	
Restricted indexation allowance*	(10,000)
Chargeable Gain	Nil

*Here the indexation allowance that would be calculated as £70,260 (as in option 1) is restricted to the amount of the unindexed gain of £10,000, so that it will not turn an unindexed gain into a loss.

Since there is neither a gain nor a loss, there is no figure to form part of the TTP for the CAP for the year ended 31/12/2019.

Option 3

	£
Proceeds on disposal	58,000
less:	
Incidental costs of disposal	(5,000)
Net proceeds	53,000
less:	
Original cost	(59,000)
Incidental costs of acquisition	(1,000)
Unindexed loss	(7,000)
less:	
Indexation allowance*	Nil
Capital Loss	(7,000)

*Here there is no indexation allowance since there is an unindexed loss that cannot be increased through indexation.

Since there is a capital loss, and no chargeable gains in the CAP to set it against, there is no figure to form part of the TTP for the CAP y/e 31/12/2019. The capital loss of £7,000 will be carried forward to set against chargeable gains in the next CAP.

links with capital allowances

As we saw in the last chapter, capital allowances are available for 'Plant and Machinery'. The following rules apply to the disposal of non-current assets where capital allowances have been claimed on the asset:

■ where the asset is sold for less than it cost, the only tax implication is through plant and machinery capital allowance computations. A capital loss will not arise

■ where a chattel is sold for more than it cost, a chargeable gain can only arise if the proceeds exceed £6,000. If the proceeds do exceed £6,000 then a chargeable gain can arise, subject to the special chattel rule that we will look at shortly. This situation is rare, since items in this category do not usually appreciate in value

DEALING WITH PART DISPOSALS

We saw earlier in the chapter that a disposal can relate to all or part of an asset. Although part disposal will not apply to many assets that are not divisible, it could apply, for example, to a piece of land.

If an asset was acquired as a whole, and then part of it is sold while the rest is retained we need to compute the gain (or loss) on the part that was disposed of. The difficulty is that although we know how much the proceeds are for that part of the asset, we probably do not know how much of the original cost of the whole asset relates to that portion.

The solution to this problem is to value the remaining part of the asset at the time of the part disposal. The original cost can then logically be apportioned by using these figures.

The formula for working out the cost of the part disposed of is:

$$\textit{Original cost of whole asset} \quad x \quad \frac{A}{(A + B)}$$

where   A = proceeds (or market value) of the part disposed of

            B = market value of the part retained

The following example will illustrate this type of calculation.

example of a gain computation involving part disposal

Fielding and Company Limited bought a piece of land for £4,000 in January 1991 to use as a car park. In February 2019 the company sold a part of the land for £3,000. At the same time the remainder of the land was valued at £9,000.

The indexation factor from January 1991 to December 2017 is 1.136.

The portion of the original cost relating to the part of the field that was sold can be calculated as:

$$£4,000 \quad \times \quad \frac{£3,000}{(£3,000 + £9,000)} \quad = \quad £1,000$$

The computation would then be carried out in the normal way:

	£
Proceeds	3,000
less cost (as calculated above)	(1,000)
indexation allowance:	
1,136 x £1,000	(1,136)
Chargeable Gain	864

IMPROVEMENT EXPENDITURE

Where expenditure after acquisition is used to enhance an asset, and the asset is then disposed of in this improved condition, the improvement expenditure forms an allowable cost in the computation.

The expenditure must be of a 'capital' nature, and examples of this could include extending a building or having an antique professionally restored. The improvement expenditure will also attract indexation allowance. This would run from the date the improvement expenditure was incurred until the earlier of the date of disposal or December 2017. A situation would therefore arise where two (or more) indexation allowances were deducted in the computation, each with different start dates, but all with the same end date. This is shown in the diagram that follows on the next page.

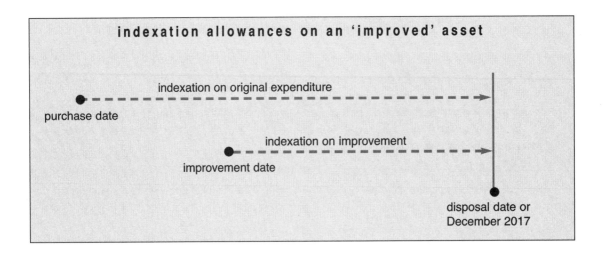

The following example illustrates how this works in practice:

example: chargeable gain involving improvement expenditure

Ledger and Company Limited bought an office building for £60,000 in September 1984. In January 1990 the company spent £40,000 extending the property. The company sold the building in April 2019 for £400,000.

The indexation factors are:

September 1984 to December 2017	2.086
January 1990 to December 2017	1.327

The calculation is as follows:

	£
Proceeds	400,000
less:	
original cost	(60,000)
improvement expenditure	(40,000)
Unindexed gain	300,000
less:	
indexation allowance on original cost	
2.086 x £60,000	(125,160)
indexation allowance on extension	
1.327 x £40,000	(53,080)
Chargeable Gain	121,760

SPECIAL RULES FOR CHATTELS

Chattels are tangible, moveable items such as furniture, portable equipment, works of art and vans.

Apart from the exemptions for all cars, and chattels bought and sold for less than £6,000, there are also some special rules about the amount of gain or loss that can occur when chattels are disposed of. Although these rules are not particularly complicated, they do need to be understood and remembered.

chattels sold at a gain for over £6,000

In this situation the gain is limited to an amount of:

5/3 (Proceeds – £6,000)

Note that in this formula both the fraction of 5/3 and the amount of £6,000 are stated in the tax legislation and will be the same in all these calculations.

'Proceeds' here refers to the gross proceeds – before the deduction of any incidental costs of disposal.

This restriction may, or may not, affect the chargeable gain. To give an illustration, suppose that gains (after any indexation) had been calculated on disposals in the following two examples:

Disposal A	Proceeds £9,000,	Gain £7,500
Disposal B	Proceeds £9,000,	Gain £2,500

In the case of Disposal A, the gain would be restricted to:

5/3 (£9,000 – £6,000) = £5,000

£5,000 would therefore be used as the chargeable gain figure. Using the same formula for Disposal B the gain would also be restricted to £5,000, but since the calculated gain is only £2,500 the restriction would be irrelevant and have no effect.

chattels sold at a loss for less than £6,000

If the chattel had been bought for less than £6,000 the transaction would be exempt from CGT, as both the cost and proceeds are less than £6,000.

If the chattel had cost more than £6,000 then the loss would be limited by using the figure of £6,000 in the gains computation **instead of the actual proceeds**. This will mean that the allowable capital loss is smaller than the actual loss incurred.

We use the phrase 'deemed proceeds' to describe substituting the actual proceeds with another figure. £6,000 is always used as the 'deemed proceeds' where the actual proceeds are less than £6,000, but the chattel was bought for more than £6,000.

For example a chattel, such as a painting that was displayed in the Boardroom, bought for £8,000 and sold for £3,000 would result in a loss calculated as:

	£
Deemed proceeds	6,000
less actual cost	(8,000)
Loss	(2,000)

Make sure that you understand the logic of this, and remember that it is the proceeds that are deemed to be £6,000. This is an area where it is easy to get confused if you are not careful.

We will now present a Case Study to consolidate an understanding of the main issues that we have covered in this chapter so far.

<table>
<tr><td>

Case Study

</td><td>

INN CREASE LIMITED: USING SPECIAL RULES

Inn Crease Limited runs a chain of hotels and pubs. During the CAP y/e 31/12/2019 the company made the disposals listed below.

The company has capital losses brought forward from the previous CAP of £20,000.

disposals:

- The company sold an antique dresser in January 2019 for £7,500. The dresser had cost £2,500 when purchased in January 1996.

- The company sold part of a plot of land for £100,000 in February 2019. It had bought the whole plot in January 1990 for £80,000. In February 2019 the market value of the remaining part of the plot of land was £300,000.

- The company sold an office building in March 2019 for £200,000. The building was bought in September 1995 for £60,000, and extended in June 2000 at a cost of £40,000.

- The company sold ten identical shoe-cleaning machines from its hotels for £100 each in January 2019. The machines had been bought for £500 each in January 1996, and plant & machinery capital allowances had been claimed on them through the main pool.

</td></tr>
</table>

- The company sold 1,000 ordinary shares in Gloxxo plc for a total of £15,000 in March 2019. The shares had been bought for £6.00 each in September 1995. These had been the only shares that it owned in Gloxxo plc.

indexation factors

The indexation factors have been calculated as follows:

January 1990 - December 2017	1.327
September 1995 - December 2017	0.847
January 1996 - December 2017	0.852
June 2000 - December 2017	0.625

required

- Calculate the chargeable gain or capital loss on each applicable disposal.
- Calculate the total chargeable gain that will be used in the taxable total profits computation for the CAP y/e 31/12/2019.

solution

Antique Dresser

	£
Proceeds	7,500
less cost	(2,500)
less indexation (0.852 x £2,500)	(2,130)
Chargeable Gain	2,870

but gain restricted to:

5/3 (£7,500 – £6,000) = £2,500

Land

Proceeds	100,000
less apportioned cost:	
£80,000 x £100,000 / £400,000	(20,000)
less indexation:	
1.327 x £20,000	(26,540)
Chargeable gain	53,460

Office building

	£
Proceeds	200,000
less cost	(60,000)
Improvement expenditure	(40,000)
less:	
indexation on cost	
£60,000 x 0.847	(50,820)
indexation on improvement	
£40,000 x 0.625	(25,000)
Chargeable gain	24,180

Shoe cleaning machines

The shoe cleaning machines are sold at a loss, and are therefore dealt with entirely through the Plant and Machinery capital allowances computation.

Shares

Proceeds	15,000
less cost	(6,000)
less indexation (0.847 x £6,000)	(5,082)
Chargeable Gain	3,918

calculation of chargeable gain for taxable total profits computation

We can now bring the chargeable gains together, and deduct the capital loss brought forward.

	£
Antique dresser	2,500
Land	53,460
Office building	24,180
Shares	3,918
	84,058
Less capital loss brought forward	(20,000)
Chargeable gain to be used in taxable total profits computation	64,058

MATCHING RULES FOR SHARES

In the Case Study on the previous pages, shares are shown as chargeable assets, and the computation for the acquisition and subsequent disposal of a block of shares is the same as for other assets.

A complication can arise when various quantities of the same type of share in the same company are bought over a period of time and then sold. The problem faced is similar to that in any inventory valuation situation – how to determine which of the shares that were bought are deemed to be the ones that were sold.

The problem is solved in this situation by the application of strict **matching rules**, in other words, matching up the shares that have been sold with the shares originally held.

When shares are sold the **matching process** is carried out by working through, in order, the following categories of acquisition, missing out any that do not apply, until all the shares sold have been matched. A separate chargeable gains computation is then used for each separate match.

■ firstly, any shares bought on the **same day** that the disposal occurs are matched with that disposal

■ secondly, any shares bought in the **nine days before the disposal** are matched with those disposed of

■ finally, any remaining shares not yet matched are deemed to have come from the **'FA 1985 pool'** of shares. This is a device for merging and indexing shares. ('FA 1985' stands for the 'Finance Act 1985' which established this procedure, explained on the next page)

The matching process is a little complicated, but forms a possible examination task. The most likely questions will involve shares matched to the FA 1985 pool because there are no very recent acquisitions.

Note that these matching rules for companies are different from the ones that relate to individuals that you may have studied and which are covered in Chapter 8 of this book.

Remember that this matching process only applies where there have been several purchases of the same type of shares in the same company. It does not apply to a mixture of different companies' shares, nor is it needed where a shareholding is bought and sold intact.

using the 'FA 1985 pool'

This device was introduced in the 1985 Finance Act, and merges (or 'pools') shares in the same company and of the same type together, and applies indexation allowances at the same time. As explained on the last page, it forms the last of the matching rules, and is used to calculate the cost of shares acquired earlier than nine days before disposal.

The pooling process is similar to the calculation of weighted average inventory valuations (as you have probably studied in Costing), but with the additional complication of indexation allowance.

The 'pool' needs to record accurate data:

- the number of shares in each transaction
- actual costs
- indexed costs

These form the three main columns of the pool working.

The pool commences with the first shares bought. The cost of these is then indexed up to the time when other shares are bought (or sold). These are added in, and the cumulative indexed cost is then re-indexed up to the date of the next share purchase or sale (or December 2017 if this is earlier). This process is repeated as often as necessary, with the last indexation occurring up to the disposal date of the shares for which we are working out the gain (or December 2017). The indexed balance in the pool is then used to calculate the cost of shares from the pool that are sold, by apportionment based on the number of shares.

We will now demonstrate how this works, using a numerical example.

example: using the FA 1985 pool

On 1/1/2019 Jay Limited sold 10,000 ordinary shares in WyeCo Ltd for £15 each, from its shareholding of 25,000. The shareholding had been built up as follows:

1/1/1988 bought 17,000 shares for £5.00 each
1/1/1993 bought 8,000 shares for £7.00 each

The relevant indexation factors are:

| January 1988 to January 1993 | 0.335 |
| January 1993 to December 2017 | 1.017 |

Since there are no acquisitions on the day of disposal, nor the nine days before that, the whole of the disposal of 10,000 shares will be matched with the pool. The pool will be built up as follows, with the disposal deducted as the latest transaction:

	Number	Cost	Indexed cost
		£	£
1/1/1988 Purchase	17,000	85,000	85,000
Indexation to Jan 1993:			
£85,000 x 0.335			28,475
			113,475
1/1/1993 Purchase	8,000	56,000	56,000
			169,475
Indexation to December 2017:			
£169,475 x 1.017			172,356
Pool Totals:	25,000	141,000	341,831
Less Disposal	(10,000)	(56,400)	(136,732)
Pool Balance after disposal	15,000	84,600	205,099

You should examine these workings carefully, and note the following:

- Indexation is applied to consecutive periods based on transaction dates or December 2017. Here the periods were:
  - January 1988 to January 1993
  - January 1993 to December 2017

- Purchases at cost are added to the cumulative indexed cost figure, and the combined amount is then re-indexed to the date of the next transaction.

- The cost figures for the disposal are a proportional amount of the pool costs before disposal, based on the number of shares.

  (eg £341,831 x 10,000 / 25,000 = £136,732)

The computation for the disposal will now be as follows:

	£
Proceeds (10,000 x £15)	150,000
less cost	(56,400)
less indexation (£136,732 – £56,400)	(80,332)
Chargeable Gain	13,268

The cost and indexation figures are shown here separately, but would total the indexed cost amount shown in the pool workings (£56,400 + £80,332 = £136,732). This is shown this way in case the indexation needs to be restricted to avoid creating a loss.

If at some future date there was another disposal of shares from the pool then the pool balances remaining would be used to determine the cost of the shares in the further disposal.

BONUS AND RIGHTS ISSUES

dealing with bonus shares

Bonus shares are additional shares given free to shareholders, based on their current shareholding. This is sometimes called a 'scrip issue' and this process may be carried out as part of a capital restructuring of a company.

For chargeable gains purposes, the bonus shares are treated as if they were acquired at the same time as the original shares that generated the issue. For example a company that owned 1,000 shares that were bought in January 2001 would be entitled to a further 200 shares if there were a bonus issue of 'one for five' shares. The total of 1,200 shares would be treated as bought in January 2001 for the amount paid for the 1,000 shares.

Bonus shares are added to the pool when they are received. Since no payment is made, there is no adjustment to the cost or indexed cost figures. The bonus share transaction date is not relevant for indexation purposes.

dealing with rights issues

A rights issue is when additional shares are sold to existing shareholders, usually at a special discounted price. For matching purposes, the shares that are bought in this way are treated as if they were bought with the original shares. However, any indexation that applies to rights issue shares will only apply from the date that they were paid for. Rights issue shares will join the pool and be treated like any other share purchase. Their cost will be added into the pool, and the date they were bought (if before December 2017) will be treated as a date to index to and from as usual.

Dealing with share transactions is one of the most complicated areas of study in this learning area, yet it is a likely assessment task. We will therefore use a further Case Study to consolidate understanding.

**Case
Study**

CHER THYME LIMITED:
MATCHING AND POOLING SHARES

Cher Thyme Limited has acquired the following quoted ordinary shares in AbCo Plc:

1/5/1985	1,000 shares at £4.00 each	£4,000
1/1/1990	Bonus issue of 1 for 4	
1/1/1992	1,750 shares at £4.20 each	£7,350
1/1/1995	Rights issue of 1 for 2 at £4.10 each	
1/12/2001	1,800 shares at £5.10 each	£9,180

On 8/12/2001 the company sold 1,000 of its shareholding of AbCo Plc

On 15/3/2019 the company sold a further 2,500 ordinary shares in AbCo Plc for £10.00 each.

required

1   Identify which shares would have already been matched against the disposal that took place on 8/12/2001.

2   State how the disposal of shares on 15/3/2019 will be matched against the acquisitions.

3   Calculate the total gain arising from the sale of shares that took place on 15/3/2019.

Indexation factors have already been calculated, and are as follows:

May 1985 - Jan 1992	0.424
Jan 1992 - Jan 1995	0.077
Jan 1995 - Dec 2001	0.188
Dec 2001 - December 2017	0.604

solution

1   The disposal of 1,000 shares on 8/12/2001 would have been matched with 1,000 of the 1,800 shares that were bought on 1/12/2001 for £5.10 each. This leaves 800 of that purchase to join the pool at that time.

2   Matching of the 15/3/2019 disposal of 2,500 shares will be against the pool, since there are no acquisitions on the same day, or any in the previous nine days.

3   To carry out the computation we must first build up the FA 1985 pool:

	Number	Cost	Indexed cost
		£	£
1/5/1985 Purchase	1,000	4,000	4,000
1/1/1990 Bonus Issue	250		
Indexation May 1985 to Jan 1992:			
£4,000 x 0.424			1,696
	1,250	–	5,696
1/1/1992 Purchase	1,750	7,350	7,350
	3,000	11,350	13,046
Indexation Jan 1992 to Jan 1995			
£13,046 x 0.077			1,005
1/1/1995 Rights issue 1 for 2	1,500	6,150	6,150
	4,500	17,500	20,201
Indexation Jan 1995 to Dec 2001:			
£20,201 x 0.188			3,798
1/12/2001 Purchase (Balance)	800	4,080	4,080
	5,300	21,580	28,079
Indexation Dec 2001 to Dec 2017:			
£28,079 x 0.604			16,960
Pool Totals	5,300	21,580	45,039
Less Disposal	(2,500)	(10,179)	(21,245)
Pool Balance after disposal	2,800	11,401	23,794

	£
Proceeds (2,500 x £10)	25,000
Less cost	(10,179)
Less indexation (£21,245 – £10,179)	(11,066)
Chargeable Gain	3,755

ROLLOVER RELIEF

Rollover relief applies when one business asset is sold, and another is bought. It is a deferral relief, which means that it postpones the impact of a chargeable gain. Since a gain can be deferred more than once, provided the rules don't change in the future, gains can sometimes be postponed almost indefinitely.

Where one business asset is replaced with another, then the gain of the first may be rolled over (deferred) into the second, so that any eventual gain on the replacement asset would include the gain deferred from the first asset.

For example, suppose a qualifying asset, such as a warehouse, is sold for £200,000, incurring a gain of £50,000. Another qualifying asset is then bought for £220,000, and the gain on the first asset is rolled over into the second, which means no tax is payable on the gain at this time.

If the second asset is sold some time later, and incurs a 'normal' chargeable gain of £100,000, the deferred gain from the first asset will increase the total chargeable gain to £150,000.

Full deferral can only occur when all the proceeds of the first asset are invested in the replacement asset(s). Any part of the proceeds that are not reinvested in the second asset will form a chargeable gain immediately.

The replacement asset must be acquired between one year before and three years after the sale of the first asset.

Both assets must be in the categories listed below, but do not have to be like-for-like replacements for each other, nor even in the same category.

This is an abbreviated list based on the type of assets involved:

- land & buildings
- immovable plant & machinery
- ships, aircraft & hovercraft

A company could, for example, sell an aircraft, and invest the proceeds in an office building and roll over the gain.

A possible assessment task involves rollover relief relating to land and buildings. You may be expected to recognise that rollover relief would benefit a company in a given situation, and calculate the position accordingly.

Companies can choose whether or not to use rollover relief.

The example on the next page illustrates how the system works.

example: rollover relief

Rollo and Company Limited purchased an office building in January 1992 for £300,000. The company sold the building in January 2019 for £800,000. A shop had been purchased for £950,000 in August 2018.

The indexation factor from January 1992 to December 2017 is 1.051.

The chargeable gain on the office building would be calculated as follows (initially ignoring any rollover relief).

	£
Proceeds	800,000
less cost	(300,000)
less indexation	
1.051 x £300,000	(315,300)
Chargeable Gain	184,700

Using rollover relief, all of this gain of £184,700 can be deferred, because all of the proceeds were invested in the shop – the shop was bought for more than £800,000. This means that there is no gain on the office building chargeable in the current CAP.

The deferral works by deducting the deferred gain of £184,700 from the purchase cost of the shop in the chargeable gains computation when the shop is ultimately disposed of.

This would make the revised 'cost' figure (£950,000 – £184,700) = £765,300. Any gain at disposal of the shop would therefore consequently be greater than if rollover relief had not been used.

If the shop had been purchased for less than £800,000, not all of the gain on the office building could have been deferred. For example, if the shop had been bought for £700,000 only £84,700 of the gain could be deferred and a £100,000 gain would be chargeable immediately.

Chapter Summary

- Chargeable gains for companies are part of the taxable total profits (TTP). Such gains arise when chargeable assets are disposed of during the chargeable accounting period (CAP). A disposal usually takes the form of the sale of the asset. All assets are chargeable unless they are exempt. Exempt assets include cars, government securities (gilts), and certain chattels.

- Each disposal uses a separate computation that compares the proceeds or market value with the original cost of the asset. Indexation allowance is also deductible based on inflation from the time of acquisition up to the earlier of the date of disposal and December 2017. Losses are set off against gains before bringing the net figure into the taxable total profits computation. Where the net result is a capital loss, the amount is carried forward to set against chargeable gains arising in the next CAP. Where capital allowances have been claimed on an asset that is disposed of, capital losses cannot arise.

- The cost of a part disposal is calculated by apportioning the cost of the whole asset. This is carried out by using the proceeds of the part disposed of as a proportion of the value of the whole asset at the time of disposal.

- Improvement expenditure that is reflected in the asset when disposed of is an allowable cost. It also attracts indexation allowance from the date of expenditure up to the date of disposal or December 2017.

- Chattels that are acquired and sold for under £6,000 are exempt. Where they are sold at a gain for over £6,000 the gain is restricted to 5/3 of the proceeds minus £6,000. Where sold at a loss for under £6,000, the loss is restricted by substituting £6,000 for the actual proceeds in the computation.

- When shares of the same type in the same company are bought and sold at different times matching rules are used to identify the shares disposed of. Firstly shares bought on the day of disposal are matched. Secondly those bought in the nine days before disposal are matched. Thirdly acquisitions are pooled (including indexation) and matched. This is known as the FA 1985 (Finance Act 1985) pool.

- Bonus and rights issues are treated as acquired at the time of the shares that they are derived from for matching purposes. They can both appear as part of the FA 1985 pool.

- Rollover relief relates to certain categories of assets. It can defer a chargeable gain where the company reinvests all or part of the proceeds of disposal in further assets. The full deferral of a gain can only occur when all of the proceeds are reinvested.

Key Terms		
	chargeable gains	these can arise when companies dispose of chargeable assets. Chargeable Gains form part of the taxable total profits (TTP)
	capital loss	this is effectively a negative chargeable gain. It results when the allowable costs of an asset exceed the sale proceeds (or market value). Indexation cannot be used to increase a loss. A capital loss is used by setting it against a gain in the same CAP, or if this is not possible, by carrying it forward to set against chargeable gains in the next available CAP
	disposal	a disposal for Capital Gains Tax purposes is the sale, gift, loss or destruction of an asset
	chargeable asset	this term is used to describe assets, the disposal of which can result in a chargeable gain or capital loss. All assets are chargeable unless they are exempt
	exempt asset	this is an asset that is not a chargeable asset. Exempt assets include cars, Gilts, and some chattels
	chattel	a tangible, moveable asset
	net proceeds	the proceeds from the sale of an asset, less any incidental costs of selling the asset
	unindexed gain	the net proceeds (or market value in some situations) less the original cost of the asset and any other allowable costs incurred. It is the subtotal of the gain computation before indexation allowance is deducted
	indexation allowance	an amount that is deductible in the gain computation that compensates for the effect of inflation on the asset between acquisition and disposal (limited to December 2017). It uses the Retail Price Index to calculate a factor that is multiplied by the historical cost of the asset

part disposal   this occurs when part of an asset is disposed of, but the remainder is retained

improvement expenditure

this term relates to capital expenditure that enhances an asset. If the enhancement is still evident at disposal then the improvement expenditure is an allowable cost

matching rules for shares

these rules determine which acquisitions of shares are identified with each disposal

bonus shares   shares issued at no cost to shareholders, the number of shares being based on their current shareholding

rights issue   shares issued by a company to its existing shareholders at a special price

rollover relief   a deferral relief available to businesses (including companies). It has the effect of postponing a chargeable gain when the proceeds of disposal have been reinvested in further assets

Activities

4.1 Analyse the following list of assets into those that are chargeable assets and those that are exempt.

		Chargeable	Exempt
(a)	Antique painting sold for £10,000		
(b)	An office block		
(c)	Shares in CIC plc		
(d)	An industrial building		
(e)	A portable machine, sold at a profit for under £6,000		
(f)	A plot of land		
(g)	A car		
(h)	Government securities		
(i)	Trading stock		

4.2 April Limited bought an office block in May 1995 for £600,000 and sold it in January 2019 for £1,300,000. The company had no other disposals in the CAP y/e 31/12/2019. April Limited had a capital loss brought forward from the previous CAP of £15,000.

The indexation factor from May 1995 to December 2017 is 0.859.

Calculate the chargeable gain that will form part of the taxable total profits for April Limited for the CAP y/e 31/12/2019.

4.3 Cee Limited bought 200 ordinary shares in Zedco plc in August 1998 for £50,000 and sold them in March 2019 for £145,000. It had no other disposals in the CAP y/e 31/12/2019.

Cee Limited had a capital loss brought forward from the previous CAP of £25,000.

The indexation factor from August 1998 to December 2017 is 0.729.

Calculate the chargeable gain that will form part of the taxable total profits for Cee Limited for the CAP.

4.4   Aye Limited made the following disposals in March 2019. These were its only disposals during CAP y/e 31/12/2019.

It sold a factory for £500,000 that had been used since it was bought new for £300,000 in September 1986.

It sold part of a piece of land for £30,000 that it had bought in January 1992. The whole piece of land had cost £50,000 at that time. At the time of the sale the remaining land was valued at £120,000.

Required:

Calculate the total chargeable gains arising from the two disposals.

The relevant indexation factors are:

September 1986 to December 2017   1.829

January 1992 to December 2017   1.051

4.5   Dee Limited made the following disposals in its CAP y/e 31/12/2019.

It sold 10,000 of its ordinary shares in Zydeco Ltd on 30/03/2019 for £60,000 in total. The shareholding in this company had been built up as follows:

1/1/1992   Bought 3,000 shares for £3.00 each

1/1/1995   Bought 12,000 shares for £3.50 each

1/1/1999   Received bonus shares on the basis of 1 for 5

1/1/2000   Sold 5,000 shares

It sold a portable antique machine to a local museum for £6,900 on 31/3/2019. The machine had been bought for £3,000 in January 2000, and capital allowances had been claimed on it since through the main pool.

Required:

- Calculate any chargeable gain made on:
  - the disposal of shares in March 2019, and
  - the disposal of the machine in March 2019
- State how the disposal of the machine will be dealt with for capital allowances.

The relevant indexation factors are:

January 1992 to January 1995   0.077

January 1995 to January 2000   0.141

January 2000 to December 2017   0.669

4.6 For each statement, tick the appropriate box.

	Chargeable asset	Exempt asset
Vintage car	☐	☐
Antique vase	☐	☐
Greyhound	☐	☐

4.7 Trevor Ltd sold a valuable picture for £12,000 in April 2019. This was bought for £4,000 in August 2000. The indexation factor from August 2000 to December 2017 was 0.631.

Complete the following computation:

£

Proceeds	☐
Cost	☐
Indexation allowance	☐
Gain	☐
Chattel restriction on gain	☐

State whether the chattel restriction will have any effect on the original gain.

4.8 Practice Ltd bought 5,000 shares in Luncheon Ltd for £15,500 in October 2001. A rights issue of 1 for 50 shares was bought in July 2003 for £2 per share. In April 2019, Practice Ltd sold all the shares for £9 per share.

Indexation factors were: October 2001 to July 2003: 0.114; July 2003 to December 2017: 0.534

What is the gain made on these shares?

	No. Shares	Cost £	Indexed cost £

Proceeds	£
Indexed Cost	£
Gain	£

5 Corporation tax – calculating the tax

this chapter covers...

In this chapter we bring together all the results of our studies of Corporation Tax in chapters 1 to 4, and learn how to calculate the Corporation Tax itself. To do this we start by reviewing the components of the computation, including an examination of deductions for gift aid.

We then go on to study how Corporation Tax is calculated.

We will then review the process and options for offsetting various losses, and consider the issues that can affect the choice of optimum loss set off. We will also review the division of profits from all sources when dealing with an accounting period of over 12 months.

The next section is concerned with completing the CT600 tax return for companies.

The chapter is completed with sections on interest and penalties and record keeping.

THE CORPORATION TAX COMPUTATION

structure of the computation

As discussed in earlier chapters, the Corporation Tax computation starts with a summary of profits from various sources that are chargeable to Corporation Tax. The computation then goes on to calculate the amount of Corporation Tax that is payable.

A separate computation will need to be carried out for each Chargeable Accounting Period (CAP), which will result in a tax liability for the period. A separate CT600 return form will also need to be completed for each CAP. A simple version of this computation is repeated here:

	Trading Income	X
+	Profits from Investments	X
+	Chargeable Gains	X
=	Taxable Total Profits	X
	Corporation Tax on taxable total profits	X

Note that 'taxable total profits' were previously known as 'profits chargeable to Corporation Tax' (PCTCT).

revision – what we have covered so far

In Chapters 2 and 3 we examined in detail how the 'Trading Income' figure is calculated, including the calculation of capital allowances for plant & machinery. In Chapter 4 we saw how chargeable gains are calculated on individual chargeable disposals and combined ready for inclusion in the Corporation Tax computation.

where we go from here

In this chapter we will be looking at the final stage of the Corporation Tax computation – bringing all the income together and working out the Corporation Tax liability. We will then see how the tax return is completed and the dates for payment. Finally we will look briefly at the sort of records that should be kept to show how the figures in the computation have been arrived at.

You may recall the summary diagram from Chapter 2, reproduced at the top of the next page. We have now looked in detail at the elements in the first three of the boxes along the top of the diagram, and will now follow the rest of the procedures over the next few pages.

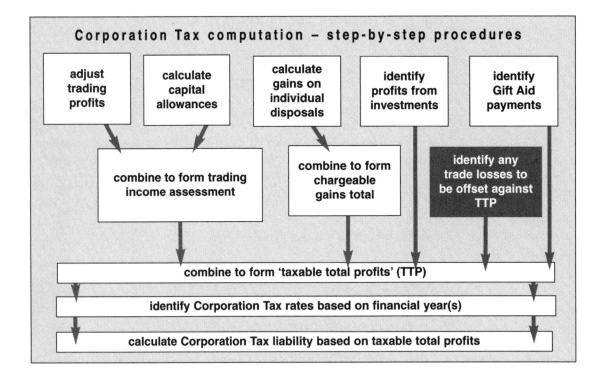

profits from investments

You will see from the above diagram that profits from investments need to be identified so that they can be incorporated into the computation. These profits could include:

- **interest received from non-trade investments**

    The gross amount of any interest receivable (ie on an **accruals basis**) during the CAP forms an investment income assessment that is brought into the main computation. Examples of the sources of interest include bank and building society deposits, debentures and Government securities ('gilts'). You can assume that any such interest in an examination task is non-trade, and should therefore be treated in this way.

- **profits from renting out property**

    The tax-adjusted profits from rental income are assessed as 'property income' on an accruals basis. You would not be expected to carry out adjustments to such figures, and would just need to incorporate the profit figure into the main computation. A little later in this chapter we will see how to deal with any losses that may arise from this type of income.

You should note that **dividends received** from other UK companies are **not** brought into the Corporation Tax computation, and are not taxed. This is because the profits from which they derive have already been taxed through the other company's computation.

gift-aid payments ('qualifying charitable donations')

Companies are entitled to make gifts to charities under the gift-aid scheme, and obtain tax relief on their payments. This operates simply by allowing the company to deduct the amount of the payment from the total profits in the Corporation Tax computation. This is known as a 'charge', and carried out as the final stage in the calculation of the taxable total profits. The **payment date determines which CAP** the gift-aid payment falls into, for example if the payment was made during a 'long' accounting period. Unlike the gift-aid scheme for individuals (that you may have come across in 'personal tax'), the company makes the payment to the charity as a gross amount, with no adjustment for tax. As we saw in Chapter 2, the company cannot use a gift-aid payment as an allowable deduction in the calculation of Trading Income profits, since this would form a duplication of tax relief.

If there are insufficient total profits to set a gift-aid payment against in the final calculation of taxable total profits, then the tax relief on the balance of the payment is lost, since it cannot be carried forward. Where trading losses are set against the taxable total profits, (as outlined in Chapter 2) this is carried out in priority to gift-aid payments, so again there is a possibility of losing the tax relief on the gift-aid payment.

We will now use a Case Study to demonstrate how the various elements are combined into a Corporation Tax computation, before looking at the tax calculation itself.

Case Study

THE BASIC COMPANY LIMITED: CALCULATING THE TTP

The Basic Company Limited has produced accounts for the year ended 31/3/2020. The accounts have been adjusted for tax purposes, and the following figures have been established:

	£
Adjusted Trading Profit (before capital allowances)	1,000,000
Capital Allowances – Plant & Machinery	163,000
Payment to Charity under Gift-Aid scheme	28,000

	£
Non-Trade Interest Receivable	55,000
Dividends Received from UK Company	90,000
Chargeable Gains	34,000
Rental Income	48,000

required

Using a Corporation Tax Computation, calculate the taxable total profits for the CAP y/e 31/3/2020.

solution

In order to complete the computation, the trading income assessment must first be established:

	£
Adjusted Trading Profits	1,000,000
less Plant & Machinery capital allowances	(163,000)
Trading Income assessment	837,000

Building on the outline computation shown at the start of this chapter, we can now combine the figures that make up the taxable total profits.

Corporation Tax Computation

	£
Trading Income	837,000
Profits from Investments:	
Non-Trade Interest Receivable	55,000
Property Income	48,000
Chargeable Gains	34,000
	974,000
less Gift-Aid payments	(28,000)
Taxable total profits	946,000

Note the structure of the computation, since you will need to use this without further guidance. Note also that the dividends received of £90,000 are left out of the calculation entirely.

In the next section we will see how the tax itself is calculated.

CALCULATING THE CORPORATION TAX LIABILITY

At the current time the calculation of Corporation Tax liability is straightforward.

The rate of Corporation Tax that applies to the Financial Years 2017, 2018 and 2019 is 19%. This rate is applied to the taxable total profits (TTP), and the result is the Corporation tax liability.

This applies to any CAP, regardless of whether it is for 12 months or a shorter period.

For example, using the data from the Basic Company Limited Case Study on pages 5.5 and 5.6, the Corporation Tax would be simply:

Taxable total profits £946,000 x 19% = Corporation tax £179,740

If the CAP had fallen into two financial years that had different rates of Corporation Tax the taxable total profits would need to be time-apportioned into the financial years and then the rates applied to each part. The total Corporation Tax for the CAP would then be these two tax amounts added together.

DEALING WITH A VARIETY OF LOSSES

Over the last few chapters we have seen how different sorts of losses can be relieved against profits.

- in Chapter 2 we saw that recent trading losses can be:
  - carried forward against future taxable total profits before Gift Aid payments, or
  - set against the current period taxable total profits before Gift Aid payments, and if this has been done,
  - then set against the taxable total profits before Gift Aid payments of the previous twelve months

- in Chapter 4 we saw that capital losses on a disposal are first set against chargeable gains arising in the same CAP, and then carried forward against chargeable gains in the future

- rental losses can be set against the current period taxable total profits and any amount not used carried forward and set against future taxable total profits before Gift Aid payments

We must therefore be careful if presented with a variety of losses to deal with each one correctly. Although the above rules are fairly straightforward, they must be learnt, since it would be easy to get confused.

We will use a Case Study now to illustrate how to deal with a variety of losses.

<table>
<tr><td>**Case Study**</td><td></td></tr>
</table>

LOSER PLC:
DEALING WITH DIFFERENT LOSSES

Loser plc has the following adjusted results for the CAPs y/e 31/3/2019, and y/e 31/3/2020.

	CAP y/e 31/3/2019	CAP y/e 31/3/2020
	£	£
Trading Profit / (Loss)	(300,000)	500,000
Rental Profit / (Loss)	(15,000)	45,000
Non-Trade Interest Receivable	425,000	210,000
Chargeable Gains / (Capital Loss)	(50,000)	120,000

The company has not received dividends from other UK companies. The company did not make any Gift Aid payments.

required

1 Explain how the rental losses and capital losses must be offset, and describe the alternative ways in which the trading loss could be offset.

2 Calculate the Corporation Tax liability for the CAPs y/e 31/3/2019 and y/e 31/3/2020, based on each alternative.

3 Recommend how the trading loss should be offset, and explain your reasoning.

solution

1 The rental loss of £15,000 is set against the taxable total profits for the year ended 31/3/2019, giving a net figure of £410,000. The capital loss must be carried forward to the next CAP, to reduce the Chargeable Gains amount. This will give a chargeable gains assessment of £120,000 – £50,000 = £70,000 in the CAP to 31/3/2020.

The trading loss could either be:

(a) set against the taxable total profits of the CAP y/e 31/3/2019; since the only profits in that period are from interest receivable less the rental loss, the trade loss would reduce the taxable total profits of the CAP to £410,000 – £300,000 = £110,000. In this situation there is no opportunity to carry the loss back to the year before, since there is sufficient taxable total profits in the y/e 31/3/2019 to utilise all the loss

(b) carried forward and set against the taxable total profits of the CAP y/e 31/3/2020 (or a later CAP); this would reduce the taxable total profits amount for that period to £825,000 – £300,000 = £525,000

2 The tax computations are as follows:

Option (a)

	CAP y/e 31/3/2019	CAP y/e 31/3/2020
	£	£
Trading Income	0	500,000
Property Income	0	45,000
Interest Receivable	425,000	210,000
Chargeable Gains	0	70,000
Less Loss on Property Income	(15,000)	–
Less Trading Loss of the year	(300,000)	–
Taxable total profits	110,000	825,000
Corporation Tax	[(1)] 20,900	[(2)] 156,750

Corporation Tax Workings:

	£
(1) Taxed at main rate:	
£110,000 x 19% =	20,900
(2) Taxed at main rate:	
£825,000 x 19% =	156,750

Option (b)

	CAP y/e 31/3/2019	CAP y/e 31/3/2020
	£	£
Trading Income	0	500,000
Property Income	0	45,000
Interest Receivable	425,000	210,000
Chargeable Gains	0	70,000
Less Loss on Property Income	(15,000)	–
Less trading loss bf	–	(300,000)
Taxable total profits	410,000	525,000
Corporation Tax	[(1)] 77,900	[(2)] 99,750

Corporation Tax Workings:

	£
(1) Taxed at main rate:	
£410,000 x 19% =	77,900
(2) Taxed at main rate:	
£525,000 x 19% =	99,750

3   Note that in this situation the total amount of Corporation Tax is the same for both options:

Option (a)   £20,900 + £156,750   = £177,650

Option (b)   £77,900 + £99,750   = £177,650

This is because the same Corporation Tax rate applies to both CAPs and all losses are set off within these two periods.

The choice of option should therefore be based on cash flow. Option (a) delays payment of Corporation Tax compared with option (b), and is therefore the recommended option.

SPLITTING ALL PROFITS FOR LONG ACCOUNTING PERIODS

In Chapter 2 we learned how to deal with the split of trading profits when a long period of account needs to be divided into two chargeable accounting periods. Now that we have also looked at the other components of taxable total profits, it is a good time to review this technique and see how other profits are split.

trading profits (before deducting capital allowances)

As discussed earlier, the trading profits for the whole long period are adjusted, and the resulting adjusted trading profit is then time apportioned.

capital allowances

Separate capital allowance computations are carried out for each CAP. The capital allowances are then deducted from the time-apportioned trading profits that were described above.

interest from non-trade investments

This income is calculated on an accruals basis, and is split based on how much relates to each period (the amount arising).

profits from renting out property

The profits from renting out property are also calculated on an accruals basis. These are split based on how much relates to each period (the amount arising).

chargeable gains

Chargeable gains are allocated to each period based on when each disposal takes place.

taxable total profits

The taxable total profits for each CAP is calculated by adding together the above elements. Any gift aid payments are deducted from the relevant figure based on the date of payment.

WHEN TO PAY CORPORATION TAX

As we noted in Chapter 1, Corporation Tax is payable nine months and one day after the end of the chargeable accounting period to which it relates, unless payments by instalment are necessary.

Whether instalment payments need to be made depend on the level of taxable profits. Only companies with profits over £1,500,000 for a twelve month CAP may need to pay by instalments (assuming no group companies).

If there are group companies then the limit of £1,500,000 is divided by the number of 'related 51% group companies' plus one (in other words including the company that we are working out the payments for).

A '51% subsidiary' is shorthand for a company where more than 50% of its ordinary share capital is beneficially owned (directly or indirectly) by another company.

The 51% group test provides these examples:

Company A is a related 51% group company of company B if:

■ A is a 51% subsidiary of B, or

■ B is a 51% subsidiary of A, or

■ A and B are both 51% subsidiaries of the same other company.

Even when a company's profits exceed the £1,500,000 limit (after adjustment if necessary under the 51% group test rules) it will **not** need to pay by instalments if **either:**

■ The current corporation tax liability is below an annual rate of £10,000, **or**

■ Provided its current profits are below £10 million, if in the **previous 12 months:**

   – it didn't exist, or didn't have a CAP, or

   – had a CAP that had either:

     • profits below the limit of £1,500,000 (or other limit), or

     • corporation tax below £10,000 per year

These rules effectively provide a brief exemption from paying by instalments when a company has seen a rapid rise in its profits.

payment by instalments

For 'large' companies that exceed the above limits, all of the company's estimated Corporation Tax liability must be paid in the following four instalments (25% in each instalment). The first instalment is due on day 14 of month seven within the CAP. The next three instalments follow at three monthly intervals. Any remaining balance of Corporation Tax (since the instalments were based on an estimate) will be payable at the normal due date, nine months and one day after the end of the CAP. Estimates should be revised each quarter if necessary.

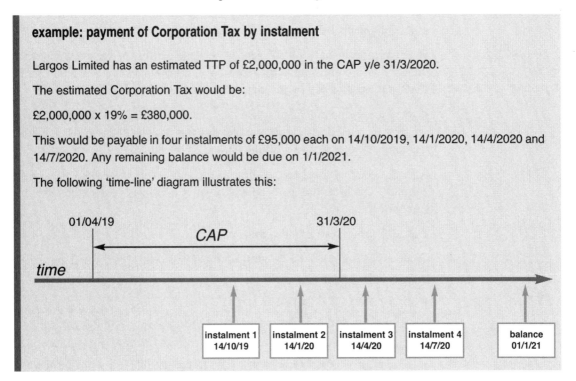

example: payment of Corporation Tax by instalment

Largos Limited has an estimated TTP of £2,000,000 in the CAP y/e 31/3/2020.

The estimated Corporation Tax would be:

£2,000,000 x 19% = £380,000.

This would be payable in four instalments of £95,000 each on 14/10/2019, 14/1/2020, 14/4/2020 and 14/7/2020. Any remaining balance would be due on 1/1/2021.

The following 'time-line' diagram illustrates this:

COMPLETION OF THE COMPANY TAX RETURN

The company tax return (the 'CT600') must be returned online by twelve months after the end of the company's accounting period from which the CAP was derived. This will be the same date as twelve months after the CAP, unless the accounting period is over twelve months long, and had to be divided into two CAPs.

The CT600 that we will be using is 'version 3'. The full eleven page form is shown in the appendix to this book. We will concentrate on pages 2 and 3 which are the most important for our studies, and relate to the majority of the tax calculation.

We will now look at the company tax calculation to see what is required, before using a Case Study to demonstrate how to complete the form.

the company tax calculation

These pages of the return are reproduced on page 5.14-5.15. It generally follows the same logic and order as a Corporation Tax computation, and is therefore relatively easy to fill in.

Notes on the completion of the main boxes in which you will need to make entries are set out below.

Page 2 Boxes

Box 145 Total turnover from trade. Enter the sales figure here.

Box 155 Trading profits
The trading income amount will be inserted here.

Box 160 Trading losses brought forward claimed against profits
This is only for trading losses that are brought forward from before April 2017 to be set against profits from the same trade.

Box 165 Net trading profits – box 155 minus box 160

Box 170 Bank, building society or other interest, and profits from non-trading loan relationships
This is for non-trade interest receivable.

Page 3 Boxes

Box 190 Income from a property business. This is for property income.

Box 210 Gross chargeable gains
The total of chargeable gains on disposals in the CAP.

Box 215 Allowable losses . . .
Insert here any capital losses from the current CAP or previous CAPs to be offset against the above gains.

Box 220 Net chargeable gains – box 210 minus box 215

Box 235 Profits before other deductions and reliefs – net sum of boxes 165 to 205 and 220

Note that where losses incurred from 1/4/2017 are set against taxable total profits (TTP) these are recorded in box 285 which is on page 4 of the form, which is not reproduced here.

About this return - continued

Accounts and computations

| 80 | I attach accounts and computations for the period to which this return relates | ☐ |

| 85 | I attach accounts and computations for a different period | ☐ |

| 90 | If you are not attaching the accounts and computations, say why not |

| |

Supplementary pages enclosed

| 95 | Loans and arrangements to participators by close companies – form CT600A | ☐ |

| 100 | Controlled foreign companies and foreign permanent establishment exemptions – form CT600B | ☐ |

| 105 | Group and consortium – form CT600C | ☐ |

| 110 | Insurance – form CT600D | ☐ |

| 115 | Charities and Community Amateur Sports Clubs (CASCs) – form CT600E | ☐ |

| 120 | Tonnage Tax – form CT600F | ☐ |

| 125 | Northern Ireland - form CT600G | ☐ |

| 130 | Cross-border Royalties – form CT600H | ☐ |

| 135 | Supplementary charge in respect of ring fence trades – form CT600I | ☐ |

| 140 | Disclosure of Tax Avoidance Schemes – form CT600J | ☐ |

| 141 | Restitution Tax – form CT600K | ☐ |

Tax calculation

Turnover

| 145 | Total turnover from trade | £ ⬚ · 0 0 |

| 150 | Banks, building societies, insurance companies and other financial concerns –
put an 'X' in this box if you do not have a recognised turnover and have not made an entry in box 145 | ☐ |

Income

| 155 | Trading profits | £ ⬚ · 0 0 |

| 160 | Trading losses brought forward set against trading profits | £ ⬚ · 0 0 |

| 165 | Net trading profits – box 155 minus box 160 | £ ⬚ · 0 0 |

| 170 | Bank, building society or other interest, and profits
from non-trading loan relationships | £ ⬚ · 0 0 |

| 172 | Put an 'X' in box 172 if the figure in box 170 is net of
carrying back a deficit from a later accounting period | ☐ |

Income - continued

175 Annual payments not otherwise charged to Corporation Tax and from which Income Tax has not been deducted £ ⬚ · 0 0

180 Non-exempt dividends or distributions from non–UK resident companies £ ⬚ · 0 0

185 Income from which Income Tax has been deducted £ ⬚ · 0 0

190 Income from a property business £ ⬚ · 0 0

195 Non-trading gains on intangible fixed assets £ ⬚ · 0 0

200 Tonnage Tax profits £ ⬚ · 0 0

205 Income not falling under any other heading £ ⬚ · 0 0

Chargeable gains

210 Gross chargeable gains £ ⬚ · 0 0

215 Allowable losses including losses brought forward £ ⬚ · 0 0

220 Net chargeable gains - box 210 minus box 215 £ ⬚ · 0 0

Profits before deductions and reliefs

225 Losses brought forward against certain investment income £ ⬚ · 0 0

230 Non-trade deficits on loan relationships (including interest) and derivative contracts (financial instruments) brought forward set against non-trading profits £ ⬚ · 0 0

235 Profits before other deductions and reliefs – net sum of boxes 165 to 205 and 220 minus sum of boxes 225 and 230 £ ⬚ · 0 0

Deductions and reliefs

240 Losses on unquoted shares £ ⬚ · 0 0

245 Management expenses £ ⬚ · 0 0

250 UK property business losses for this or previous accounting period £ ⬚ · 0 0

255 Capital allowances for the purposes of management of the business £ ⬚ · 0 0

260 Non-trade deficits for this accounting period from loan relationships and derivative contracts (financial instruments) £ ⬚ · 0 0

We will now use a Case Study to show how the main boxes on pages 2 and 3 are completed.

COMPLETION PLC:
FILLING IN THE CT600

Completion plc has the following Corporation Tax computation for the year ended 31 December 2019. It has no group companies.

	£	£
Adjusted Trading Profits	600,000	
Assessable Trading Income		600,000
Property Income		120,000
Interest Receivable		110,000
Chargeable Gains	175,000	
Less capital loss brought forward	(35,000)	
		140,000
Taxable total profits		970,000
Corporation Tax:		
£970,000 x 19%		184,300

required
Complete, as far as information permits, pages 2 and 3 of the company tax return form CT600 for Completion plc for the CAP y/e 31/12/2019.

solution

The completed form is shown on the next page (the two pages have been condensed for reproduction in this book).

Tax calculation
Turnover

| 145 | Total turnover from trade | £ ⬚⬚⬚⬚⬚⬚⬚⬚⬚⬚⬚⬚⬚⬚⬚⬚⬚⬚⬚⬚⬚ · 0 0 |

| 150 | Banks, building societies, insurance companies and other financial concerns – put an 'X' in this box if you do not have a recognised turnover and have not made an entry in box 145 | ⬚ |

Income

| 155 | Trading profits | £ 6 0 0 0 0 0 · 0 0 |

| 160 | Trading losses brought forward set against trading profits | £ · 0 0 |

| 165 | Net trading profits – box 155 minus box 160 | £ 6 0 0 0 0 0 · 0 0 |

| 170 | Bank, building society or other interest, and profits from non-trading loan relationships | £ 1 1 0 0 0 0 · 0 0 |

| 172 | Put an 'X' in box 172 if the figure in box 170 is net of carrying back a deficit from a later accounting period | ⬚ |

| 175 | Annual payments not otherwise charged to Corporation Tax and from which Income Tax has not been deducted | £ · 0 0 |

| 180 | Non-exempt dividends or distributions from non–UK resident companies | £ · 0 0 |

| 185 | Income from which Income Tax has been deducted | £ · 0 0 |

| 190 | Income from a property business | £ 1 2 0 0 0 0 · 0 0 |

| 195 | Non-trading gains on intangible fixed assets | £ · 0 0 |

| 200 | Tonnage Tax profits | £ · 0 0 |

| 205 | Income not falling under any other heading | £ · 0 0 |

Chargeable gains

| 210 | Gross chargeable gains | £ 1 7 5 0 0 0 · 0 0 |

| 215 | Allowable losses including losses brought forward | £ 3 5 0 0 0 · 0 0 |

| 220 | Net chargeable gains – box 210 minus box 215 | £ 1 4 0 0 0 0 · 0 0 |

Profits before deductions and reliefs

| 225 | Losses brought forward against certain investment income | £ · 0 0 |

| 230 | Non-trade deficits on loan relationships (including interest) and derivative contracts (financial instruments) brought forward set against non-trading profits | £ · 0 0 |

| 235 | Profits before other deductions and reliefs – net sum of boxes 165 to 205 and 220 minus sum of boxes 225 and 230 | £ 9 7 0 0 0 0 · 0 0 |

INTEREST AND PENALTIES

interest

Where tax is paid after the due date (or a lower amount is paid than is due) interest is charged. This applies both to large companies that need to pay by instalments, and other companies that should pay nine months and one day after the end of the CAP. The interest rates are laid down by HM Revenue & Customs. The rates charged are currently 1.75% for underpaid quarterly instalments and 3.25% on late final payments.

If a company overpays its Corporation Tax (or pays early) interest is payable to the company (although the interest rates are generally lower than amounts charged on overdue tax – it is currently 0.5%). Interest that is paid to the Company is taxable, but interest payable is an allowable deduction against non-trading interest.

penalties for not telling HMRC your company is liable for Corporation Tax

HMRC must be made aware that the company is liable to pay tax (for example if the company has just started trading). This must be done within three months of the start of business activities. This is usually done on a 'new company details' form.

If HMRC are not informed, then a penalty can arise. The penalty will be based on a percentage of the 'potential lost revenue' which is the Corporation tax that would be due. The penalty ranges from 0% (if 'reasonable care was taken) to 100% (if the act was deliberate and concealed) of the potential lost revenue.

This is the same system that applies to errors in tax returns and is explained on the next page.

late return penalties

There are also penalties for failure to submit a Corporation Tax Return on time. These are divided into flat amount and percentage penalties:

■ the initial penalties are £100 for submitting up to three months late and £200 for submitting more than three months late. These can increase for repeated occurrences

■ in addition 10% of the Corporation Tax relating to the return period can be charged where the return is 6-12 months late, increasing to 20% for over 12 months

penalties system for errors in tax returns and documents

A company can amend a return that it has submitted up to 12 months after the filing date. A system for penalties applies for incorrect information stated in tax returns and documents. This is based on a percentage of the extra tax due, depending on the behaviour that gave rise to the error. If the error is:

- due to **lack of reasonable care**, the penalty will be between 0% and 30% of the extra tax due

- **deliberate**, the penalty will be between 20% and 70% of the extra tax due, and if

- **deliberate and concealed**, the penalty will be between 30% and 100% of the extra tax due

The percentage can be reduced if the taxpayer tells HMRC about the error(s), helps them work out the extra tax, and gives HMRC access to check the figures.

If the taxpayer made an error despite taking 'reasonable care' then no penalty will arise.

This system also applies to Income Tax.

failure to keep records

There can be a penalty for not keeping the required records for the correct length of time of up to £3,000 per chargeable accounting period for companies.

HMRC enquiries

HMRC may open an 'enquiry' into a company's tax return, either at random, or because they believe that income and / or expenses may be misstated. The company must be notified about an enquiry within 12 months of the submission of the tax return.

The enquiry can lead to requests for documents to be produced to HMRC. There is an initial penalty for failure to supply the requested documents of £300 plus £60 per day that the failure continues.

The company may amend their return within 12 months of the filing date (as noted earlier), but any change in the amount of tax due will not take effect until any enquiry is completed.

On completion of an enquiry, HMRC will issue a closure notice and make any necessary amendments to the tax due. The company has 30 days to appeal this decision.

Where there has been an enquiry into a business where there is complexity, avoidance or large amounts of tax at risk, a part of the enquiry can be closed while the rest remains open. This is done by the issue by HMRC of a 'Partial

Closure Notice' (PCN). This will provide greater certainty about the tax owed on individual discrete matters.

KEEPING RECORDS

general principles

Accounting records must be retained by a business, including a company, or its agent (for example an accountant) for at least six years after the end of the accounting period. This period is extended if an enquiry is taking place.

A business will normally archive appropriate accounting records automatically for six years to satisfy the requirements of a variety of statutes, including the Companies Acts and the Limitation Act (which allows legal action to be brought on a contract for up to six years after a breach of that contract). Documents such as invoices, for example, are evidence of contracts of sale.

These records will need to be made available for a number of interested parties – and particularly in the unfortunate event of an inspection or investigation being made:

■ auditors (when an audit is required)

■ HM Revenue & Customs for both Corporation taxes and VAT

■ Department of Work & Pensions

Typical records include:

■ ledger accounts and daybooks - manual or computerised

■ financial documents, eg invoices, credit notes, bank statements, cheque book stubs

■ payroll records

■ VAT records

records relating to tax computations

A company will need to keep for at least six years, as part of the general archiving process, a number of records which specifically relate to Corporation Tax matters. These include:

■ statements of profit or loss (income statements) and statements of financial position (balance sheets)

■ taxation working papers, including capital allowance computations

■ copies of tax returns

■ invoices relating to allowable expenses and the acquisition of non-current (fixed) assets

■ details of non-trade income

■ non-current asset schedules

time limits for assessments and claims

Where a company discovers an error in a previous year's tax return and wants to adjust the return (perhaps to claim a tax repayment) the time limit is four years from the end of the tax year.

The same four year limit applies to HMRC when they discover errors in returns (as discussed earlier), provided the company has taken reasonable care. If the errors are the result of careless behaviour by the company the time limit is six years, and if the behaviour was deliberate the time limit is twenty years.

Chapter Summary	■ The Corporation Tax computation for a chargeable accounting period (CAP) involves combining profits from various sources, and deducting any payments made to charity under the gift aid scheme.
	■ A single rate of Corporation Tax of 19% currently applies to the taxable total profits (TTP).
	■ Property income losses are initially set against the taxable total profits of the current period, with any remaining balance carried forward to be set against the first available taxable total profit. Capital losses can only be carried forward to offset against income of the same type. There are various options for dealing with trade losses.
	■ Corporation Tax is payable a maximum of nine months and one day after the end of the CAP. For 'large' companies, instalments may need to be paid, based on the estimated tax payable.
	■ The company tax return (CT600) is due to be submitted twelve months after the end of the accounting period.
	■ Appropriate records must be kept for at least six years from the end of the accounting period.

Key Terms

taxable total profits (TTP)

this is the figure used as the basis for calculation of Corporation Tax for a limited company. It includes trading income, profits from investments, and chargeable gains, and is charged after gift-aid payments have been deducted. It is calculated for each chargeable accounting period (CAP) within which the company operates

chargeable accounting period (CAP)

this is the period for which the TTP must be calculated. It is the same as the period for which the company produces financial accounts, unless that period is for more than twelve months. In that case the financial accounting period is divided into two CAPs

gift-aid

a system which allows payments that companies have made to charity to be deducted in the final calculation of taxable total profits. This provides the company with tax relief on the payment and is known as a 'charge'

CT600

the self-assessment Corporation Tax return for limited companies. One form must be completed for each CAP

Activities

5.1 The Management Company Limited has produced accounts for the year ended 31/3/20. The accounts have been adjusted for tax purposes, and the following figures have been established.

	£
Adjusted Trading Profit (before capital allowances)	1,120,000
Capital Allowances – Plant & Machinery	63,000
Payment to Charity under Gift-Aid scheme	45,000
Non-Trade Interest Receivable	60,000
Dividends Received from UK Company	90,000
Chargeable Gains	48,000
Rental Income	23,000

Required:

Using a Corporation Tax Computation, calculate the taxable total profits for the CAP, and the Corporation Tax payable.

Carry out all calculations to the nearest £.

5.2 The Resource Company Limited has produced accounts for the year ended 31/3/20. The accounts have been adjusted for tax purposes, and the following figures have been established.

	£
Adjusted Trading Profit (before capital allowances)	1,420,000
Capital Allowances – Plant & Machinery	205,000
Payment to Charity under Gift-Aid scheme	8,000
Non-Trade Interest Receivable	12,000
Dividends Received from UK Company	27,000
Chargeable Gains	88,000
Capital Loss brought forward from previous year	18,000
Rental Income	92,000

Required:

Using a Corporation Tax Computation, calculate the taxable total profits for the CAP, and the Corporation Tax payable.

Carry out all calculations to the nearest £.

5.3   The Quick Company Limited has the following tax-adjusted results for the CAP y/e 31/12/19.

	£
Trading Loss	120,000
Chargeable Gains	90,000
Non-trade Interest Receivable	40,000
Rental Income	35,000
Gift-Aid Payment	10,000

The company also has capital losses brought forward of £8,000, and rental losses brought forward of £13,000.

The company wishes to obtain any relief for the offset of its trading loss as quickly as possible, and will therefore set it against the TTP of the current CAP.

Required:

Using a Corporation Tax Computation, calculate the taxable total profits for the CAP, and the Corporation Tax payable.

Carry out all calculations to the nearest £.

State an alternative option that may be available to this company for offsetting its trading loss.

5.4   Trade Trader Ltd has an unadjusted income statement for the year ended 30/9/2019 as follows:

	£	£
Sales		720,000
less cost of sales		400,000
Gross profit		320,000
Interest receivable		50,000
Profit on disposal of non-current assets		50,000
Rental income receivable		40,000
		460,000
less expenses:		
Discounts allowed	11,000	
Salaries and wages	70,000	
Depreciation	41,000	
Bad debts written off	12,000	
Rates and insurance	13,000	
Postage and stationery	10,000	
Administration expenses	14,000	
Advertising	18,000	
Travel and entertaining	20,000	
		209,000
Net Profit		251,000

Notes:

- Administration includes £1,000 directors' speeding fines incurred while on company business.

- Advertising consists of:
  - gifts of CDs with company logos to 1000 customers totalled £8,000
  - gifts of food hampers with company logos to 400 other customers totalled £10,000

- Travel and entertaining is made up as follows:

	£
Employees' travel expenses	7,400
Employees' subsistence allowances	3,600
Entertaining customers	6,000
Entertaining staff on company trip to theme park	3,000
	20,000

The interest receivable is non-trade.

The profit on sale of non-current assets resulted in a chargeable gain of £41,000.

The rental income is assessable as Property Income, and the figure in the accounts can be used for tax purposes.

Capital allowances for the period have been calculated at £11,000.

Required:

1   Adjust the net profit shown to arrive at the trading income assessment for Corporation Tax purposes.

2   Calculate the taxable total profits.

3   Calculate the Corporation Tax payable.

4   Complete pages 2 and 3 of tax return CT600 as far as possible.
     (A blank form is reproduced in the Appendix of this book or may be downloaded from the Student Resource pages of www.osbornebooks.co.uk or from www.hmrc.gov.uk)

Carry out all calculations to the nearest £.

5.5 Mastermind Limited is changing its accounting dates, and to accommodate this has produced one long set of financial accounts, from 1/4/2018 to 31/7/2019.

Capital allowances have already been calculated for each of the two CAPs as follows:

CAP 1/4/2018 to 31/3/2019   £8,000

CAP 1/4/2019 to 31/7/2019   £2,500

The financial accounts for the 16 months to 31/7/2019 are as follows:

	£	£
Sales		293,000
less cost of sales		155,000
Gross profit		138,000
add		
bad debts recovered		3,100
discounts received		2,000
		143,100
less expenses:		
Salaries and wages	68,500	
Rent, rates, and insurance	9,200	
Depreciation etc.	10,000	
General expenses	15,630	
Interest payable	8,300	
Bad debts written off	12,400	
Selling expenses	15,000	
		139,030
Net Profit		4,070

The following information is also provided:

- depreciation etc is made up as follows:

  - Depreciation   £45,000

  - Loss on sale of computer   £19,500

  - Profit on sale of Building   £54,500

- general expenses include debt recovery fees of £800

- selling expenses include:

– Entertaining customers	£1,930
– Gifts of diaries to customers (£6 each, with company advert)	£600

The profit on the sale of the building resulted in a chargeable gain of £45,000 on 1/6/2019.

There were no other chargeable gains in either CAP.

Required:

- Adjust the financial accounts for the 16-month period, before deduction of capital allowances.

- Time-apportion the adjusted profit figure into CAPs.

- Calculate the trading income assessment for each CAP.

- Calculate the taxable total profits for each CAP.

- Calculate the Corporation Tax payable in respect of each CAP.

Carry out all calculations to the nearest £.

5.6   Tick the appropriate box for each of the following statements:

	True	False
(a) If a company is five months late in submitting their tax return, they will receive a fixed penalty of £200.		
(b) Penalties for errors made by companies in their tax return vary from 20% to 100%.		
(c) If a company fails to keep records for the appropriate period of time, they can be fined £3,000.		
(d) A company with a period of account ending on 30 April 2019 must keep their records until 30 April 2025.		

6 Income tax – trading profits

this chapter covers...

In this chapter we turn our attention to the trading profits of sole traders and partnerships – these are taxed under Income Tax. Some of the treatment of these profits is similar to those examined under Corporation Tax, but there are many important differences.

We start by learning about what is considered 'trading' and therefore come under the rules that we are going to study. The factors that help determine that a business is being carried out are called the 'badges of trade'. We also consider the implications of using 'personal service companies'.

We then go on to examine the normal basis of assessment for trading income, and also learn about allowable and non-allowable expenditure for sole traders and partners and see where it differs from the situation for limited companies.

Next we examine the calculation of capital allowances, and see the similarities and important differences compared with Corporation tax.

Finally we will look at offset of trading losses for sole traders and partnerships. Here again there are similarities, but also important differences between the Income Tax rules and those for Corporation Tax.

INTRODUCTION TO BUSINESS TAXATION OF INDIVIDUALS

In this book so far we have provided an introduction to the taxes that apply to business in the UK, and looked in detail at the way that Corporation Tax is applied to various types of profits of limited companies.

In the remaining chapters of this book we are going to examine how the trading profits and gains of business are subject to Income Tax and Capital Gains Tax. This applies to organisations that have not been formed as limited companies, but are operated by individuals who are sole traders or partners.

The business activities of these individuals are not legally separate from their personal financial interests, and therefore they are subject to Income Tax and Capital Gains Tax on their income and gains from all sources. The learning area 'Personal Tax' (covered in Osborne Books' *Personal Tax* text) examines how Income Tax and Capital Gains Tax is calculated. In this book we will examine the impact of these taxes on individuals' **business** profits and gains.

WHAT IS TRADING?

In order to appreciate the way that Income Tax applies to those who operate a trade, we must first understand exactly what constitutes **trading** from a tax point of view. Nearly all of us buy and sell things from time to time (for example we may change our cars regularly), but we usually wouldn't think of ourselves as traders. It is important to distinguish between a trading and non-trading situation, since:

■ trading carried out by an individual is assessable to Income Tax as 'Trading Income'

■ non-trading activities may be subject to Capital Gains Tax, or may be outside the scope of all taxation

HM Revenue & Customs use several tests known as 'the badges of trade' to help decide whether they believe an activity should be classed as trading. The result of each of these tests will provide evidence in one direction or the other, and the final decision will be judged on the overall weight of evidence. These tests are described below.

the badges of trade

■ **profit motive**

Where profit is clearly the driving force behind the activity, then this is a strong indicator that the activity may constitute trading.

■ **subject matter of the activity**

Where the items bought and sold are of no personal use to the individual then this is further evidence of trading, and this case is strengthened if the individual already works in a situation where such items are traded. Where, however the items are used by the individual or can provide personal pleasure then this would be evidence that the activity is not trading.

■ **length of ownership**

Where items are sold shortly after acquisition then this is an indicator of trading. Where they are held for a long period it may provide evidence that it is not trading.

■ **frequency of transactions**

Where there is a series of similar transactions, then this indicates trading. A single transaction is less likely to be considered as trading.

■ **supplementary work**

Where the individual carries out work on the items (eg repairs) to make them more saleable, this is evidence of trading.

■ **reasons for acquisition and sale**

An intentional purchase and planned sale will provide evidence of trading. An item that was given to the individual, or one that was sold quickly to raise money to pay personal debts is less likely to constitute trading.

These tests will also apply (as far as possible) when considering whether the provision of a service amounts to a business.

We will now illustrate the use of these indicators with a Case Study.

Case Study

DAN THE BANGER MAN: BADGES OF TRADE

Dan works as an Assistant Accountant, but in his spare time will often be found working on one of his cars in his garage. He usually owns a couple of cars at the same time – one to drive around in and one that he is repairing. He goes to a car auction about once every six weeks and buys a car that needs a little work, provided it is at a good price. After he has repaired the car he usually keeps it for a few weeks to use, before advertising it in his local paper and selling it, so that he can obtain the best price. Dan regards this activity as his hobby.

r e q u i r e d

Using the badges of trade, identify:

• the points that indicate that Dan is trading

• the points that suggest non-trading

Explain what conclusion you would reach from the balance of evidence.

solution

The badges of trade can be interpreted as follows:

*   **Profit motive**

    Dan seems to deliberately buy and sell at a profit. He buys only at auction, and sets his own selling price through his adverts. This indicates trading.

*   **Subject matter**

    Dan gets personal use from the cars that he buys, and this could indicate that he is not trading. The fact that he is not employed in the car trade helps this argument.

*   **Length of ownership**

    After repairing the cars, Dan only keeps them for a few weeks. Such a short time indicates trading.

*   **Frequency of transactions**

    The buying and selling of cars seems to be a regular activity, with purchases being made about every six weeks. This indicates trading.

*   **Supplementary work**

    Repairing the cars counts as supplementary work, and Dan deliberately buys cars that need work carrying out. This indicates trading.

*   **Reason for acquisition and sale**

    Acquisition appears to be planned with the ultimate sale in mind. This indicates trading.

In conclusion . . .

Overall, nearly all indicators point to trading. The only point that indicates the opposite is that Dan uses the cars before sale. The fact that he views his activity as a hobby is not relevant in the face of such evidence.

It is likely that HM Revenue & Customs would wish to assess his income from this activity as Trading Income.

notification of starting trading

When an individual starts trading he/she must notify HM Revenue and Customs. The time limit is within six months of the end of the tax year for Income Tax and NIC purposes. HMRC will then arrange to tax the income as 'Trading Income' under the self-assessment system as described in the next section.

trading allowance

Where it has been established that an individual is trading (although on a small scale) a tax-free trading allowance of up to £1,000 may be available. This is an automatic deduction from gross trading income (ie sales) which is an alternative to normal allowable expenses. It can therefore eliminate taxable profits from gross trading income of up to £1,000.

Where gross trading income is over £1,000, the trading allowance can still be used instead of the normal allowable expenses if they are less than £1,000. This will reduce the taxable amount.

Where gross trading income is less than £1,000, but allowable expenses are more than income, it will be beneficial to elect not to claim the trading allowance. In this way a loss can be established that can be offset using the rules that will be explained later.

The trading allowance is only available to individuals. It is not available to partnerships or limited companies. There is also an equivalent 'property allowance' that can be used by individuals who receive small amounts of rental income.

EMPLOYED OR SELF EMPLOYED?

In these chapters we are mainly concerned with self-employed individuals or those in partnership. Before we look at these situations in detail we must ensure that we can distinguish between workers who are employed (and therefore pay Income Tax and National Insurance through PAYE) and those who are self-employed and invoice for their work and account for their own Income Tax and NIC.

The distinction is whether the contract that applies is one **of service** (when the person is an **employee**), or a contract **for services** (a **self-employed** relationship). These can be confusing phrases, but if you think a contract:

- **of service** could apply to a servant (where the employee serves the employer)
- **for services** could apply to someone who invoices 'for services rendered' and is self employed

In some cases it can be difficult to establish whether the person is employed or self employed, and HMRC have produced leaflets and an online 'Employment Status Indicator' tool to help.

The following are indicators that help provide evidence in one direction or the other.

Indicators of employment	Indicators of self employment
Need to do the work yourself	Can employ helper or substitute
Told how, where and when to do work	Decide yourself how, when and where to do work
Work set hours and paid regular wage with sick pay and holidays	Choose work hours and invoice for work done
No risk of capital or losses	Risk own capital and bear losses from work that is not to standard
Employer provides equipment	Provide own equipment
Work for one employer (but sometimes more)	Work for several people or organisations

USE OF 'PERSONAL SERVICE COMPANIES'

We saw in the last section that there are various indicators that can influence the decision as to whether an individual is an employee or self-employed. Where an individual would normally be classed as an employee, but actually charges for their work through an '**intermediary**' special rules, known as IR35 can apply. Intermediaries are often known as 'personal service companies'.

An example of the type of situation that we are considering would be when a worker (Mr Jones) appears to work as an employee for an organisation (Aye Company). Instead of being paid as an employee of Aye Company, Mr Jones arranges for his own company (Jones Limited) to invoice Aye Company. Mr Jones then arranges for Jones Limited to pay him, possibly as an employee of Jones Limited, and / or through dividends.

IR35 legislation was brought in some years ago to prevent this kind of disguise of the true situation – that Mr Jones is effectively an employee of Aye Company.

When IR35 legislation applies, a comparison is made between

■ the amount of Income Tax and National Insurance that Jones Limited pays on behalf of Mr Jones (if any), with

■ the amount of Income Tax and National Insurance that Aye Company would have paid to HMRC if Mr Jones had been treated as their employee.

Where the first amount is lower, the difference will form a **deemed employment income tax charge** (or deemed employment payment) that will be levied on the intermediary (in this case Jones Limited).

This ensures that there is no tax saving through the use of intermediaries when used to disguise employment.

The issues that we examined in the last section can be used to determine whether the individual should be treated as an employee. This will assess what the relationship would be if there were no intermediary involved. If the individual is found to be effectively an employee, although he / she is being paid through an intermediary, then IR35 will apply.

Under the IR35 rules, an intermediary could be:

■ a limited company in which the worker or his family controls at least 5%

■ a partnership in which the worker or his family is entitled to at least 60% of the profits

If IR35 applies to a situation, but the intermediary does not conform to the rules, penalties and interest will apply.

We will now use a Case Study to illustrate how the various rules could apply.

LONE STARR LIMITED:
USE OF AN INTERMEDIARY

situation

Sue Starr is the sole shareholder of Lone Starr Limited. The company provides marketing services to various large organisations.

Sue has recently been approached by MegaRetail to help carry out a two year review of their marketing strategy. She will work with a small team of MegaRetail employees and have access to the company's IT equipment. Sue will be provided with an office at MegaRetail headquarters, where she will work three days every week, leaving her free to work from home for other clients the rest of the time.

Sue plans to invoice MegaRetail £4,000 per month for her services through Lone Starr Limited. She will then decide on how much dividend payments she wished to receive from Lone Starr Limited.

required

- Outline the points that indicate whether or not (in the absence of the intermediary Lone Starr Limited) Sue would be treated as an employee of MegaRetail.

- Explain the implications if HMRC decided that IR35 rules applied to the contract with MegaRetail.

solution

The points that imply employment with MegaRetail are:

- Sue will use an office at MegaRetail and use their IT equipment

- She will work set days alongside people who are employees of MegaRetail

- She appears to need to carry out the work herself and cannot provide a substitute

The points that may imply she would not be an employee are:

- Sue carries out work for other clients alongside the proposed contract with MegaRetail

- The contract is not permanent (although some employment contracts are fixed term)

If HMRC decide that IR35 rules apply then Lone Starr Limited will be charged with the Income Tax and NIC that would apply if she was an employee of MegaRetail. This is known as a deemed employment charge, and would be based on the £4,000 per month that Lone Starr Limited is charging MegaRetail.

Any tax saving that she would have made by taking her money out as dividends would therefore be eliminated. Penalties and interest would apply if Sue did not operate within the legislation.

THE BASIS OF ASSESSMENT OF TRADING PROFITS

Trading profits (both for sole traders and those in partnership) and professional profits are assessed to Income Tax as 'Trading Income'.

The trading income assessment for a sole trader will form part of his/her income that is taxable under Income Tax, and will be incorporated into the personal Income Tax computation. We examined this briefly in Chapter 1, and you may also have studied it in the 'personal tax' learning area.

The assessable trading profits of a partnership are divided between the partners according to the partnership agreement, and each partner's share then forms part of their individual Income Tax computation.

basis period for assessment

Sole traders and partnerships can produce their annual accounts up to any date in the year that they choose. Once the business is established, most accounting years will consistently follow the same pattern.

Income Tax is assessed based on tax years (6 April to the following 5 April), so that all income (both business and personal) can be brought together and the tax calculated. This means that a link must be established between the profits that are generated in an accounting period and a particular tax year. This mechanism is part of the basis of assessment, and is known as the **basis period**.

For a continuing business this link is very straightforward. The normal basis of assessment for trading income is the adjusted profits for the accounting period that ends in the tax year. So for a business that produces its accounts each year to 31 December, the basis period for the tax year 2019/20 would be the accounting period 1/1/2019 to 31/12/2019.

The term 'adjusted profits' refers to profits (on an accruals basis) that have been adjusted for tax purposes, and incorporate any capital allowances. This procedure is very similar to the one that we studied in Chapters 2 and 3 in connection with Corporation Tax for limited companies.

The procedure that we need to use is summarised in the diagram on the next page. This diagram will also be useful later on, when we examine the more complicated basis of assessments that apply to businesses when they are starting trading or ceasing trading.

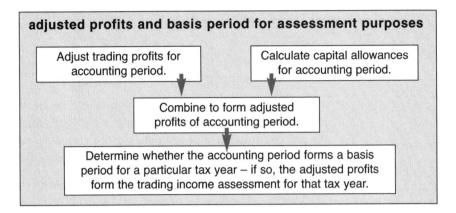

ADJUSTING THE TRADING PROFITS OF AN ACCOUNTING PERIOD

The procedure for adjusting profits for sole traders and partnerships is very similar to the one used for companies in Chapter 2. This means that you can use a lot of the knowledge gained in that area and apply it to this situation. We will firstly review the way that the procedure works, and then identify the main differences that you will encounter when dealing with trading under Income Tax rules in comparison with Corporation Tax.

review of adjusting profits

The object of adjusting the financial accounts is to make sure that:

■ the only income that is credited is trading income

■ the only expenditure that is deducted is allowable trading expenditure

When we adjust profits, we will start with the profit from the financial accounts, and:

■ deduct any income that is not trading income, and

■ add back any expenditure that has already been deducted but is not allowable

adjusting income

Provided that the 'sales' amount relates entirely to trading, this figure will not need adjusting. Other income may or may not be taxable, but if it does not fall under trading income, then it will need to be adjusted for in the trading profit calculation. The following examples of non-trading income that were given in Chapter 2 are also valid in this situation:

■ non-trading interest receivable

■ rent receivable

■ gains on the disposal of non-current (fixed) assets

■ dividends received

adjusting expenditure

We will only need to adjust for any expenditure accounted for in the financial accounts profit if it is not allowable. We do this by adding it back to the financial accounts profit. Expenditure that is allowable can be left unadjusted in the accounts.

The general rule for expenditure to be allowable in a trading income computation is that it must be:

■ revenue rather than capital in nature, and

■ 'wholly and exclusively' for the purpose of the trade

Expenditure that has a 'dual purpose' is therefore strictly speaking not allowable in its entirety (for example travel expenses for a trip combining a business conference and a holiday). However, expenditure that can be divided into a part that was wholly business and a part that is wholly private could be apportioned and have the business portion allowed. This could apply to motoring expenses.

Members of the sole trader or partner's family are sometimes employed in their business – for example spouses or children. This will be an allowable expense provided the amount paid is reasonable for the work carried out. For example, paying a son or daughter £40,000 per year for occasional help in the office would not be an allowable deduction (but £5,000 may be). If a relative is employed then PAYE would need to be applied to their earnings in the normal way.

adjusting accounts of companies and individuals

■ **issues not arising for sole traders and partnerships**

The following items will not appear in the accounts that we will be adjusting for Income Tax purposes:

– dividends payable

– Corporation Tax

– payments to directors

The special rules that we saw relating to qualifying research and development expenditure by companies do not apply to sole traders or partnerships.

■ **issues arising only for sole traders and partnerships**

– private expenditure of the owner(s) – this is non-allowable expenditure.

This could arise where entirely private expenditure had been paid through the business accounts (eg a personal electricity bill), or where certain expenditure needs to be apportioned between business and personal use. This latter situation is possible for expenditure such as motor expenses where business and private mileage could be used to apportion the total cost. As we will see later, there is a similar adjustment that is made to capital allowances on items with some private use.

– drawings of the owner(s) – these are not allowable deductions.

If the accounts have been produced following normal good accounting practice, then drawings will not appear before the net profit figure, and therefore no adjustment will be necessary. However some accounts may have been prepared to include drawing in the profit calculation, possibly under the heading of 'wages' and here the figure must be added back in the adjustment.

– taking trading goods out of the business for private use – this is also non-allowable, but requires particular care.

In contrast to normal accounting practice, these goods need to be accounted for tax purposes at their normal selling price. This means that any profit that would have been made by selling the goods normally through the business is still assessable. If there is no other specific information to guide you, the normal mark-up profit percentage (from the accounts) should be added to the cost price when adjusting the accounts.

We will now summarise some common expenditure items that are allowable and non-allowable in the form of a table. We will then illustrate the points by means of a Case Study.

Allowable expenditure	Non-allowable expenditure
Revenue expenditure wholly & exclusively for trade	Capital expenditure and private revenue expenditure
Cost of sales	Goods for private use
Staff salaries & wages (including relatives if amount paid is in line with work carried out). (including employers' NIC)	Drawings of owner(s), (including self-employed NIC, pension payments and Income Tax). Excessive payments for employing relatives.
Entertaining staff	Entertaining customers or suppliers
Certain gifts to customers (up to £50 each p.a., not food, drink, tobacco or vouchers)	All other gifts to customers
Trade bad debts written off	Non-trade bad debts written off
Increases in specific bad debt provisions	Increases in general bad debt provisions
Staff fines for minor motoring offences (eg parking)	All other fines for lawbreaking (owners and staff)
Capital allowances	Depreciation

Case Study

THE SOLE TRADER:
ADJUSTING TRADING PROFITS

Rachel Sole is a fishmonger, operating under the trade name of 'The Sole Trader'.

Her draft accounts for the year are as follows:

	£	£
Sales		64,000
less cost of sales:		
Opening inventory (stock)	6,000	
Purchases	30,000	
	36,000	
less closing inventory (stock)	4,000	
		32,000
Gross profit		32,000
add: building society interest rec'd		600
		32,600
less expenses:		
Rent, Rates & Insurance	1,500	
Part Time Employee's Wages	5,500	
Employers' NIC for Part Time Employee	112	
Depreciation on Fittings	1,250	
Increase in General Provision for Bad Debts	550	
General Expenses	1,450	
Purchase of new Freezer Cabinet	1,000	
Wages drawn for self	15,100	
Personal pension contribution for self	400	
		26,862
Net Profit		5,738

Notes:

1   Rachel pays the combined electricity bill for the shop and her private flat out of her personal bank account. The amount relating to the shop is calculated at £250.

2   Rachel took fish from her shop throughout the year to eat at home. The purchases figure in the accounts of £30,000 is after deducting the £1,000 cost price of this fish. Rachel's normal mark-up is 100% on cost.

3   Capital allowances have been calculated at £2,500 for the accounting period.

required

Calculate the trading income assessment for Rachel.

solution

	£
Net Profit per accounts	5,738

Add Back:

Expenditure that is shown in the accounts but is not allowable

	£
Depreciation	1,250
Increase in General Bad Debt Provision	550
Capital expenditure (freezer)	1,000
Drawings	15,100
Personal pension contributions	400
Adjustment to reflect profit in goods taken for own use	1,000
	25,038

Deduct:

Income that is not taxable as trading income	£	
Building Society Interest Received	600	
Allowable expenditure not shown in accounts		
Electricity for business	250	
Capital Allowances	2,500	
		(3,350)
Trading Income Assessment		21,688

Note:

The adjustment for notional profit on the fish taken out of inventory is based on the normal mark up of 100% of cost. This increases the value of the fish taken out of the business to its normal selling price. The mark up could also have been calculated from the accounts, where gross profit/cost of sales = 100%.

If the transaction deducting the fish at cost from the purchases had not been recorded in the accounts already, a total adjustment of £2,000 would have been required.

CAPITAL ALLOWANCES UNDER INCOME TAX

You will be relieved to learn that the calculation of capital allowances for plant & machinery under Income Tax is nearly identical to the system under Corporation Tax. Before you study this section, you may find it useful to revise capital allowances as they apply to Corporation Tax.

There are three main issues that are important regarding the capital allowances for a sole trader or partnership.

- Capital allowances are calculated for the accounting period, and are treated as allowable expenditure. If the accounting period is for less than 12 months, or between 12 months and 18 months, writing down allowances only are time apportioned. This is consistent with the treatment under Corporation Tax, although you will recall that CAPs over 12 months long do not exist under that system. The change in WDA rate for the special rate pool from 8% to 6% (and the calculation of a hybrid rate) also applies under Income Tax, but the date that the change applies from is 6th April 2019. However, for the calculation of hybrid rates April 6th to 30th can be treated as a whole month.

- The same annual investment allowance (AIA) that is available to limited companies is also available to sole traders and partnerships for acquisitions of plant and machinery. The limit of £200,000 or £1,000,000 or a hybrid figure for a 12-month period (time-apportioned for shorter or longer accounting periods) is also the same as for companies.

- Assets that have some private use by the owner(s) of the business are treated in a special way for plant & machinery capital allowances purposes, since only the business proportion of any allowance can be claimed. The general rule is that any asset with part private use must be held in a 'single asset pool', and the initial calculations of the allowances and balances carried forward are carried out as normal. However, only the business proportion of all allowances and charges that apply to that asset can be claimed. So, a car with part private use would need to enter its own single asset pool. The writing down allowance on the car would be calculated as normal, but only the business proportion of the allowance would be claimed as a capital allowance.

  If an asset with part private use (other than a car) was acquired then it would be entitled to the Annual Investment Allowance (AIA). However only the business proportion of the AIA could be claimed. For the purpose of determining whether expenditure breaches the AIA limit, the whole of the expenditure on assets with part private use is counted – not just the business proportion. However the taxpayer can choose which assets to claim AIA on if the total expenditure is over the limit.

  This is the main practical difference between preparing capital allowances under Income Tax and Corporation Tax, and can cause confusion. Remember that companies do not have private use, and therefore no private use adjustment applies.

The 'small pools allowance' that can sometimes be used to write off the main pool or the special rate pool applies under Income Tax as well as Corporation Tax.

We will now use a Case Study to illustrate some of the issues that we have discussed. When you are reading it, make sure, in particular, that you can understand how the private use of assets by the partners (or sole traders) affects the computation.

Case Study

CAPITOL IDEAS:
CAPITAL ALLOWANCES

Capitol Ideas is the trading name of a partnership owned and run by James and Jo Capitol. The business produces accounts to 31 March each year. The adjusted trading profit for the accounting period of 12 months to 31/3/2020 has already been calculated at £84,000 before deduction of capital allowances for plant & machinery.

The capital allowance computation for the last accounting period closed with written down values as follows:

- main pool   £30,000
- single asset pool for car (a BMW) with 25% private use by Jo   £15,000

During the accounting period the following assets were acquired and disposed of:

- a new pick-up truck was bought for £20,000. This was to have 20% private use by James
- the BMW was sold for £14,000
- a used Audi car was bought for £25,000. This was to replace the BMW, and also had 25% private use by Jo. Emissions level is 100g/km
- a machine in the main pool was sold for £2,000
- a computer system was bought for £5,000
- a Ford car for staff use was bought for £11,000. Emissions level is 105 g/km

All disposal proceeds were less than original cost.

required

- Using a plant & machinery capital allowance computation, calculate the allowances for the accounting period y/e 31/3/2020.

- Calculate the adjusted trading profits for the accounting period (after capital allowances), and state for which tax year these will form the trading income assessable profits.

solution

The capital allowance computation is shown below. The notes that follow provide explanations.

	Main pool	Car (BMW) 25% private	Car (Audi) 25% private	Capital allowances
	£	£	£	£
WDV bf	30,000	15,000		
add				
Acquisitions				
without FYA or AIA:				
Ford Car (105g/km)	11,000			
Audi Car (100g/km)				
(25% private use)			25,000	
Acquisitions qualifying for AIA:				
Computer 5,000				
AIA claimed (5,000)	0			5,000
Pick up truck 20,000				
AIA claimed (20,000)x 80%				16,000
less				
Proceeds of Disposals:				
Machine	(2,000)			
BMW		(14,000)		
	39,000	1,000	25,000	
WDA 18%	(7,020)		(4,500) x 75%	10,395
Balancing Allowance		(1,000) x 75%		750
WDV cf	31,980	0	20,500	
Total Capital Allowances				32,145

- The only additions that do not attract AIA or FYAs are the two cars. The Audi has 25% private use so is kept separate, while the Ford joins the main pool. Both cars have emission levels of 110g/km or less and so are entitled to 18% writing down allowances.

- The limit of AIA on purchases is £1,000,000. The £5,000 cost of the computer can be claimed in full, and the whole £20,000 cost of the truck is eligible for AIA. The £20,000 is then restricted for the 20% private use.

- The disposal proceeds of the machine are deducted from the main pool.

- The WDA on the Audi is £4,500 x 75% business use. Note that the full £4,500 is used to calculate the WDV carried forward.

- The disposal of the BMW was for less than the WDV brought forward. There is therefore a balancing allowance, but this is restricted to the business use of 75%. If a balancing charge had arisen it would also have been restricted to the proportion of business use.

Calculation of trading income assessment:	**£**
Adjusted trading profits (before capital allowances)	84,000
Capital allowances (as above)	(32,145)
Trading income assessment for tax year 2019/20	51,855

This amount will be then divided between the partners.

DEALING WITH TRADING LOSSES

In Chapters 2 and 5 we saw how trading losses for a limited company can be offset to reduce the amount of Corporation Tax that is payable. We will now examine the equivalent rules that apply to sole traders and partnerships under Income Tax. You will need to take particular care with loss provisions, since the rules under Income Tax and Corporation Tax are not identical, and this can lead to confusion.

In this section we will examine losses that occur in continuing businesses that are using normal twelve month accounting periods. If, once profits for an accounting period have been tax-adjusted and any capital allowances deducted, the result is a minus figure a '**trading loss**' will have arisen. This will have two implications:

- the trading income assessment for the relevant tax year will be zero (not the negative profit figure). This is the tax year in which the accounting period ends – ie the basis period
- the amount of the negative profit figure will form the trading loss, and the individual can choose how to set it off

The choices available are as follows:

1   The trading loss can be carried forward to reduce profits from the same trade in the future. If this option is chosen the loss must be used up as quickly as possible. If the following year's profit from the same trade is less than the loss, then that profit will be reduced to nil and the balance of the loss carried on forward. This will occur as many times as is necessary to offset the whole loss.

2   The trading loss can be used to reduce (or eliminate) the total taxable income in the tax year of the loss. This set off would be against taxable income from all sources for the relevant tax year.

2(a)   If the trading loss has been set off against total taxable income for the year of the loss, the taxpayer can then set any remaining loss against capital gains of the same year. This extension of the claim is optional.

3   Whether or not option (2) above is chosen, the loss can be carried back against the total taxable income from all sources in the tax year preceding the tax year of the loss. If the tax payer has sufficient loss and wishes to set against both these tax years, he/she can choose which year to set off the loss first.

3(a)   If the trading loss has been set off against the total taxable income for the year preceeding the loss, the taxpayer can opt to extend the claim to set the loss against any capital gains for that year.

The set off against capital gains in 2(a) and 3(a) is before the annual exempt amount is deducted (see Chapter 8).

Note that one important difference between Income Tax loss set off and the rules under Corporation Tax is that under Income Tax the order of options 2 and 3 are entirely the taxpayer's choice.

Since the set offs under all the options take place before the personal allowance (currently £12,500) is deducted, there is a danger that this tax-free amount will be wasted in some situations.

The following diagram illustrates the main options using as an example a sole trader making up accounts to the 31 December each year. A loss arises in the year ended 31/12/2019, which forms the basis period of the tax year 2019/20.

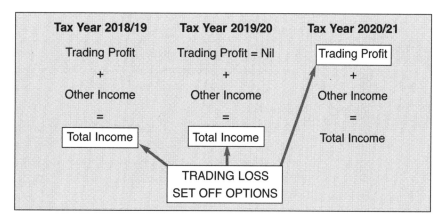

'Other Income' could include property income, employment income, savings income, and dividend income.

Case Study

DOWNHILL TRADING: TRADING LOSS OPTIONS

Downhill Trading is a business operated by Dawn Hill, who sells skiing equipment. The business has the following tax-adjusted trading results for the three twelve-month accounting periods to 31/12/2019. Dawn also has other taxable income for the tax years 2017/18 - 2019/20 as stated below.

Accounting periods	y/e 31/12/17	y/e 31/12/18	y/e 31/12/19
	£	£	£
Trading Profit/(Loss)	12,000	(15,000)	16,000
Tax Years	**2017/18**	**2018/19**	**2019/20**
	£	£	£
Other Income	4,000	5,000	5,500

Dawn does not have any capital gains.

required

State the options available for offsetting the £15,000 trading loss incurred in the y/e 31/12/2018. Demonstrate the effects on the relevant total income figures, and comment briefly on the implications of each option.

solution

The tax year of the loss will be 2018/19, since the accounting period y/e 31/12/2018 ends in (ie is the basis period for) this tax year. The other two accounting periods (y/e 31/12/2017 and y/e 31/12/2019) form the basis periods for 2017/18 and 2019/20 respectively.

We will show the options one by one, but with all the three tax years' details shown in columnar form for reference. There are four options in this situation.

Option A

The trading loss could be carried forward and set against the trading income assessment of 2019/20. Since this profit is larger than the loss the whole loss could be offset in this way. The three years would look as follows:

	2017/18	2018/19	2019/20
	£	£	£
Trading Profits	12,000	0	16,000
less loss relief			**(15,000)**
			1,000
Other Income	4,000	5,000	5,500
Total Income	16,000	5,000	6,500

An advantage of this option is that there is sufficient total income in each tax year to utilise at least some of Dawn's personal allowances. However Dawn would have to wait until the tax for 2019/20 was payable until she felt the tax benefit of the loss in cash saved.

Option B

The trading loss could be set against the other income of the tax year of the loss (2018/19). Due to the size of the loss this will not be sufficient to offset the whole loss. The balance of the loss could then be carried back to the previous tax year and set against the total income. This would give the following figures.

	2017/18	2018/19	2019/20
	£	£	£
Trading Profits	12,000	0	16,000
Other Income	4,000	5,000	5,500
	16,000	5,000	1,500
less loss relief	**(10,000)**	**(5,000)**	
Total Income	6,000	–	21,500

A disadvantage of this approach would be that the personal allowance in 2018/19 is wasted, since there is no income in that tax year. However, Dawn would get a tax refund for 2017/18 almost immediately, assuming that she had already paid Income Tax based on total income of £16,000.

Option C

The trading loss could be set against the other income of the tax year of the loss (2018/19), as in option B. The balance of the loss could then be carried forward to the next tax year and set against the profits of the same trade only. This would give the following figures.

	2017/18	2018/19	2019/20
	£	£	£
Trading Profits	12,000	0	16,000
less loss relief			**(10,000)**
			6,000
Other Income	4,000	5,000	5,500
	16,000	5,000	11,500
less loss relief	**–**	**(5,000)**	
Total Income	16,000	–	11,500

A disadvantage of this approach would be that the personal allowance in 2018/19 is wasted, since there is no income in that tax year. Dawn would pay no tax for that year, but would have to wait to feel any further tax effect of the loss until payment of the 2019/20 tax.

Option D

The trading loss could be set against the other income of the previous tax year (2017/18). This would accommodate the whole loss. This would give the following figures:

	2017/18	2018/19	2019/20
	£	£	£
Trading Profits	12,000	0	16,000
Other Income	4,000	5,000	5,500
	16,000	5,000	21,500
less loss relief	**(15,000)**	–	
Total Income	1,000	5,000	21,500

A disadvantage of this approach would be that most of the personal allowance in 2017/18 is wasted, since there is only £1,000 of income in that tax year. However Dawn would get a tax refund for the tax paid for that year almost immediately, assuming she had already paid Income Tax based on a total income of £16,000.

Chapter Summary

- Trading profits of sole traders and partners are subject to Income Tax, and are included in their computations along with personal income. Evidence indicators called 'badges of trade' are used to establish whether an individual is trading or not.

- There are indicators that can help establish whether an individual is employed or self-employed. Where they would be considered employed, but use an intermediary in the form of a personal services company, then IR35 rules can apply to counteract tax avoidance.

- The normal basis of assessment for the trading income of a business is the adjusted profits (after capital allowances) of the accounting period that ends in the tax year. The accounts of sole traders and partnerships are tax-adjusted in a similar way to those of a limited company. Specific expenditure that is non-allowable in arriving at trading profit includes owners' drawings, private expenditure, and trading goods taken from the business for private use.

- Capital allowances for plant & machinery can be claimed by the self-employed in a similar way to companies. Cars that have a private use element by the business owners need to be kept in a single asset pool, and only the business proportion of the capital allowances can be claimed. The business use part of other assets bought can form a claim for AIA or FYA.

- Where the adjusted trading profits (after capital allowances) result in a negative figure, the trading income assessment is zero, and a trading loss is formed that can be relieved in several ways. It may be carried forward and set off against the first available profits of the same trade. It may alternatively be set against the total income of the tax year in which the loss was incurred, and / or the previous tax year. Claims against total income of year of loss and previous tax years can also be extended against capital gains.

Key Terms

badges of trade indicators that are used to determine whether an activity constitutes trading, and should therefore be taxed as such

intermediary an organisation used to act in between a worker and client (for example a personal services company)

IR35 the rules that are used to prevent tax avoidance through the use of an intermediary to disguise employment status

basis period the term that describes the link between accounting periods and tax years. For a continuing business, the basis period for a particular tax year is the 12-month accounting period that ends in that tax year

adjusted trading profits trading profits that have been adjusted for tax purposes by excluding income not taxable as trading income and non-allowable expenditure

trading income assessment
the taxable trading profit for the tax year. It is made up of adjusted trading profits for the basis period, after deducting any capital allowances

plant & machinery one of the major non-current asset categories for capital allowance purposes. It includes vehicles and computers

annual investment allowance (AIA)
this is an allowance that can be claimed against the whole cost of most plant and machinery, with the exception of cars. The maximum that can be claimed is £200,000 or £1,000,000 or a hybrid figure for a 12-month period. This limit is reduced for shorter periods

first year allowances 100% First Year Allowances are available on new low-emission cars in the CAP in which the acquisition takes place

writing down allowances allowances are available at 18% of the pool value for plant and machinery. This figure relates to 12-month accounting periods, and is time-apportioned for shorter periods and longer periods up to 18 months. 8% or 6% or a hybrid % writing down allowances are available on the balance on the 'special rate pool'

written down value (plant & machinery)
this term relates to the balance at the end of an accounting period that remains in a plant & machinery pool. It represents the part of the pool value that has not yet been claimed as allowances, and is carried forward to the next accounting period

balancing allowance (plant & machinery)
this allowance can be claimed when an asset is sold for less than the written down value (unrelieved expenditure) in a single asset pool

balancing charge (plant & machinery)
this is the opposite of an allowance, and occurs when the disposal proceeds of an asset in a single asset pool are more than the written down value (unrelieved expenditure). It is in effect a reclaiming of allowances previously obtained

trading loss this occurs when the adjusted trading profits after deducting capital allowances produces a negative figure. the negative figure is the trading loss, whilst the trading income assessment is zero

loss relief the offsetting of the trading loss against profits or total income etc (plus capital gains if elected), according to legislation. This may be against future profits from the same trade, or against total income of the current and / or previous tax year

Activities

6.1   Michelle Flatley has moved home seven times in the last five years, and currently lives in a house valued at £500,000. Her first property was a small studio apartment that she was left by her uncle. It was valued at £40,000. After carrying out some renovations she moved in, and stayed three months before selling the property for £60,000 and investing the proceeds in her next flat. She has continued this procedure with all the properties that she has owned, always renovating with a view to a prospective buyer, and always making a profit by timing the sale carefully.

Required:

Using each of the 'badges of trade', explain the issues that provide evidence that she is trading, and those that point to non-trading.

6.2   The following items appear in a sole trader's income statement (profit and loss account), before the net profit figure. You are calculating an adjusted trading profit for tax purposes. State in each case whether:

- the item should be added to the net profit, or
- the item should be deducted from the net profit, or
- the item should be ignored

1   depreciation of vehicles

2   loss on sale of non-current assets

3   building society interest received

4   dividends received

5   owner's drawings

6   profit on sale of non-current asset

7   increase in general provision for bad debts

8   gifts of food hampers (with company adverts) to customers, costing £45 per recipient.

9   decrease in specific bad debt provision

10   owner's self-employed National Insurance contribution

11   employers' National Insurance contributions regarding employees

12   owner's private expenses

6.3   Vikram Singh is in business as a sole trader. The unadjusted income statement for the year ended 31/1/2020 is as follows:

	£	£
Sales		700,000
less cost of sales		420,000
Gross profit		280,000
Bank interest received		12,000
Rental income		10,000
		302,000
less expenses:		
Salaries and wages	78,000	
Depreciation	22,000	
Loss on sale of non-current assets	4,000	
Administration expenses	11,600	
Advertising	8,000	
Overdraft interest payable	2,000	
Travel and entertaining	10,000	
Pension contributions	7,400	
Bad debts and provisions	15,000	
		158,000
Net Profit		144,000

Notes:

- Salaries and wages include £18,000 drawn by Vikram.
- Advertising includes:
  - gift-vouchers given to 100 top customers £3,000
  - gifts of diaries with company logos to 200 other customers £1,000
- Travel and entertaining is made up as follows:

	£
Employees' travel expenses	2,000
Vikram's business travel expenses	3,500
Entertaining customers	4,500
	10,000

- Pension contributions consist of:

Contribution regarding employees	5,000
Contribution regarding Vikram	2,400
	7,400

- Bad debts and provisions is made up of:

Trade bad debts written off	10,400
Increase in specific bad debt provision	4,600
	15,000

- Capital allowances for the accounting period have been calculated at £23,000.

Required:

Adjust the net profit shown to arrive at the trading income assessment for the tax year 2019/20.

6.4   Candies & Cakes is the trading name of a shop owned and run by John Candy. The business produces accounts to 31 March each year. The adjusted trading profit for the accounting period of twelve months to 31/3/2020 has already been calculated at £12,000 before deduction of capital allowances for plant & machinery.

The capital allowance computation for the last accounting period closed with written down values as follows:

- main pool   £25,000
- single asset pool for car with 40% private use by John   £10,000

During the accounting period the following assets were acquired and disposed of:

- a new 'low emission' car was bought for £26,000. This was to have 40% private use by John
- the original car used partly privately by John was sold for £4,000
- a computer system was bought for £2,000
- a food processor was sold for £200
- a new shop counter was bought for £3,000

All disposal proceeds were less than original cost.

Required:

- Using a plant & machinery capital allowance computation, calculate the allowances for the accounting period y/e 31/3/2020.
- Calculate the adjusted trading profit or loss for the accounting period (after capital allowances).
- Explain any alternative options that are available to John, following the results of the last task.

6.5   Stan and Anne have run their partnership manufacturing business for many years, producing accounts up to the 31 March each year. At the start of April 2019 the following written down balances were brought forward for Plant & Machinery capital allowance purposes:

Main Pool	£66,300
Electronic Machine (short life asset)	£2,000
Car (80% business use BMW)	£16,000

The income statement for the year ended 31/3/2020 was as follows:

	£	£
Sales		1,200,000
less cost of sales:		
Raw materials	300,000	
Direct labour	450,000	
Factory overheads	200,000	
		950,000
Gross profit		250,000
less:		
Administration salaries	50,000	
Selling & distribution expenses	15,000	
Depreciation etc	40,000	
General expenses	35,000	
		140,000
Net profit		110,000

Notes:

- The direct labour relates to 20 employees of the partnership, and includes £5,000 employers' National Insurance contributions.

- The administration salaries include £20,000 drawn by Stan, and £25,000 drawn by Anne. All private motor expenses are included in these drawings.

- The 'depreciation etc' figure is made up as follows:

	£
Depreciation on plant & cars	32,000
Loss on sale of BMW car sold for £12,000	3,000
Depreciation on Factory	6,000
Gain on sale of Vauxhall car, sold for £4,000	(1,000)

- A used Range Rover (80% business use) was bought for £28,000 to replace the BMW. It has emissions of 200 g/km.

- A Ford Focus was bought to replace the Vauxhall. It had 100% business use and cost £19,000. It has emissions of 105 g/km.

- There were no other acquisitions or disposals of non-current assets.

- General expenses include the following items:

	£
Bad Debts written off	3,000
Reduction in General Bad Debt Provision from £12,000 to £8,000	(4,000)
Office Party for all 20 employees	1,500
Entertaining customers	2,000

Calculate:

- The Plant & Machinery Capital Allowances for the accounting period.

- Trading Income assessment for the partnership for 2019/20, after incorporating the above capital allowances.

6.6   Mr Chang is a sole trader. His business has the following income statement:

	£	£
Sales		1,210,210
less Cost of sales:		808,480
Gross profit		401,730
less:		
Wages and salaries	125,778	
Rent, rates and insurance	59,221	
Repairs to plant	8,215	
Advertising and entertaining	19,077	
Accountancy and legal costs	5,710	
Motor expenses	53,018	
Telephone and office costs	14,017	
Depreciation	28,019	
Other expenses	92,460	405,515
Loss		(3,785)

Notes:

- Wages and salaries include:

	£
Mr Chang	30,000
Mr Chang's wife, who works in the marketing department	18,000

- Advertising and entertaining includes:

	£
Gifts to customers:	
Bottles of wine costing £15 each	2,250
40 diaries carrying the business's logo	400
Staff Christmas party for 20 employees	1,485

- Motor expenses include those relating to:

	£
Delivery vans	10,403
Sales manager's car	6,915
Mr Chang's car expenses	
(the car is only used for private mileage)	5,700

- Other expenses include:

	£
Cost of staff training	3,550
Subscription to a golf club for Mr Chang	220

- Capital allowances have already been calculated at £9,878

Required:

Complete the adjusted trading profits computation.

7 Income tax – further issues

this chapter covers...

In this chapter we examine some of the more complex issues connected with the income of sole traders and partnerships.

We commence with the rules regarding basis of assessment for these organisations when trading starts. The initial tax years do not use the normal rules, but instead special rules apply which must be learnt. A further set of rules apply in the final tax year when trading ceases.

We will then examine the basis period rules that apply when there is a change in accounting date.

The chapter then looks specifically at partnerships, and the rules for dividing the profits of the partnership between the partners is explained and illustrated. These include the rules that apply when partners join or leave a partnership.

The next sections are concerned with National Insurance for sole traders and partners, followed by payment dates for Income Tax and a summary of penalties for non-compliance.

Finally we examine the relevant tax forms for sole traders and partnerships, and illustrate their completion.

WHEN BUSINESSES START TRADING

In the last chapter we saw that the basis of assessment that applies when businesses have been trading for some time is the profits of the twelve month accounting period that ends in the tax year. This normal basis is known as the 'current year basis'. We now need to examine the special rules that operate before the normal basis can apply – in the first years of a new business. These rules apply to both sole traders and partnerships, and are designed so that all the profits throughout the life of a business are certain to be assessed in at least one particular tax year. We do not have an equivalent situation for limited companies, since under Corporation Tax each chargeable accounting period is assessed separately, with no need for basis periods.

A major issue to note is that right from the start of the business, accounts will be produced for the accounting periods that the business owners decide upon. These accounts will then be adjusted for tax purposes, including calculating capital allowances for the accounting period. Only when that has been carried out does the procedure relating to basis periods that we will now examine come into play.

We must initially determine which is the tax year in which the new business will first be assessed to Income Tax. The rule for this is straightforward – the first tax year in which a new business' profits are assessed is the tax year in which the business starts. Starting with this tax year, there are rules about exactly what profits from what period of time will be assessed in each of the first tax years. Because different businesses will have different accounting periods we will need to apportion the tax-adjusted trading profits (after capital allowances) to match these basis periods.

basis periods in the opening years

In the following summary that covers the majority of situations, 'accounting date' refers to a date up to which accounts are produced.

	Tax year	Basis period
1	the tax year in which the business starts	from the start date to the next 5 April
2	the next (second) tax year	the 12 month period that ends on the accounting date in the second tax year
		or (if that's impossible because the accounting period isn't long enough)
		the first 12 months of the business
3	the third tax year	normal 'current year basis' - the 12 month accounting period that ends in the third tax year

For example, if a new business starts trading on 1 January 2017, and produces annual accounts each year to 31 December, the following would apply.

The first tax year – the tax year in which business starts – is 2016/17.

The basis period for the tax year 2016/17 will be 1/1/2017 - 5/4/2017.

The second tax year will be the next year, 2017/18.

The basis period for the tax year 2017/18 will be the 12 months to 31/12/2017.

This is the 12-month period ending on the accounting date in the second tax year.

The third tax year will be the next year, 2018/19.

The basis period for the tax year 2018/19 will be the 12 months to 31/12/2018.

This is the normal 'current year' basis – the 12-month accounting period that ends in the third tax year.

This is demonstrated on the following time-line diagram.

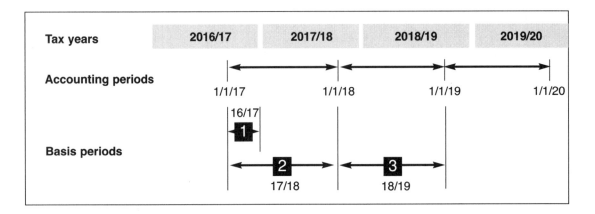

You can see that in this example there is a period of time that relates to two basis periods: the period 1/1/2017 to 5/4/2017 forms the basis period for 2016/17, but is also part of the year ended 31/12/2017 that forms the basis period for 2017/18. This is a common occurrence, and is known as an overlap period. The profits arising in that period are known as overlap profits. These profits are effectively assessed twice – once in each tax year. When the business ceases trading the overlap profits can reduce the final trading income assessment.

The rules and examples used so far will enable you to deal with the vast majority of situations for a new business. The only exception occurs when a business starts in one tax year and then produces a long first set of accounts that end in the third tax year. Since there is no accounting end date in the second tax year the previous summary does not apply. Instead, this is dealt with as follows:

■ the basis period for the second tax year is 6 April to 5 April – ie the actual tax year

■ the basis period for the third tax year is the 12 months leading up to the accounting date in the third tax year

The following diagram gives a comprehensive view of all possibilities for the **second tax year** in the form of a flowchart.

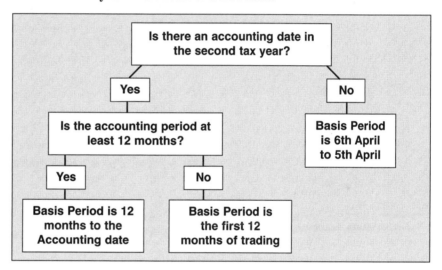

time-apportionment of trading profits

Each accounting period for the business will have adjusted trading profits. These profit figures will incorporate capital allowances that will have been worked out based on the same accounting period. The adjusted trading profits will then need to be matched to the basis periods that we have just examined, using time-apportionment where necessary. When carrying out time-apportionment, note that:

■ we will use whole months – each one assumed to be 1/12 of a calendar year

■ the few days between 31 March and 5 April can be ignored – so for example the period 1 January to 5 April will be treated as exactly three months

We will follow both these practices in all examples. These calculation methods are acceptable by HM Revenue & Customs.

example: time-apportionment of profits

Using the data from the previous example we will now show how the time-apportionment of profits is carried out.

The adjusted trading profits for the business (after capital allowances) have been calculated as:

1 January 2017 - 31 December 2017   £24,000

1 January 2018 - 31 December 2018   £30,000

Using the basis periods calculated earlier, these profits are used to form trading income assessments for the first few tax years of the business as follows:

Tax year	Basis period	Trading income assessment
2016/17	1/1/2017 - 5/4/2017	£24,000 x 3/12 = £6,000
2017/18	1/1/2017 - 31/12/2017	= £24,000
2018/19	1/1/2018 - 31/12/2018	= £30,000

The overlap profits are those arising from the period 1/1/2017 - 5/4/2017, and are £6,000, which is assessed both on its own for 2016/17, and as part of the £24,000 assessment for 2017/18. This £6,000 is deductible in the calculation of the assessable profit for the final tax year of the business when trading ceases.

Different combinations of business start dates and accounting periods will produce various basis periods and amounts of overlap profits. If accounts are always produced up to 31 March, there will not be any overlap profits. The key to accurate calculations is to learn and follow the rules outlined earlier in this chapter, being especially careful to identify each tax year accurately. Mistakes can also easily be made by incorrectly counting months when carrying out time-apportionment. If you find it helpful to sketch a time-line diagram, then this can form part of your workings.

The following Case Study illustrates a variety of possible situations. Examine it carefully to make sure that you could arrive at the same results without assistance.

Case Study

FRESHER AND CO:
ASSESSING NEW BUSINESSES

Fresher and Company is an accountancy practice that has several new clients who have recently commenced trading.

John Able started trading on 1 July 2016. He produced accounts with adjusted trading profits (after capital allowances) as follows:

1/7/2016 - 30/6/2017	£18,000
1/7/2017 - 30/6/2018	£30,000
1/7/2018 - 30/6/2019	£33,000

The partnership of Joe and Jo Barclay started trading on 1 December 2016. They produced accounts with adjusted trading profits (after capital allowances) as follows:

1/12/2016 - 31/3/2017 (4 months)	£20,000
1/4/2017 - 31/3/2018	£50,000
1/4/2018 - 31/3/2019	£60,000

Karen Cabot started trading on 1 October 2016. She produced accounts with adjusted trading profits (after capital allowances) as follows:

1/10/2016 - 30/6/2017 (9 months)	£27,000
1/7/2017 - 30/6/2018	£42,000
1/7/2018 - 30/6/2019	£47,000

David Daley started trading on 1 November 2016. He produced accounts with adjusted trading profits (after capital allowances) as follows:

1/11/2016 - 31/12/2017 (14 months)	£28,000
1/1/2018 - 31/12/2018	£26,000
1/1/2019 - 31/12/2019	£29,000

Edgar Evans started trading on 1 January 2017. He produced accounts with adjusted trading profits (after capital allowances) as follows:

1/1/2017 - 31/7/2018 (19 months)	£47,500
1/8/2018 - 31/7/2019	£36,000
1/8/2019 - 31/7/2020	£48,000

required

For each of the clients, calculate the assessable profits for each of their first three tax years, and show the amount of any overlap profits, and how it has arisen.

solution

John Able

Tax year	Basis period	Trading income assessment	
2016/17	1/7/2016 - 5/4/2017	£18,000 x 9/12	= £13,500
2017/18	1/7/2016 - 30/6/2017		= £18,000
2018/19	1/7/2017 - 30/6/2018		= £30,000

The overlap profits are £13,500, and relate to the nine month period 1/7/2016 - 5/4/2017, which is assessed in both 2016/17 and 2017/18. The following diagram shows the periods.

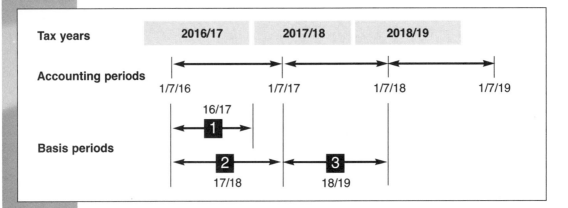

Joe and Jo Barclay

Tax year	Basis period	Trading income assessment
2016/17	1/12/2016 - 5/4/2017	= £20,000
2017/18	1/4/2017 - 31/3/2018	= £50,000
2018/19	1/4/2018 - 31/3/2019	= £60,000

There are no overlap profits for this business, since the accounting date of 31 March has been chosen. The diagram on the next page shows the periods.

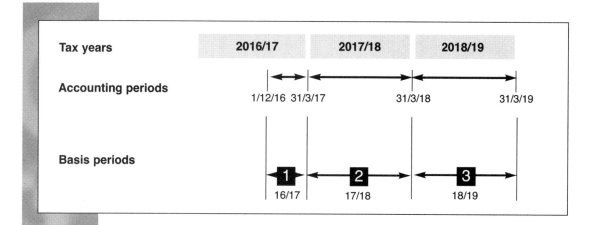

Karen Cabot

Tax year	Basis period	Trading income assessment	
2016/17	1/10/2016 - 5/4/2017	£27,000 x 6/9	= £18,000
2017/18	1/10/2016 - 30/9/2017	£27,000 +	
		(£42,000 x 3/12)	= £37,500
2018/19	1/7/2017 - 30/6/2018		= £42,000

This situation is a little more complicated than those seen so far.

- Note that the apportionment for the first tax year is 6/9 since the first accounting period is for only nine months.

- For the second tax year there is no 12-month accounting period ending in the tax year, because the accounting period is only nine months. This means that the alternative of the first 12 months of the business must be used.

- The overlap profits are for nine months and total £28,500, and arise from two separate periods:

    1/10/2016 - 5/4/2017 (profits of £18,000), and

    1/7/2017 - 30/9/2017 (profits of £42,000 x 3/12 = £10,500)

The diagram on the next page shows the periods.

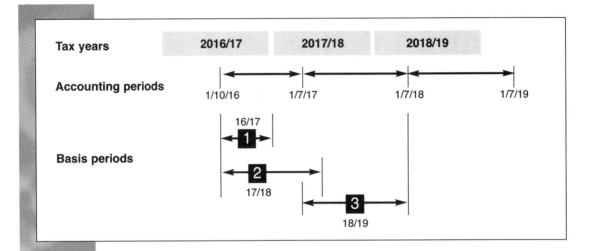

David Daley

Tax year	Basis period	Trading income assessment	
2016/17	1/11/2016 - 5/4/2017	£28,000 x 5/14	= £10,000
2017/18	1/1/2017 - 31/12/2017	£28,000 x 12/14	= £24,000
2018/19	1/1/2018 - 31/12/2018		= £26,000

The overlap profits are 3/14 x £28,000 = £6,000, and relate to the period 1/1/2017 - 5/4/2017, which is assessed in both 2016/17 and 2017/18.

The fact that 5 + 12 = 17 months of the 14-month period profits have been assessed confirms the three months that have been assessed twice. The following diagram shows the periods.

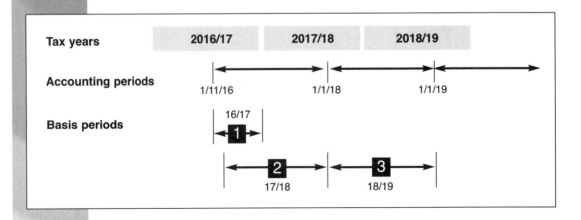

Edgar Evans

Note that we have a situation here where there is no accounting date in the second tax year, and we will therefore follow the special rules noted earlier that apply to the second and third tax years.

Tax year	Basis period	Trading income assessment	
2016/17	1/1/2017 - 5/4/2017	£47,500 x 3/19	= £7,500
2017/18	6/4/2017 - 5/4/2018	£47,500 x 12/19	= £30,000
2018/19	1/8/2017 - 31/7/2018	£47,500 x 12/19	= £30,000

The overlap profits are 8/19 x £47,500 = £20,000, and relate to the period 1/8/2017 - 5/4/2018, which is assessed in both 2017/18 and 2018/19. The second and third years are therefore where the overlap occurs in this situation.

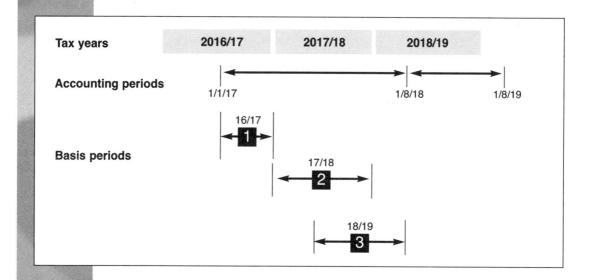

WHEN BUSINESSES STOP TRADING

basis periods

When a business closes down and stops trading, the last tax year in which the business is taxed is the tax year in which trading ceases. For this tax year only there is a special rule regarding the basis period, so that no period of time is missed out for assessment purposes.

The basis period for the final tax year is from the end of the basis period of the previous tax year to the date that the business ceases ie all profits that have not yet been assessed.

The previous year will have been assessed on the normal current year basis, so this means that the final basis period will run from the accounting date in that tax year to the date the business stops. The profits of this final period will be reduced by any overlap profits that are brought forward from the start of the business.

Take, for example, a sole trader who has been in business for several years, making accounts up to 31 December. He ceases trading on 30 June 2019, with the following adjusted profits (after capital allowances) for the final accounting periods:

1/1/2018 - 31/12/2018	£25,000
1/1/2019 - 30/6/2019 (6 months)	£15,000

There are overlap profits of £6,000 brought forward from when he started the business.

The assessable profits for the last two tax years of the business are:

Tax year	Basis period	Trading income assessment	
2018/19	1/1/2018 - 31/12/2018		£25,000
2019/20	1/1/2019 - 30/6/2019		£15,000
		less overlap profits	(£6,000)
			£9,000

The mechanism for basis periods at the beginning and end of a business, and the way that overlap profits are deducted in the final tax year means that over the whole life of the business all profits are assessed. Therefore,

total adjusted profits over the life of the business

= total assessments over the life of the business

As well as showing that the system has some fairness, this also gives us a useful way to check total assessments if we are presented with data for a business from start to finish. The following Case Study will demonstrate this.

HOLE TRADING:
ASSESSMENTS THROUGHOUT A BUSINESS

Hole Trading is a shop run by Roger Hole that specialises in caving equipment. The business started on 1/6/2015, and ceased trading on 31/12/2018. The accounts were produced annually up to 31 May, and the adjusted profits (after capital allowances) were as follows:

	£
1/6/2015 - 31/5/2016	18,000
1/6/2016 - 31/5/2017	36,000
1/6/2017 - 31/5/2018	24,000
1/6/2018 - 31/12/2018 (7 months)	21,000
Total	99,000

required

Calculate the trading income assessments for each tax year in which the business will be assessed.

solution

2015/16	1/6/2015 - 5/4/2016	£18,000 x 10/12	= £15,000
2016/17	1/6/2015 - 31/5/2016		= £18,000
	(overlap profits 1/6/2015 - 5/4/2016 £15,000)		
2017/18	1/6/2016 - 31/5/2017		= £36,000
2018/19	1/6/2017 - 31/12/2018	£24,000 + £21,000	= £45,000
		less overlap profits	(£15,000)
			£30,000

The trading income assessments for the four years that the business is taxed total (£15,000 + £18,000 + £36,000 + £30,000) = £99,000. This agrees with the total adjusted profits over the life of the business.

capital allowances when a business ceases

Capital allowances are calculated separately for each accounting period of a business, and the result forms part of the adjusted trading profits of each accounting period.

When a business ceases capital allowances will need to be calculated for the final accounting period, but special care must be taken since:

- there can be <u>no</u> WDA, FYA or AIA in this last period
- all remaining assets will have been disposed of by the business
- balancing allowances and / or balancing charges will occur for all pools (including the main pool) since there can be no written down values to carry forward

Where there is partial private use of assets any allowances or charges will need to reflect only the business proportion of the asset use. However, you may remember that balancing allowances and charges are not time-apportioned if we have long or short accounting periods, so at least that will not create a complication.

Any asset bought from the business by the owner of the business must be included as a disposal at open market value.

Case Study

S. TOPP TRADING:
CAPITAL ALLOWANCES AT END OF TRADE

Steve Topp has been running his business for many years, with an accounting date of 31 December.

The written down values carried forward at 31 December 2018 were:

Main Pool	£32,000
Car (80% business use)	£16,000

The business ceased trading on 30/6/2019. The adjusted trading profit for the period 1/1/2019 to 30/6/2019 was £40,000, before deducting capital allowances. There is also £10,000 overlap profit from the start of the business available for set off.

Steve managed to sell all the remaining business assets (except the car) for £14,000. He bought the car from the business himself to use privately for a market value figure of £17,000.

required

- Calculate the plant & machinery capital allowances for the accounting period 1/1/2019 to 30/6/2019.
- Calculate the trading income assessment for the final tax year of the business.

solution

Plant & machinery capital allowances computation

	Main pool	Single asset pool car (20% private use)	Capital allowances
	£	£	£
WDV bf	32,000	16,000	
Disposals	(14,000)	(17,000)	
	18,000	(1,000)	
Balancing allowances	(18,000)		18,000
Balancing charge		1,000 x 80%	(800)
WDV cf	0	0	
Total Capital Allowances			17,200

Trading Income assessment working:

	£
Accounting period 1/1/2019 - 30/6/2019:	
Adjusted trading profits (before capital allowances)	40,000
less capital allowances	(17,200)
	22,800

Tax Year 2019/20	**Basis period 1/1/2019 - 30/6/2019:**	
	Adjusted Profit (as above)	22,800
	Less overlap profits	(10,000)
	Trading Income assessment	12,800

CHANGE OF ACCOUNTING DATE

Sole traders and partnerships are permitted to change their accounting date (the date that their accounts are made up to) under certain circumstances:

- the period for the first accounts ending on the new date must not exceed 18 months
- HMRC must be notified of the change in accounting date by 31 January following the tax year of change (the normal filing date for an online tax return)

■ changes in accounting date are not normally permitted more than once in every five years, unless HMRC are satisfied that the change is for valid commercial reasons

The period from the old accounting date (which will be the end of the last basis period) to the new accounting date is known as the relevant period.

When an accounting date is changed the basis period for the tax year in which the change occurs will end on the new accounting date.

■ where the new accounting date is **less than 12 months** from the old accounting date (ie the relevant period is less than 12 months) the **basis period will be for 12 months up to the new accounting date**. This will create an **overlap period** – based on the number of months that the relevant period is below 12. This overlap profit will be added to any overlap profit created when the business started and the total will be deducted when the business ceases (or maybe earlier if there is another change of accounting date)

■ where the new accounting date is **more than 12 months** from the old accounting date, the basis period for the tax year of change will be the **period from the end of the last basis period to the new accounting date**. To compensate for this long basis period, **previous overlap profits** equal to the number of months that this relevant period exceeds 12 months **can be deducted**. This will reduce the overlap profit carried forward that will be deducted when the business ceases (or possibly on a later change of accounting date)

To understand how this system operates, we will now extend two of the examples that we used earlier.

example 1: relevant period less than 12 months.

John Able (see pages 7.7 and 7.8) has used an accounting date of 30 June. He has overlap profits brought forward of £13,500 relating to a nine month period.

Assume that he decides to change his accounting date to 30 April in 2021. His accounts showed tax-adjusted profits as follows:

12 months to 30 June 2020	£42,000
10 months to 30 April 2021	£37,000

The year of change is 2021/22 and the relevant period is 10 months.

The basis periods and trading income assessments will be:

2020/21	1/7/2019 - 30/6/2020		£42,000
2021/22	1/5/2020 - 30/4/2021	2/12 x £42,000	
		+ £37,000	£44,000

The overlap profits created here relating to the period 1/5/2020 to 30/6/2020 are £7,000. These will be added to the existing overlap profits of £13,500, and the total of £20,500 will be carried forward.

example 2: relevant period more than 12 months.

Edgar Evans (see pages 7.7 and 7.11) has used an accounting date of 31 July. He has overlap profits brought forward of £20,000 representing an 8 month period.

Assume that he decides to change his accounting date to 30 September in 2021. His accounts showed tax-adjusted profits as follows:

12 months to 31 July 2020	£48,000
14 months to 30 September 2021	£57,400

The year of change is 2021/22 and the relevant period is 14 months. This exceeds 12 months by 2 months, and so 2 months' previous overlap profits can be offset.

The basis periods and trading income assessments will be:

2020/21	1/8/2019 - 31/7/2020		£48,000
2021/22	1/8/2020 - 30/9/2021	£57,400	
Less part of original overlap profits £20,000 x 2/8		(£5,000)	
			£52,400

The overlap profits remaining to be carried forward are now (£20,000 – £5,000) = £15,000.

DIVIDING TRADING PROFITS BETWEEN PARTNERS

We have seen throughout the last two chapters that a partnership is taxed in the same way as a sole trader. It uses the same adjustment mechanism for trading profits; capital allowances are calculated in exactly the same way, and basis periods throughout the business are also identical.

The way in which partners decide to divide their profits is entirely their choice, and is stated in their partnership agreement. The division agreed will not only apply to the actual profits that the partnership generates, but also to the amount that is assessable on each partner for Income Tax purposes.

simple profit splits

If a partnership is made up of two individuals who agree to share profits and losses equally, then the calculation of each partner's trading income assessment is straightforward. The adjusted trading profits for the partnership (after capital allowances) is simply halved, and each partner is assessed on this figure.

So, for example, suppose the ongoing partnership of Sue and Adam had adjusted profits for the accounting period of 12 months to 31/12/2019 of £40,000 (after capital allowances). If their agreement was to divide profits and losses equally then the trading income assessment for Sue for the tax year 2019/20 would be £20,000, and the assessment for Adam for the same tax year would also be £20,000. Note that the current year basis of assessment is used here, just as it is for sole traders.

The simplest split is to agree a percentage that each partner will be entitled to. This could be a straightforward 50%:50% as just mentioned, or could be any other figures that the partners feel is fair. A partnership of three individuals may, for example agree that a 60%:30%:10% split is fair in their particular circumstances. These divisions could also be expressed as ratios – 50%:50% would be shown as 1:1, while 60%:30%:10% could be expressed as 6:3:1.

more complex profit splits

Some partnerships may, however, agree a more complex division of profits and losses. They may for example agree that out of the profits,

- 'salaries' are to be provided for some or all partners, and/or
- 'interest on capital' should be paid to partners based on their investment in the partnership

Both these types of appropriation would be made out of the total profits that the partnership has made. The larger these payments are, the less profit will remain to be shared by the partners by using the agreed percentages or ratios.

For tax purposes the starting point would always be the adjusted profits of the accounting period (after capital allowances), and this is the amount that the combined trading income assessments of each partner must total. Any salaries or interest on capitals are allocated first, and then the remaining profit (or loss) is shared amongst the partners. Note that partners' salaries and interest on capitals are trading profits, and are taxed as part of trading income. Partners' salaries are not assessed as employment income, which only relates to employees.

If a profit sharing arrangement changes, the agreement that is in existence during the accounting period is the one that applies to dividing the tax-adjusted profits of that accounting period.

The Case Study that follows shows how individual partners' assessments are calculated for an ongoing partnership where the normal 'current year basis' is operating. We will then go on to look at some other situations.

Case Study

PENN, QUILL AND WRIGHT: PARTNERS' ASSESSMENTS

John Penn, Daisy Quill and Sue Wright have been trading in partnership for several years. The partnership produces accounts each year up to the 30 June. Their partnership agreement states that the following salaries, rates of interest on capitals, and shares of remaining profits or losses should apply:

	Salary (pa)	Interest on capital	Share of profit/loss
John Penn	£10,000	5%	30%
Daisy Quill	£15,000	5%	20%
Sue Wright	–	5%	50%

The partnership accounts for the twelve month accounting period to 30/6/2019 shows tax-adjusted profits of £95,000 (after deducting capital allowances):

The capital accounts balances for the partners are:

John Penn	£100,000
Daisy Quill	£50,000
Sue Wright	£250,000

required

Calculate the trading income assessments for each of the three partners that will be based on the adjusted profits for this period, and state the tax year that the assessments will be for.

solution

The following calculation shows how the adjusted profits are divided up:

	John Penn	Daisy Quill	Sue Wright	Total remaining
	£	£	£	£
Adjusted Profits				95,000
Salaries	10,000	15,000	0	(25,000)
Balance Remaining				70,000
Interest on Capitals	5,000	2,500	12,500	(20,000)
Balance Remaining				50,000
Share of Balance	15,000	10,000	25,000	(50,000)
	30,000	27,500	37,500	

The calculation follows the same principles that are used for dividing profits for financial accounting purposes (with which you may be familiar) – the only difference is that here our starting point is the adjusted profits after capital allowances.

Notes:

- Salaries and interest on capitals are deducted from the original adjusted profit first, leaving a balance of £50,000 to be shared using the profit sharing percentages.
- Interest on capitals are calculated using the individual partners' balances on their capital accounts.
- The overall amounts allocated to each partner of £30,000, £27,500, and £37,500 total the original adjusted profit figure of £95,000.

The trading income assessments for each partner for 2019/20 (since the accounting period ends in that tax year) will be:

John Penn	£30,000
Daisy Quill	£27,500
Sue Wright	£37,500

partnership losses

If a partnership incurs a trading loss, each partner's share of the loss can be dealt with independently. This means that each partner has the same choices of how their own share of the trading loss should be relieved as a sole trader. The individual partners could all choose different ways to relieve their own loss, according to their personal circumstances.

when partnerships start or cease trading

When a partnership is first formed and starts trading, the basis periods that apply to each partners' share will be exactly the same as if they were sole traders. Therefore the rules that we saw earlier in the chapter for commencing or ceasing trading or changing accounting date apply to both sole traders and partnerships.

CHANGES IN A PARTNERSHIP

when the profit sharing agreement changes

Depending on when the existing partners decide to alter their profit sharing agreement, there are two possible implications:

- if the change is made with effect from a normal accounting date (ie the start/end of an accounting period), then the new arrangement will simply apply to the new accounting period. This will mean that the new share of profits will apply entirely to the basis period of a new tax year

■ if the change is made during an accounting period, the adjusted profits (after capital allowances) will first have to be time-apportioned into the two parts of the period – before and after the change. Each part of the profits will then be divided amongst the partners according to the agreement in force at the time, and the two parts for each partner added together to form their assessment for the tax year

when a new partner joins a partnership

When a new partner joins an established partnership (or a partnership is formed by an individual joining an established sole trader) the new partner is treated as if they had started a new business on the date that they joined. There will need to be a new profit sharing agreement that incorporates the additional partner, and this will operate from the date the new partner started.

The new partner will be subject to the opening basis of assessment rules, but the established partners (or established sole trader) will carry on applying the normal 'current year' basis to their shares of the adjusted profits. The new partner may therefore have personal overlap profits that will be carried forward until they leave the partnership, or the partnership ceases trading, or maybe changes accounting date.

If the new partner starts on a normal accounting date for the partnership the situation is not too complicated, as the following example shows.

example: introduction of a new partner at the start of an accounting period

Rose and Daisy have been in partnership for several years, sharing profits and losses equally. They have always made their accounts up to 31 December each year. On 1 January 2020 they are joined by Bud, and the partnership agreement is changed to Rose 40%, Daisy 40%, Bud 20% from that date. They have never used salaries or interest on capitals as part of their profit sharing arrangement.

The first accounting year of the revised partnership (the year ended 31 December 2020) produced adjusted profits (after capital allowances) of £120,000.

For both Rose and Daisy their share of the profits for the y/e 31/12/2020 will be £120,000 x 40% = £48,000 each. The figure will form their trading income assessments for 2020/21 under the normal 'current year basis' rules.

Bud will be treated as if he started a new business on 1 January 2020. His share of the profits for the accounting year ended 31/12/2020 of 20% x £120,000 = £24,000 will be used to calculate the assessments for his first two tax years:

Bud's assessment for the tax year 2019/20 will use the basis period 1/1/2020 - 5/4/2020. His assessment for 2019/20 will therefore be £24,000 x 3/12 = £6,000.

His assessment for the tax year 2020/21 will use the basis period 1/1/2020 - 31/12/2020. His assessment for 2020/21 will therefore be £24,000.

This means that Bud will have overlap profits of £6,000, (relating to the period 1/1/2020 - 5/4/2020) that he will carry forward.

a partner joining partway through an accounting period

If the new partner joins partway through an accounting period, the adjusted profits of the period must first be time-apportioned into the parts either side of that date. Each existing partner's assessment will then be generated by adding together their shares from each part of the period, just as if they had simply changed their profit sharing arrangement. The new partner will be treated as if he had started a new business on the date he joined. The following example will illustrate the situation.

example: introduction of a new partner partway into an accounting period

Oak and Ash have been in partnership for several years, sharing profits and losses equally. They have always made their accounts up to 31 December each year. On 1 October 2019 they are joined by Elm, and the partnership agreement is changed to Oak 40%, Ash 40%, Elm 20% from that date. They have never used salaries or interest on capitals as part of their profit sharing arrangement.

The year ended 31 December 2019 produced adjusted profits (after capital allowances) of £120,000. The year ended 31 December 2020 produced adjusted profits (after capital allowances) of £180,000.

The first step is to time-apportion the adjusted profits into the periods before and after Elm joined:

1/1/2019 - 30/9/2019	£120,000 x 9/12 = £90,000
1/10/2019 - 31/12/2019	£120,000 x 3/12 = £30,000

Oak and Ash

For the existing partners, Oak and Ash, they will each have a share of the profits for the whole accounting year made up of:

1/1/2019 - 30/9/2019	£90,000 x 50%	=	£45,000, plus
1/10/2019 - 31/12/2019	£30,000 x 40%	=	£12,000
			£57,000

For both Oak and Ash this figure will form the assessment for 2019/20 under the normal rules.

For 2020/21 their assessments will each be based on £180,000 x 40% = £72,000.

Elm

The new partner, Elm will be treated as if he started a new business on 1 October 2019.

He has a share of the profits for the period 1/10/2019 - 31/12/2019 of

20% x £30,000 = £6,000.

He has a share of the profits for the period 1/1/2020 - 31/12/2020 of

20% x £180,000 = £36,000.

These amounts will be used to calculate the assessments for his first two tax years:

Elm's assessment for his first tax year – 2019/20 will use the basis period 1/10/2019 - 5/4/2020.

His trading income assessment for 2019/20 will therefore be made up of:

1/10/2019 - 31/12/2019		£6,000, plus
1/1/2020 - 5/4/2020 £36,000 x 3/12	=	£9,000
		£15,000

His assessment for the tax year 2020/21 will use the basis period 1/1/2020 - 31/12/2020. His assessment for 2020/21 will therefore be £36,000.

Elm will have overlap profits of £9,000, (relating to the period 1/1/2020 - 5/4/2020) that he will carry forward until either he leaves the partnership, or it ceases trading, or the accounting date is changed.

when a partner leaves a partnership

If a partner leaves then the treatment follows the same logic as we have just seen. It is only the leaving partner that has the closing basis period rules applied to his/her share of the profits. The individual's own overlap profits (if any) would be deducted from their final share of profits. The existing partners carry on as normal.

The following example illustrates the situation.

example: partner leaving a partnership

Reddy, Eddy and Go have been in business for several years, sharing profits equally, and making accounts up to 31 December. Go decides to leave the partnership on 30 June 2020.

The partnership had the following adjusted profits (after capital allowances) for their accounting periods.

1/1/2019 - 31/12/2019	£75,000
1/1/2020 - 31/12/2020	£60,000

Go has personal overlap profits of £1,000 brought forward from when he started in partnership.

For **Go**, the assessable profits for his last two tax years of the business are:

Tax year	Basis period	Trading income assessment	
2019/20	1/1/2019 - 31/12/2019	£75,000 x 1/3	= **£25,000**
2020/21	1/1/2020 - 30/6/2020	£60,000 x 6/12 x 1/3	= £10,000
		less overlap profits	(£1,000)
			£9,000

NATIONAL INSURANCE FOR THE SELF-EMPLOYED

As we saw in Chapter 1, sole traders and partners are liable to Class 2 and Class 4 National Insurance contributions.

■ Class 2 contributions are payable at a flat rate of £3.00 per week (unless the 'small profits threshold' applies), and in addition

■ Class 4 contributions are payable on the profits above £8,632 per year

The profits for self-employed NIC purposes are the same ones that are used for Income Tax purposes – the assessable trading profits. For partners this refers to their personal share of the assessable profits, not those relating to the whole partnership.

Where an individual's profits are less than £6,365 then Class 2 contributions need not be paid.

The rates for Class 4 contributions are:

9% of profits for the year between £8,632 and £50,000, plus

2% of profits above £50,000.

If profits are below £8,632 then there are no Class 4 contributions.

A REVIEW OF INCOME TAX PAYMENT DATES

In Chapter 1 we saw that the final date for payment of Income Tax is 31 January following the end of the tax year (eg 31/1/21 for 2019/20). We also discussed briefly the timing of payments on account that are sometimes due. We will now look a little more closely at these interim payments.

payments on account

The two payments on account are calculated as follows:

Each payment on account is based on **half** the Income Tax and NIC amount due for the **previous** year, (after deducting tax paid under PAYE and other Income Tax deducted at source).

Suppose, for example, that a partner only had trading income, and no other income. If his Income Tax and NIC liability for 2018/19 was £7,000, none of this would have been paid by deduction at source.

This means that for 2019/20 he would need to make two payments on account. Each of the two payments on account would be:

1/2 x £7,000 = £3,500.

These payments on account for 2019/20 would be made on 31/1/20 and 31/7/20. If the Income Tax amount for each year is quite similar, there would not be much left to pay (or have refunded) on the final date of 31/1/21.

Payments on account do not have to be made if either:

■ the amount of tax payable the previous year was less than £1,000 (excluding tax deducted at source), or

■ more than 80% of the tax due the previous year was collected at source

Payments on account can also be reduced or eliminated if the taxpayer makes a claim that his tax for the coming year will be less than for the previous year.

INTEREST AND PENALTIES

Interest on tax is payable on late payments, and also on any underpayment of the amount due on account. The rate is 3.0% at the time of going to press.

Penalties are also payable for:

1. Late submission of tax return:

■ a £100 penalty for missing the deadline – regardless of the amount of tax involved

■ for returns over three months late – an additional daily penalty of £10 per day up to a 90 day maximum of £900

■ for returns over six months late – an additional £300 or 5% of the tax due if this is higher

■ for returns over 12 months late – a further £300 or 5% of the tax due if this is higher

There are very limited 'reasonable excuses' for late returns; for example a fire or flood destroying paperwork or a serious illness.

The tax return submission deadlines are:

■ 31 October following end of tax year for paper-based returns

■ 31 January following end of tax year for online submission

2. Late payment of the balancing payment by more than 30 days:

■ 5% of the tax due plus

■ further 5% of the tax due if still unpaid by 31 July

■ a third 5% of the tax due if payment has still not been made 12 months after it was due

Note that the penalties are in addition to the interest charges.

incorrect returns

If after submitting a tax return, the taxpayer discovers that he has made an error or omission, he should notify HM Revenue & Customs as soon as possible. If the alteration results in less tax being payable than was originally thought, the taxpayer will receive a refund. Where additional tax is due this will of course need to be paid, plus interest that will run from the normal payment date.

If a taxpayer (or his agent) finds that they have made a mistake on a tax return they have normally got 12 months from 31 January following the end of the tax year to correct it. For the tax year 2019/20 amendments can therefore be made by 31 January 2022.

HMRC can still be told about errors after the above date, but then they must be notified to HMRC in writing. Such notifications must be made within four years of the end of the tax year. This means the deadline relating to the tax year 2019/20 is 5 April 2024.

The following system for penalties applies for incorrect information stated in tax returns and documents. This is based on a percentage of the extra tax due, depending on the behaviour that gave rise to the error.

If the error is:

■ due to **lack of reasonable care**, the penalty is between 0% and 30% of the extra tax due

■ **deliberate**, the penalty is between 20% and 70% of the extra tax due, and if

■ **deliberate and concealed**, the penalty is between 30% and 100% of the extra tax due.

The penalty also depends on whether the disclosure was prompted or unprompted. This gives the following series of penalty rates:

Type of behaviour	Unprompted disclosure	Prompted disclosure
Reasonable care	No penalty	No penalty
Careless	0% to 30%	15% to 30%
Deliberate	20% to 70%	35% to 70%
Deliberate and concealed	30% to 100%	50% to 100%

The percentage can be reduced if the taxpayer tells HMRC about the error(s), helps them work out the extra tax, and gives HMRC access to check the figures. If the taxpayer took 'reasonable care' there is no penalty.

These penalties also apply if a taxpayer fails to notify HMRC that he has self employed income that is subject to tax.

This system also applies to Corporation Tax, as we saw earlier. The system for 'enquiries' is also the same as for Corporation Tax.

failure to keep records

There can be a penalty for not keeping the required records for the correct length of time of up to £3,000 per tax year for individuals.

COMPLETING THE TAX RETURN PAGES

The tax return for individuals has to be completed and submitted at the latest by 31 January that follows the end of the tax year – for example 31 January 2021 for the tax year 2019/20. This assumes online submission. The completed tax return contains information about the individual's income from all sources, and supplementary pages are used for those with specific types of income. In studying this learning area, we are concerned with the supplementary pages that relate to sole traders and partners, and you may be asked to complete these in your assessment.

We have illustrated all the return pages with the 2018/19 versions, since the 2019/20 versions were not available when this book was published.

self-employment pages

There are two alternative versions of the supplementary self-employment pages:

■ the 'full' version is 6 pages long and is suitable for dealing with situations with any level of turnover, and where there are complexities, for example businesses that are starting or ceasing

■ the 'short' version is 2 pages long and can only be used for sole traders where (amongst other conditions):

- – Turnover is less than £85,000 p.a. (2018/19 limit)
- – The accounting period is the same as the basis period.
- – There is no claim to set off overlap profits.

Completion of the 'full' version of these supplementary pages could form an assessment task.

self-employment (full)

The page that you are most likely to be asked to complete is page SEF 2 and this (2018/19 versions) is reproduced on the next page. The whole form is shown in the appendix to this book.

The following commentary gives an overview of the main issues. Later on, we will demonstrate how the page is completed by using a Case Study.

Page SEF 2 contains boxes for a comprehensive analysis of the statement of profit or loss (income statement). It provides two columns for expenses,

■ the one on the left (boxes 17 - 30) for total expenses (ie taken from the income statement, before adjusting for any disallowable amounts), and

■ the one on the right (boxes 32 - 45) for any disallowable items. Both columns have total boxes (31 for total expenses and 46 for total disallowable amounts)

Business expenses

Please read the 'Self-employment (full) notes' before filling in this section.

Total expenses	Disallowable expenses
If your annual turnover was below £85,000, you may just put your total expenses in box 31	Use this column if the figures in boxes 17 to 30 include disallowable amounts

17 Cost of goods bought for resale or goods used

£   . 0 0

32

£   . 0 0

18 Construction industry – payments to subcontractors

£   . 0 0

33

£   . 0 0

19 Wages, salaries and other staff costs

£   . 0 0

34

£   . 0 0

20 Car, van and travel expenses

£   . 0 0

35

£   . 0 0

21 Rent, rates, power and insurance costs

£   . 0 0

36

£   . 0 0

22 Repairs and maintenance of property and equipment

£   . 0 0

37

£   . 0 0

23 Phone, fax, stationery and other office costs

£   . 0 0

38

£   . 0 0

24 Advertising and business entertainment costs

£   . 0 0

39

£   . 0 0

25 Interest on bank and other loans

£   . 0 0

40

£   . 0 0

26 Bank, credit card and other financial charges

£   . 0 0

41

£   . 0 0

27 Irrecoverable debts written off

£   . 0 0

42

£   . 0 0

28 Accountancy, legal and other professional fees

£   . 0 0

43

£   . 0 0

29 Depreciation and loss or profit on sale of assets

£   . 0 0

44

£   . 0 0

30 Other business expenses

£   . 0 0

45

£   . 0 0

31 Total expenses (total of boxes 17 to 30)

£   . 0 0

46 Total disallowable expenses (total of boxes 32 to 45)

£   . 0 0

The following Case Study will revise some of the main issues relating to a sole trader that we have examined, and show how in practice the full version supplementary pages are completed.

MARK UPP:
A COMPREHENSIVE PROBLEM

Mark Upp commenced in business as a market trader on 1 January 2020. He produced a set of accounts for the period 1/1/2020 - 31/12/2020 as follows:

	£	£
Sales		90,000
less cost of sales:		45,000
Gross profit		45,000
less expenses:		
Insurance	2,500	
Part Time Employees' Wages & NIC	6,500	
Depreciation	3,250	
Motor Expenses	1,000	
General Expenses	3,000	
Bank Interest	1,000	
		17,250
Net Profit		27,750

Notes:

1 Mark has agreed that his car is used 75% for business purposes and 25% privately. The motor expenses figure in the accounts relates to both business and private mileage. The car was bought for £13,000 on 1/1/2020. It has emissions of 105 g/km.

2 Mark took goods from his market stall shop throughout the year to use privately. The cost of sales figure in the accounts of £45,000 is after deducting the £2,000 cost price of these goods. Mark's normal mark-up is 100% on cost.

3 Mark bought his portable stall for £6,400 when he commenced business. It qualifies as plant & machinery.

required
- Calculate the capital allowances claimable by Mark for the accounting year ended 31/12/2020.
- Calculate the adjusted profits for the same period, after taking into account the capital allowances.
- Calculate the trading income assessment for Mark for 2019/20.

- Calculate the Class 4 National Insurance contributions payable by Mark for 2019/20.
- Complete the full version supplementary page SEF2 of the tax return for Mark for 2019/20.

solution

Capital Allowances

AIA is claimable on the portable stall of £6,400.

	Main pool	Single asset pool car (25% private)	Capital allowances
	£	£	£	£
WDV bf		–	–	
Additions				
without FYAs:				
Car			13,000	
WDA 18%			(2,340) x 75%	1,755
Acquisition - stall	6,400			
AIA claimed	(6,400)	0		6,400
WDV cf		–	10,660	
Total Capital Allowances				8,155

Adjustment of Profits

	£	£
Net Profit per accounts		27,750
Add Back:		
Expenditure that is shown in the accounts but is not allowable		
Depreciation		3,250
Private motor expenses (£1,000 x 25%)		250
Adjustment to reflect profit in goods taken for own use		2,000
		33,250
Deduct:		
Allowable expenditure not shown in accounts		
Capital Allowances	8,155	
		(8,155)
Adjusted Profits for y/e 31/12/2020		25,095

Trading Income assessment for 2019/20

This is Mark's first tax year for the business. The basis period is:
1/1/2020 - 5/4/2020

This is apportioned from the adjusted profits as:
£25,095 x 3/12 = £6,274

Class 4 National Insurance

This is calculated based on the trading income. As his income is below £8,632 there is no Class 4 NIC payable for 2019/20.

Supplementary tax return page

This is shown on the next page.

Make sure that you can understand where the data has been obtained for each box that has been completed.

Note that we have used the 2018/19 version of the form here as the 2019/20 version was not available when this book was published.

Business expenses

Please read the 'Self-employment (full) notes' before filling in this section.

Total expenses

If your annual turnover was below £85,000, you may just put your total expenses in box 31

Disallowable expenses

Use this column if the figures in boxes 17 to 30 include disallowable amounts

Box	Description	Total expenses	Box	Disallowable expenses
17	Cost of goods bought for resale or goods used	£ 45000 · 0 0	32	£ · 0 0
18	Construction industry – payments to subcontractors	£ · 0 0	33	£ · 0 0
19	Wages, salaries and other staff costs	£ 6500 · 0 0	34	£ · 0 0
20	Car, van and travel expenses	£ 1000 · 0 0	35	£ 250 · 0 0
21	Rent, rates, power and insurance costs	£ 2500 · 0 0	36	£ · 0 0
22	Repairs and maintenance of property and equipment	£ · 0 0	37	£ · 0 0
23	Phone, fax, stationery and other office costs	£ · 0 0	38	£ · 0 0
24	Advertising and business entertainment costs	£ · 0 0	39	£ · 0 0
25	Interest on bank and other loans	£ 1000 · 0 0	40	£ · 0 0
26	Bank, credit card and other financial charges	£ · 0 0	41	£ · 0 0
27	Irrecoverable debts written off	£ · 0 0	42	£ · 0 0
28	Accountancy, legal and other professional fees	£ · 0 0	43	£ · 0 0
29	Depreciation and loss or profit on sale of assets	£ 3250 · 0 0	44	£ 3250 · 0 0
30	Other business expenses	£ 3000 · 0 0	45	£ · 0 0
31	Total expenses (total of boxes 17 to 30)	£ 62250 · 0 0	46	Total disallowable expenses (total of boxes 32 to 45) £ 3500 · 0 0

PARTNERSHIP TAX RETURN

Each partnership needs to complete a tax return (the SA800) which records the profits of the partnership as a whole, as well as the amount of profit allocated to each partner.

Each partner would also complete partnership supplementary pages on their own individual tax returns, but we do not need to consider those pages for our studies.

We need to be able to complete page 6 of the short version of the partnership tax return, and the 2018/19 version is reproduced on the following page. The whole form is shown in the appendix.

Page 6 is where the allocation of the partnership profits commences. The left side of the page is for a summary of the partnership profits, and the right side is the allocation of those profits to the first partner.

The following boxes in particular may need to be completed in an examination:

Box 11   Profit from a trade or profession – this is the profit of the partnership after adjustments for disallowable expenses and capital allowances etc.

Box 13   Income from untaxed savings – this is for the amount of interest received from banks etc.

Box 24   CIS deductions – this is for tax deductions made from amounts received by the partnership. It relates to the construction industry where there is a scheme set up so that sub-contractors (eg the partnership) receive amounts after deduction of tax (in a similar way to PAYE).

Box 24A   Other tax taken off – this is unlikely to apply in your tasks.

Box 29   Partnership charges – these are amounts paid out by the partnership that individual partners can claim relief for. These must be for wholly commercial reasons, but the detail of these is beyond the scope of your studies.

Partnership Statement (short) for the year ended 5 April 2019

Please read these instructions before completing the Statement

Use these pages to allocate partnership income if the only income for the relevant return period was trading and professional income or untaxed interest and alternative finance receipts from UK banks and building societies. Otherwise you must download the 'Partnership Statement (Full)' pages to record details of the allocation of all the partnership income. Go to www.gov.uk/taxreturnforms

Step 1   Fill in boxes 1 to 29 and boxes A and B as appropriate. Get the figures you need from the relevant boxes in the Partnership Tax Return. Complete a separate Statement for each accounting period covered by this Partnership Tax Return and for each trade or profession carried on by the partnership.

Step 2   Then allocate the amounts in boxes 11 to 29 attributable to each partner using the allocation columns on this page and page 7, read the Partnership Tax Return Guide, go to www.gov.uk/taxreturnforms
If the partnership has more than 3 partners, please photocopy page 7.

Step 3   Each partner will need a copy of their allocation of income to fill in their personal tax return.

PARTNERSHIP INFORMATION

If the partnership business includes a trade or profession, enter here the accounting period for which appropriate items in this statement are returned.

Start **1** / /

End **2** / /

Nature of trade **3**

MIXED PARTNERSHIPS

Tick here if this Statement is drawn up using Corporation Tax rules **4**

Tick here if this Statement is drawn up using tax rules for non-residents **5**

Individual partner details

6 Name of partner

Address

Postcode

Date appointed as a partner
(if during 2017–18 or 2018–19) Partner's Unique Taxpayer Reference (UTR)
7 / / **8**

Date ceased to be a partner
(if during 2017–18 or 2018–19) Partner's National Insurance number
9 / / **10**

Partnership's profits, losses, income and tax credits	Tick this box if the items entered in the box had foreign tax taken off ▼	Partner's share of profits, losses, income and tax credits
		Copy figures in boxes 11 to 29 to boxes in the individual's Partnership (short) pages as shown below

● for an accounting period ended in 2018 to 2019

from box 3.83	Profit from a trade or profession	**A**	**11** £	Profit **11** £	Copy this figure to box 8
from box 3.82	Adjustment on change of basis		**11A** £	**11A** £	Copy this figure to box 10
from box 3.84	Loss from a trade or profession	**B**	**12** £	Loss **12** £	Copy this figure to box 8
from box 3.94	Disguised remuneration		**12A**	**12A**	Copy to box 15

● for the period 6 April 2018 to 5 April 2019*

from box 7.9A	Income from untaxed UK savings	**13** £	**13** £	Copy this figure to box 28
from box 3.97	CIS deductions made by contractors on account of tax	**24** £	**24** £	Copy this figure to box 30
from box 3.98	Other tax taken off trading income	**24A** £	**24A** £	Copy this figure to box 31
from box 3.117	Partnership charges	**29** £	**29** £	Copy this figure to box 4, 'Other tax reliefs' section on page Ai 2 in your personal tax return

* If you're a 'CT Partnership' see the Partnership Tax Return Guide

PENN, QUILL AND WRIGHT: PARTNERSHIP TAX RETURN

John Penn, Daisy Quill and Sue Wright have been trading in partnership for several years. They produce accounts each year up to 30 June. Their individual trading income assessments have already been calculated for 2019/20 as follows (see Case Study on pages 7.19 – 7.20):

John Penn	£30,000
Daisy Quill	£27,500
Sue Wright	£37,500

These profit figures are based on the accounting year ended 30 June 2019, which recorded an adjusted profit for tax purposes (after capital allowances) of £95,000.

In addition to the above trading income, the partnership also receives untaxed savings interest, which is split equally amongst the partners. This totalled £3,000 for the tax year 2019/20.

required

Complete (as far as information permits) page 6 of the partnership tax return for 2019/20, relating to the partnership and John Penn share.

solution

See next page.

Note that we have used the 2018/19 version of the form here as the 2019/20 version was not available when this book was published.

Partnership Statement (short) for the year ended 5 April 2019

Please read these instructions before completing the Statement

Use these pages to allocate partnership income if the only income for the relevant return period was trading and professional income or untaxed interest and alternative finance receipts from UK banks and building societies. Otherwise you must download the 'Partnership Statement (Full)' pages to record details of the allocation of all the partnership income. Go to www.gov.uk/taxreturnforms

Step 1   Fill in boxes 1 to 29 and boxes A and B as appropriate. Get the figures you need from the relevant boxes in the Partnership Tax Return. Complete a separate Statement for each accounting period covered by this Partnership Tax Return and for each trade or profession carried on by the partnership.

Step 2   Then allocate the amounts in boxes 11 to 29 attributable to each partner using the allocation columns on this page and page 7, read the Partnership Tax Return Guide, go to www.gov.uk/taxreturnforms
If the partnership has more than 3 partners, please photocopy page 7.

Step 3   Each partner will need a copy of their allocation of income to fill in their personal tax return.

PARTNERSHIP INFORMATION
If the partnership business includes a trade or profession, enter here the accounting period for which appropriate items in this statement are returned.

Start   **1**   1 / 7 /18

End   **2**   30 / 6 / 19

Nature of trade   **3**

MIXED PARTNERSHIPS

Tick here if this Statement is drawn up using Corporation Tax rules **4**

Tick here if this Statement is drawn up using tax rules for non-residents **5**

Individual partner details

6   Name of partner   JOHN PENN

Address

Postcode

Date appointed as a partner
(if during 2017–18 or 2018–19) Partner's Unique Taxpayer Reference (UTR)

7   /   /   **8**

Date ceased to be a partner
(if during 2017–18 or 2018–19) Partner's National Insurance number

9   /   /   **10**

Partnership's profits, losses, income and tax credits

Tick this box if the items entered in the box had foreign tax taken off ▼

Partner's share of profits, losses, income and tax credits

Copy figures in boxes 11 to 29 to boxes in the individual's Partnership (short) pages as shown below

● for an accounting period ended in 2018 to 2019

from box 3.83	Profit from a trade or profession	**A** **11** £ 95000	Profit **11** £ 30000	Copy this figure to box 8
from box 3.82	Adjustment on change of basis	**11A** £	**11A** £	Copy this figure to box 10
from box 3.84	Loss from a trade or profession	**B** **12** £	Loss **12** £	Copy this figure to box 8
from box 3.94	Disguised remuneration	**12A**	**12A**	Copy to box 15

● for the period 6 April 2018 to 5 April 2019*

from box 7.9A	Income from untaxed UK savings	**13** £ 3000	**13** £ 1000	Copy this figure to box 28
from box 3.97	CIS deductions made by contractors on account of tax	**24** £	**24** £	Copy this figure to box 30
from box 3.98	Other tax taken off trading income	**24A** £	**24A** £	Copy this figure to box 31
from box 3.117	Partnership charges	**29** £	**29** £	Copy this figure to box 4, 'Other tax reliefs' section on page Ai 2 in your personal tax return

* If you're a 'CT Partnership' see the Partnership Tax Return Guide

SA800 2019   PARTNERSHIP TAX RETURN: PAGE 6

KEEPING RECORDS

Sole traders and partnerships need to keep records relating to their trading for five years after the online tax return is due to be submitted. For the tax year 2019/20 the return is due on 31 January 2021, and so the records must be kept until 31 January 2026. This date would be extended if HM Revenue & Customs were holding an enquiry into the taxpayer.

The records kept would be very similar to those retained by a limited company, as explained earlier. The records should be able to back up the information on the tax return, and would include:

- statement of profit or loss (income statement) and statements of financial position (balance sheets)
- cash books and bank statements
- account ledgers or working papers
- invoices relating to allowable expenses and the acquisition of non-current (fixed) assets
- non-current asset schedules
- taxation working papers, including capital allowance computations
- copies of tax returns

Chapter Summary

■ When sole traders or partnerships commence trading they are subject to special basis period rules. The first tax year in which they are assessed is the year into which the start date falls. The basis period for this tax year is from the date of commencement until the following 5 April. The following tax year will usually have as its basis period as either the 12 months ending on the accounting date in that tax year, or if that is impossible, the first 12 months of the business. Overlap profits may arise that have been assessed twice, and these can be relieved on cessation.

■ When sole traders or partnerships cease trading the final tax year will be the one in which the final date of trading falls. The basis period for this tax year will be from the last day of the basis period of the previous tax year to the date of cessation.

■ Change of accounting date is permitted subject to certain criteria. The new accounting date is used as the end of the basis period. Depending how long the relevant period is there could be additional overlap profits generated, or previous overlap profits offset.

■ Trading profits and losses for a partnership are divided amongst the partners according to the profit sharing agreement that is in force during the accounting period. This could include the allocation of salaries and/or interest on capitals, as well as a share of remaining profits or losses. These amounts all form part of the individual partners' trading income assessment.

■ When an individual partner joins or leaves a partnership they are subject to the opening or closing basis of assessment rules, just like a sole trader. The basis periods for the other partners are not affected.

■ Both sole traders and partners are subject to Class 2 and Class 4 National Insurance contributions. Class 2 is a flat rate, whereas Class 4 is based on profits.

■ Income Tax is payable by the 31 January following the end of the tax year. Payments on account are often also required. These are payable on the previous 31 January, and 31 July, and are based on the last year's Income Tax.

■ There are separate supplementary pages in the Income Tax return for sole traders and there is a separate partnership tax return. These must be completed for each tax year and submitted with the rest of the tax return by the 31 October or 31 January following the end of the tax year, the later date relating to online returns.

Key Terms		
	accounting date	the date to which the accounts are made up. Sole traders and partnerships can choose their regular accounting dates without restriction
	accounting period	the period for which the business produces its accounts
	basis period	the link between accounting periods and tax years. For a continuing business, the basis period for a particular tax year is the twelve month accounting period that ends in that tax year. There are special basis period rules when businesses start and cease trading, which may require time-apportionment of adjusted trading profits after capital allowances
	adjusted trading profits	the trading profits that have been adjusted for tax purposes by excluding income not taxable as trading income, and non-allowable expenditure
	trading income assessment	the taxable trading profit for the tax year. It is made up – after deducting any capital allowances – of adjusted trading profits for the basis period
	relevant period	the period between the end of the previous basis period and the new accounting date when there is a change of accounting date

Activities

7.1 Rashid started in business as a sole trader on 1 December 2016. He made his accounts up to 30 November each year from then on. His adjusted profits (after capital allowances) for his first two years trading were as follows:

1/12/2016 - 30/11/2017   £48,000

1/12/2017 - 30/11/2018   £30,000

Required:

State what the first three tax years will be for the business, and calculate the trading income assessments for each of these tax years.

State the amount of any overlap profits, and the period in which they arose.

7.2 Zorah started in business as a sole trader on 1 February 2017. She made her accounts up to 31 December each year, with the first set of accounts relating to 11 months. Her adjusted profits (after capital allowances) for the first two accounting periods were as follows:

1/2/2017 - 31/12/2017   £33,000

1/1/2018 - 31/12/2018   £48,000

Required:

State what the first three tax years will be for the business, and calculate the trading income assessments for each of these tax years.

State the amount of any overlap profits, and the period in which they arose.

7.3 Adam has been in business as a sole trader for many years, with an accounting date of 30 June. On 31 May 2019 he ceased trading. He had overlap profits brought forward from the start of his business of £5,000. His adjusted profits (after deducting capital allowances) for the last three accounting periods of the business were as follows:

1/7/2016 - 30/6/2017   £40,000

1/7/2017 - 30/6/2018   £36,000

1/7/2018 - 31/5/2019   £20,000

Required:

Calculate the trading income assessment for each of the tax years 2018/19 and 2019/20.

7.4 Clive has been in business for many years, with an accounting date of 31 December. He has £6,000 overlap profits brought forward, representing 3 months.

He decided to change his accounting date to 28 February, and the 14 month accounts to 28 February 2020 show adjusted trading profits of £56,000.

Calculate the basis period and the trading income assessment for 2019/20 and state the overlap profits to be carried forward.

7.5 David has been in business for many years, with an accounting date of 31 December. He has £6,000 overlap profits brought forward, representing 3 months.

He decided to change his accounting date to 30 September, and the 9 month accounts to 30 September 2019 show adjusted trading profits of £36,000.

The accounts y/e 31 December 2018 showed adjusted profits of £60,000.

Calculate the basis period and the trading income assessment for 2019/20 and state the overlap profits to be carried forward.

7.6 Alice and Bob have been in partnership for several years, sharing profits and losses equally. They have always made their accounts up to 31 December each year. On 1 October 2019 Colin joined the partnership, and the partnership agreement was changed to Alice 45%, Bob 40%, Colin 15% from that date.

The year ended 31 December 2019 produced adjusted profits (after capital allowances) of £96,000. The year ended 31 December 2020 produced adjusted profits (after capital allowances) of £108,000.

Required:

Calculate separately the trading income assessments for the tax years 2019/20 and 2020/21 for each of the partners, and note any overlap profits for Colin.

7.7 Mark, Norma and Olga had been trading in partnership for many years, sharing profits and losses equally. They had always used 31 March as their accounting date. On 31 March 2020 Olga left the partnership. She had no overlap profits brought forward from when she joined the partnership.

The partnership accounts for the year ended 31/3/2020 were as follows:

	£	£
Sales		180,000
less cost of sales:		55,000
Gross profit		125,000
less expenses:		
Rent	12,500	
Employees' Wages & NIC	16,500	
Depreciation	12,250	
Motor Expenses	8,000	
General Expenses	3,000	
Bank Interest	1,750	
		54,000
Net Profit		71,000

Notes:

1 There were the following written down values for plant & machinery capital allowances purposes as at 31/3/2019:

General Pool	£35,000
Car (30% private use by Olga)	£16,000

Olga bought the car from the partnership on 31/3/2020 for the market value of £10,000. There were no other transactions in non-current assets during the period.

2 The motor expenses shown in the accounts include £500 relating to private mileage by Olga.

3 General Expenses includes:

Increase in General Provision for Bad Debts	£200
Gift Vouchers as presents for customers	£400

Required:

- Calculate the capital allowances claimable by the partnership for the accounting year ended 31/3/2020 (Plant & Machinery).

- Calculate the adjusted profits for the same period, after taking into account the capital allowances.

- Calculate the trading income assessment for Olga for 2019/20.

- Calculate the Class 4 National Insurance contributions payable by Olga for 2019/20.

- Complete page 6 of the partnership tax return for the partnership, with the profit appropriated to Olga. Note that adjustment for overlap profits are not taken into account on this form.

(Blank pages of the 2018/19 version are reproduced in the Appendix of this book or may be downloaded from the Resource pages of www.osbornebooks.co.uk or from www.gov.uk)

7.8   John was an employee for many years, paying Income Tax through PAYE. During the tax year 2017/2018 he left his job and became self-employed. The Income Tax liability and NIC has been accurately calculated for each of the tax years 2017/18 and 2018/19 as follows:

2017/18   £8,500 (including £2,300 paid via PAYE)

2018/19   £11,000 (none paid via PAYE)

Based on the above figures, complete the following table by inserting the amounts that John was due to pay relating to the tax years 2017/18 to 2019/20 on the dates shown. Insert zeros in any cells that do not apply.

Payment date	31 Jan 2018 £	31 July 2018 £	31 Jan 2019 £	31 July 2019 £	31 Jan 2020 £	31 July 2020 £
Tax year 2017/18						
Tax year 2018/19						
Tax year 2019/20						
Totals due						

7.9   Shaun Slapp has been in business for many years as a self-employed plasterer, running his business from home. He produces accounts each year to 30 November. His accounts for the year ended 30/11/2019 are as follows:

	£	£
Sales		55,000
less cost of materials		11,000
Gross profit		44,000
less expenses:		
Van running costs	6,300	
Depreciation	2,800	
Wages of part time employee	9,800	
Insurance	1,200	
Accountancy costs	600	
Entertaining	1,000	
Telephone and Postage	800	
		22,500
Net Profit		21,500

The van is used 20% privately, and the van expenses include this element. The telephone and postage costs are 75% business and 25% private. Capital allowances have already been calculated at £4,200 after taking account of private use of the van. It has been agreed that the amount of costs not shown in the above accounts that relate to heating and lighting the room in his house that is used as his business office is £150 per year.

Shaun has an unrelieved trading loss of £6,000 brought forward from 2018/19.

Required:

Calculate the trading income assessment for Shaun for 2019/20 after taking account of the brought forward loss.

7.10 Adrian started trading on 1 February 2018. He makes up his accounts to 31 December each year. The profits were calculated at:

	£
Period to 31 December 2018	66,000
Year to 31 December 2019	81,000
Year to 31 December 2020	90,000

(a) The tax year in which he started trading was (select one):

2016/17   2017/18   2018/19   2019/20

(b) His taxable profits in his first tax year of trading were (select one):

£5,500   £6,000   £11,000   £12,000

(c) His taxable profits in his second tax year of trading were (select one):

£66,000   £72,750   £81,000   £90,000

(d) His taxable profits in his third tax year of trading were (select one):

£66,000   £72,750   £81,000   £90,000

(e) His overlap profits were £ _____

(f) His overlap profits are deducted (select one):

- from his first year profits

- from the profits in the third year of trading

- from the profits in the final year of trading, or on change of accounting date

- from any profits chosen by Adrian

7.11   State whether each of the following statements is true or false.

		True	False
(a)	A loss made by a sole trader can only be relieved against trading profits made in the same tax year.		
(b)	For a loss made by a sole trader to be relieved in the preceding tax year, it must first have been relieved in the current tax year.		
(c)	To be relieved in future years, a loss made by a sole trader must be relieved against the profits arising from the same trade.		
(d)	A loss made by a sole trader can be relieved against total income arising in future years.		
(e)	A sole trader can restrict the amount of loss carried back to any year so the personal allowances are not lost.		
(f)	A sole trader can only offset a trading loss against capital gains of the same year if the loss is first set against total income of that year.		

8 Capital gains tax for individuals

this chapter covers...

In this final chapter we examine the impact of Capital Gains Tax on disposals of business assets made by individuals. We start by reviewing the basis of assessment and how the gains are calculated and the tax liability worked out.

We then go on to compare this system of tax for individuals to the one that applies to companies under Corporation Tax. Here we need to be especially careful as some rules are the same, but some are quite different.

We then see how to deal with shares and share pools, and the disposal of a business including goodwill. We learn about the reliefs that are specific to the business assets of individuals – entrepreneurs' relief, investors' relief, and gift relief.

Finally we briefly discuss record keeping in connection with Capital Gains Tax.

CAPITAL GAINS TAX – A PERSONAL AND BUSINESS TAX

We saw in Chapter 4 that any chargeable gains that a limited company generates are assessable to Corporation Tax.

Any chargeable gains that an individual makes are instead taxable under Capital Gains Tax (CGT). This tax can apply to the disposal of both **personal** and **business** assets. The disposal of personal assets under CGT is dealt with in the learning area 'Personal Tax' (covered in Osborne Books' *Personal Tax*). In this book we need to see its impact on business assets.

Some of the issues that were covered when we examined chargeable gains for limited companies also apply to sole traders. We will begin by examining the differences between disposals under Capital Gains Tax for sole traders and Corporation Tax for limited companies, and note any common ground. It is very important to distinguish clearly between these taxes, and be careful always to apply the correct rules.

basis of assessment

Capital Gains Tax is applied to individuals by using the same tax years as those used for Income Tax. The basis of assessment for Capital Gains Tax is the chargeable gains less capital losses arising from **disposals** that occur during the **tax year** (not in the basis period of the business). Both the definition of a disposal, and the types of asset that are exempt or chargeable are identical to those applicable under Corporation Tax. Most of the situations that we will come across will be based on the sale or gift of an asset. The interaction of capital allowances with chargeable gains is the same as was described for limited companies.

Two situations where disposals do not give rise to Capital Gains Tax are:

■ disposals arising because the owner has died

■ any disposal between spouses (husband and wife) or civil partners

HOW IS CAPITAL GAINS TAX CALCULATED?

annual exempt amount

Unlike limited companies, all individuals are entitled to an **annual exempt amount** (or annual exemption) for each tax year. This works in a similar way to a personal allowance under Income Tax. The exempt amount is deducted from the total net gains that have been calculated on the individual assets that have been disposed of during the year. Capital Gains Tax is then worked out on the balance.

The exempt amount is £12,000 in 2019/20. The exempt amount can only be used against capital gains, and is not set against income. It cannot be carried back or forward and used in another tax year.

Once the exempt amount has been deducted from the total net gains, the balance is subject to Capital Gains Tax. The rates of Capital Gains Tax are 10% and 20% for gains on all assets with the exception of those relating to disposals of residential property (which we are not concerned with).

Although Capital Gains Tax is a separate tax from Income Tax, it uses the same band structure. Gains are treated as if they were added on top of taxable income, and the 10% rate is applied to gains falling within the basic rate band and the 20% rate applies to gains within the higher or additional rate bands.

If an individual is already a higher rate or additional rate taxpayer then any gains will always be taxed at 20%. Where the taxpayer pays Income Tax only at the basic rate then any gains will be taxed at the lower rates provided they do not exceed the basic rate band of £37,500 when added to taxable income. Where they do exceed this amount the excess will be taxed at the higher rates.

The following example will illustrate the situation.

example

Raymond has total taxable income in 2019/20 of £33,000 after deducting his personal allowance. He made capital gains of £25,000 before deducting his exempt amount.

Raymond has taxable gains of £25,000 – £12,000 (exempt amount) = £13,000.

He has £37,500 – £33,000 = £4,500 remaining in his basic rate band after accounting for his taxable income. Therefore £4,500 of his gains will be taxed at 10%, and the remainder taxed at 20%, as follows:

£4,500 x 10%	£450.00
£8,500 (the remainder of the £13,000) x 20%	£1,700.00
Total Capital Gains Tax	£2,150.00

THE COMPUTATION OF EACH GAIN

The standard format that we saw in Chapter 4 in the treatment of Corporation Tax is largely applicable to disposals by individuals chargeable to Capital Gains Tax.

However, Capital Gains Tax computations for individuals are much simpler than the equivalent computations for companies, since for individuals there is no indexation allowance whatsoever.

The basic computation format is as follows:

		£
	Proceeds on disposal	X
	less	
	Incidental costs of disposal	(x)
=	Net proceeds	X
	less	
	Original cost	(x)
	Incidental costs of acquisition	(x)
=	Gain	X

transfer to spouse or civil partner

When an asset is transferred to a spouse or civil partner no capital gain arises, as mentioned earlier. This is achieved by treating the disposal proceeds as the amount needed to generate exactly zero gain or loss.

For example if a wife had bought an asset some time ago for £10,000, (with no other costs) and gave it to her husband, the disposal proceeds would be treated as £10,000 so that no gain would arise. This would also mean that if the husband later sold the asset, his cost would also be considered to be £10,000, and any gain calculated on that basis.

A transfer between spouses or civil partners is often known as being made on a 'no gain, no loss' basis.

transfer to a 'connected person'

When an asset is sold to a connected person at less than market value, the market value is used in the computation of gains. This also applies to **all gifts** (whether to a connected person or not).

The following relatives of the person disposing of the asset are 'connected persons', and so are the relatives' spouses or civil partners:

■ ancestors and spouse's ancestors (parent, grandparent, etc)

■ siblings and spouse's siblings (brother, sister)

■ lineal descendants and spouse's lineal descendants (child, grandchild etc)

In addition, any business partners of the person disposing of the asset are also connected persons, plus their spouses, civil partners and relatives (as defined above).

If a loss is incurred on a disposal to a connected person, the loss cannot be set against general gains, but can only be set against gains made on other disposals to the same person.

exempt assets

The following are the main examples of assets that are exempt from Capital Gains Tax:

- trading inventory (stock)
- cars
- chattels bought and sold for £6,000 or less
- government securities (gilts)
- animals
- gifts to charities
- disposals made on the death of a taxpayer

You will notice that most of the items on this list are the same as those that were exempt under Corporation Tax.

dealing with capital losses

Capital losses arise from disposals in the same way as gains.

Once losses have been calculated they are dealt with as follows:

- firstly they are set against gains arising in the same tax year, until these are reduced to zero, then
- any unused loss is carried forward to set against the next gains that arise in future tax years

The key to offsetting losses is to remember that the order of calculation is:

1 firstly offset losses in the year
2 then deduct annual exempt amount

to arrive at the amount subject to Capital Gains Tax.

offsetting against gains arising in the same tax year

Any losses that arise during a tax year are offset against capital gains arising from disposals in the same tax year. When dealing with losses arising in the same tax year there can be no safeguarding of the annual exempt amount. If there are sufficient losses the gains will be reduced to zero, wasting the exempt amount, before carrying forward any balance of loss.

offsetting against gains in a later tax year

This will only occur when there are insufficient gains in the same tax year to offset the loss (or no gains at all). The loss must be offset as soon as possible, by using any gains that occur in the next tax year. The system is very similar to the one just described, except that in these circumstances an amount of gain equal to the annual exempt amount is not offset, and any loss balance carried on forward again. This provides protection against wasting the exempt amount.

The Case Study that follows demonstrates the main issues that we have examined so far.

Case Study	

JOHN GAIN TRADING: CAPITAL GAINS TAX

John Gain has been in business as a sole trader for several years. During the tax year 2019/20 he disposed of the following business assets:

He sold a piece of land for £20,000. He had bought the land in June 2000 for £30,000 and was originally going to extend his factory onto it. However he was refused planning permission, and decided to sell it.

He sold a shop for £100,000. He had bought it for £72,000 in September 2005.

He sold a factory building for £300,000. He had bought it new in December 1990 for £120,000. John is a higher rate Income Tax payer.

required

Calculate the gain or loss on each disposal, and John's total Capital Gains Tax liability for 2019/20.

solution

Disposal of Land	£
Proceeds	20,000
Less Cost	(30,000)
Loss	(10,000)

Disposal of Shop	£
Proceeds	100,000
Less Cost	(72,000)
Gain	28,000

Disposal of Factory	£
Proceeds	300,000
Less Cost	(120,000)
Gain	180,000

Summary	£
Gain on shop	28,000
Gain on factory	180,000
Less loss on land	(10,000)
Net gains	198,000
Less annual exempt amount	(12,000)
Amount subject to CGT	186,000

Capital Gains Tax   £186,000 x 20% = £37,200

ISSUES THAT ARE COMMON TO COMPANIES AND INDIVIDUALS

The following techniques and rules that we examined in Chapter 4 in respect of limited companies and Corporation Tax are also applicable to individuals under Capital Gains Tax. We will note them here in outline only – if you need further explanation you should refer back to the earlier chapter.

■ **links with capital allowances**

The issues outlined for companies are valid here. They are:

- Where losses occur on items where capital allowances have been claimed, no capital loss arises.

- Gains on chattels can only arise if the proceeds exceed £6,000, and this is subject to the chattels rules (dealt with below).

■ **part disposals**

These are dealt with in exactly the same way as for limited companies. The original cost of the whole asset is apportioned based on the proceeds of the part disposed of and the market value of the remainder at the time of the part disposal.

■ **improvement expenditure**

This follows the same logic under CGT rules as it does for chargeable gains under Corporation Tax. However, since there is no indexation allowance, the calculation is much simpler.

■ **chattels**

The special rules for chattels are identical to those for companies:

- The gain on chattels sold for over £6,000 cannot exceed 5/3 of (Gross proceeds minus £6,000).

- The capital loss on chattels sold for under £6,000 is limited by substituting £6,000 for the actual proceeds in the computation.

■ **rollover relief**

This is applicable to the same classes of business assets owned by individuals as owned by companies and in addition it is available for **goodwill** acquisitions and disposals by individuals. The rules work in exactly the same way, and defer the gain when the proceeds of one disposal are reinvested in another qualifying asset.

MATCHING RULES FOR SHARES

We saw earlier on that shares are chargeable assets, and that the computation for the acquisition and subsequent disposal of a block of shares is the same as for other assets.

The complication that can arise is when various quantities of the same type of share in the same company are bought and sold. The problem faced is similar to that in any inventory valuation situation – how to determine which of the shares that were bought are deemed to be the same ones that were sold. The dilemma is solved in this situation by the application of strict **matching rules**.

When some shares are sold the matching process is carried out by working down the following categories of acquisition, skipping any that do not apply, until all the shares sold have been matched. A separate CGT computation is then used for each separate match.

Note that these rules that apply to individuals are **not** the same as those that apply to companies under Corporation Tax.

1 Firstly, any shares bought on the **same day** that the disposal occurs are matched with that disposal.

2 Secondly, any shares bought in the **30 days after** the disposal are matched with those disposed of, (matching the earliest first if more than one acquisition). This probably seems illogical – selling something before it is bought!

3 Thirdly, any remaining shares not yet matched are deemed to have come from the 'FA 1985 pool' of shares. This is a device for merging shares.

The above order of matching is illustrated in the diagram below. The numbers in the diagram relate to the numbered stages described above.

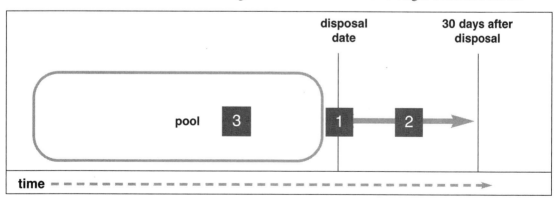

Remember that this matching process only applies where there have been several purchases of the same type of shares in the same company. It does not apply to a mixture of different company's shares, nor is it needed where a shareholding is bought and sold intact.

USING THE 'FA 1985 POOL'

This device was introduced in the 1985 Finance Act, and merges (or 'pools') shares in the same company and of the same type together. As we just saw, it occurs as the last of the matching rules, and is used to calculate the cost of shares acquired before the disposal date.

This is the same principle as the pool used for Corporation Tax gains, but is simpler here because there is no indexation allowance.

The pool needs to keep data relating to:

■ numbers of shares and

■ actual costs

These form the two main columns of the pool working.

The pool commences with the first shares bought. It then moves forward in time, adding each subsequent purchase of shares to provide cumulative numbers and costs of shares in the pool.

When any shares from the pool are disposed of, a proportion of the cumulative cost at the time of disposal is deducted from the pool, based on the numbers of shares. This cost amount that is deducted from the pool is then used in the gains calculation and compared with the proceeds in the normal way.

We will now demonstrate how the process works using a numerical example.

Although shares could be eligible for entrepreneurs' relief (see later) we will assume that it does not apply in this example.

---

example

On 1/1/2020 Julie sold 10,000 ordinary shares in WyeCo Ltd for £10 each, from her shareholding of 25,000. Her shareholding had been built up as follows:

1/1/1988 bought 17,000 shares for £5.00 each

1/1/1993 bought 8,000 shares for £7.00 each.

Since there are no acquisitions on or after 1/1/2020, the whole of the disposal of 10,000 shares will be matched with the pool. The pool will be built up as follows, with the disposal deducted as the latest transaction:

	Number	**Cost**
		£
1/1/1988 Purchase	17,000	85,000
1/1/1993 Purchase	8,000	56,000
Pool Totals	25,000	141,000
Less Disposal	(10,000)	(56,400)
Pool Balance after disposal	15,000	84,600

You should note the following:

• the cost figure for the disposal is a proportional amount of the pool costs before disposal, based on the number of shares (eg £141,000 x 10,000 / 25,000 = £56,400)

The computation for the disposal will now appear as follows:

	£
Proceeds (10,000 x £10)	100,000
Less cost	(56,400)
Gain	43,600

If at some future date there was another disposal of shares from the pool then the pool balance remaining would be used to determine the cost of the shares in the further disposal.

BONUS AND RIGHTS ISSUES

Bonus and rights issues were examined under Corporation Tax in Chapter 4. Here the principles are the same, but we will again explain the methods fully.

dealing with bonus shares

Bonus shares are additional shares given free to shareholders based on their current shareholding. This is sometimes called a 'scrip issue' and may be carried out as part of a capital restructuring of the company.

For CGT purposes the bonus shares are treated as if they were acquired at the same time as the original shares that generated the issue. For example, a shareholder who owned 1,000 shares that were bought in January 2001 would be entitled to a further 200 shares if there were a bonus issue of 'one for five' shares. The total of 1,200 shares would be treated as bought in January 2001 for the amount paid for the 1,000 shares.

In virtually all situations, bonus shares are added to the pool when they are received. Since no payment is made, there is no adjustment to the cost figure.

If the bonus shares are received based on several acquisitions of original shares, the bonus shares will still be added into the pool, since the original shares will also be in the pool.

dealing with rights issues

A **rights issue** is the situation where additional shares are sold to existing shareholders, usually at a special price. For matching purposes, the shares that are bought in this way are treated as if they were bought with the original shares.

Rights issue shares will join the pool and be treated like any other share purchase. Their cost will be added into the pool.

We will now use a Case Study to make sure the principles relating to various matters studied are clear.

Case Study

CHER BYERS:
GAINS INCLUDING SHARES AND POOLING

Cher had acquired the following quoted ordinary shares in AbCo Limited (an unquoted company). We will assume that entrepreneurs' relief doesn't apply.

1/5/1985	1,000 shares at £4.00 each	£4,000
1/1/1990	Bonus issue of 1 for 4	
1/1/1992	1,750 shares at £4.20 each	£7,350
1/1/1995	1,500 shares at £4.10 each	£6,150 (Rights issue)
1/12/2001	1,800 shares at £5.10 each	£9,180

On 15/11/2001 she had sold 1,000 of her shareholding.

On 15/5/2019 she sold a further 2,500 ordinary shares in AbCo Limited for £10.00 each.

required

1   Identify which shares would have already been matched against the disposal that took place on 15/11/2001.

2   Show how the disposal of shares on 15/5/2019 will be matched against the acquisitions, and

3   Calculate the total gain arising from the sale of shares that took place on 15/5/2019.

solution

Task 1

The disposal of 1,000 shares on 15/11/2001 would have been matched with 1,000 of the 1,800 shares that were bought on 1/12/2001 for £5.10 each (shares bought in the 30 days after disposal). This leaves 800 of that purchase to join the pool.

Task 2

Matching of the 15/5/2019 disposal of 2,500 shares will be entirely against the pool, since there were no shares of that type bought on 15/5/2019 or the following 30 days.

Task 3

We will first need to build up the pool to May 2019, so that we can calculate the balances.

		Number	**Cost**
			£
1/5/1985	Purchase	1,000	4,000
1/1/1990	Bonus Issue	250	–
1/1/1992	Purchase	1,750	7,350
1/1/1995	Rights Issue	1,500	6,150
1/12/2001	Balance of Purchase (1,800 less 1,000 already matched)	800	4,080
		5,300	21,580
15/5/2019	Disposal	(2,500)	(10,179)*
	Pool balance after disposal	2,800	11,401

*The cost of the shares disposed of is calculated as:
  (2,500 / 5,300) x £21,580 = £10,179

We can now calculate the gain on the disposal of shares, using the cost figure calculated in the pool.

	£
Proceeds	25,000
less cost	(10,179)
Gain	14,821

DEALING WITH THE DISPOSAL OF A BUSINESS

We have already seen how trading profits are calculated when a business ceases trading, and how the capital allowances for the last accounting period are calculated.

In addition to these implications, if a sole trader sells his or her business, then Capital Gains Tax will apply **individually** to **each chargeable asset** that is included in the business. The sale of the business can therefore result in a number of separate capital gains computations.

The current assets and current liabilities of a business are not chargeable assets, which leaves **non-current (fixed) assets** and **goodwill** as items on which CGT may be assessable.

non-current assets

As we have already seen, land and buildings are chargeable assets, and could easily form part of a business that is being disposed of. Chattels bought and sold for under £6,000 are exempt, and so are cars. Other plant and machinery could theoretically give rise to a capital gain, but since it is rarely sold for more than it cost is unlikely to do so. Any plant and machinery disposed of for less than original cost would simply be dealt with through the capital allowances computation as we have seen previously.

goodwill

Goodwill is an intangible asset that may exist if the business is sold as a going concern. It arises when the buyer is prepared to pay more for the business as a whole than the market value of the net assets of the business. This could be, for example, because of the businesses' customer base that the new owner wishes to continue selling to. Where a sole trader has built up the business himself the goodwill is unlikely to be shown in the business statement of financial position (balance sheet), and will often have an original cost of zero for CGT purposes. If you are faced with a situation where the proceeds relating to the goodwill is not stated, you will need to calculate it as the balance of the proceeds that do not relate to any other assets.

ENTREPRENEURS' RELIEF

Entrepreneurs' Relief applies to individuals who dispose of:

- all or part of a trading business
- shares in a 'personal trading company'
- assets of an individual's or partnership's business that has now ceased

All assets must have been owned for at least 24 months prior to sale. The owner of shares in a personal trading company must have held the shares for at least 24 months and be employed in the company during that time.

The relief is available for qualifying gains up to a 'lifetime limit' and applies a tax rate of 10% to these gains (instead of 20%). The lifetime limit is £10,000,000 of gains.

Where qualifying gains occur (and are therefore taxed at 10% if within the lifetime limit) they are treated as using up the basic rate band. Therefore any other gains that do not qualify for entrepreneurs' relief will be more likely to be taxed at 20%. However, where there are both qualifying and non-qualifying gains, the taxpayer can set the annual exempt amount as far as possible against the non-qualifying gains. This will be most tax-efficient.

Claims for entrepreneur's relief must be made within 12 months of the online filing date for the tax year.

conditions for entrepreneurs' relief

The qualifying conditions have to have been met for at least a **two year** period that ends on the **earlier** of:

■ the date of disposal of the asset(s)

■ the date of cessation of the business

The conditions (which are summarised below) depend on the type of disposal:

■ disposal of whole or part of a business

The business must have been owned by the sole trader who is making the claim, or by a partnership of which the claimant was a member. The disposal must be of either the whole business or a distinct part of a business.

■ disposal of assets following cessation of a business

The business that has ceased must have been owned by the sole trader who is making the claim, or by a partnership of which the claimant was a member. The cessation of the business cannot be more that three years before the disposal of the assets.

■ disposal of shares in a personal limited company

The claimant must have held at least 5% of the ordinary shares in the company that provide entitlement to:

• at least 5% of the voting rights, and

• at least 5% of the company's distributable profits, and

• at least 5% of the company assets available for distribution to equity holders in a winding up

The company must normally be a trading company, and the claimant must have been an officer or employee of the company.

Case Study

DUNN TRADING: DISPOSAL OF A BUSINESS

Jo Dunn had been in business as a sole trader since January 1995. She ceased trading on 31/1/2020, and on that date sold her business as a going concern for a total of £500,000.

The summarised statement of financial position of the business on 31/1/2020 was as follows:

	£
Premises	200,000
Plant & Machinery	20,000
Net Current Assets	80,000
Total Net Assets	300,000

The premises were bought in January 1995. No depreciation had been charged on the premises in the accounts. The plant and machinery value is based on amounts after depreciation has been charged. Capital allowances had been claimed on all plant and machinery.

It was agreed with the purchaser of the business that the premises were to be valued at £350,000 in the sale, and that the plant and machinery and the net current assets were valued at the amounts shown in the statement of financial position.

Jo has never made a claim for Entrepreneurs' Relief before this disposal.

required

Calculate the CGT arising on the sale of the business, assuming that the disposals qualify for Entrepreneurs' Relief.

solution

The first step is to allocate the sale proceeds to the individual assets, including any balance of proceeds to goodwill, and determine which assets are chargeable.

	£	
Premises	350,000	Chargeable
Plant & Machinery	20,000	Proceeds < Cost. Dealt with through capital allowance computation
Net Current Assets	80,000	Exempt
Goodwill	50,000	Chargeable
Total Proceeds	500,000	

The goodwill is calculated as the balancing figure, after accounting for the other assets. The computations are then carried out individually on the chargeable assets.

		£
Premises		
	Proceeds	350,000
	Less Cost	(200,000)
	Gain	150,000
Goodwill		
	Proceeds	50,000
	Less Cost	0
	Gain	50,000
Summary		
	Gain on premises	150,000
	Gain on goodwill	50,000
	Total Gains	200,000
	Less Annual Exempt Amount	(12,000)
	Amount subject to CGT	188,000
	CGT £188,000 x 10%	18,800

Since the total of qualifying gains is £200,000, this is below the lifetime limit of £10,000,000 and the gains are taxed at 10%.

INVESTORS' RELIEF

Investors' Relief works in a similar way to Entrepreneurs' Relief in that it:

■ reduces the Capital Gains Tax rate to 10%, and

■ has a lifetime cap for each individual investor of £10 million.

However, Investors' Relief is aimed at external investors in 'new' ordinary shares in unlisted trading companies.

To qualify for the relief the investor must not be an employee (or connected to an employee) of the company. In addition, the shares must meet the following conditions:

■ The shares must be ordinary shares in a trading company (or the holding company of a trading group)

■ The shares must have been issued by the company on or after 17 March 2016, and subscribed for by the investor in exchange for cash

■ The shares must have been held continuously for at least 3 years (and until at least 6 April 2019) before disposal

Shares that are owned can be categorised as either:

■ Qualifying – meeting all above conditions, or

■ Potentially qualifying – would qualify, but not yet held for 3 years), or

■ Excluded – cannot qualify, as do not meet all the conditions

Claims for Investors' Relief for 2019/20 must be made by 31 January 2022.

---

example

John disposed of the following shares on 30 June 2019. All the shares were ordinary shares in trading companies that did not employ John, or anyone connected with him.

1   500 shares in XY Ltd purchased in April 2016. The shares were originally issued in January 2016.

2   100 shares in AB Ltd purchased when issued in May 2016.

3   250 shares in CD Ltd purchased when issued in February 2016

4   150 shares in FG Ltd purchased when issued in January 2017

Required

State whether each of these share disposals will qualify for Investors' Relief.

Solution

1   500 shares in XY Ltd purchased in April 2016. The shares were originally issued in January 2016.

   Excluded, so do not qualify – shares issued before 17 March, and were not bought 'new' by John

2   100 shares in AB Ltd purchased when issued in May 2016.

   Qualify – all conditions met

3   250 shares in CD Ltd purchased when issued in February 2016

   Excluded, so do not qualify – shares issued before 17 March

4   150 shares in FG Ltd purchased when issued in January 2017

   Do not qualify – shares disposed of before being held for 3 years

GIFT RELIEF

We saw earlier in our studies that the gift of an asset is a disposal for Capital Gains Tax purposes. This means that even though the donor (the person giving the item) has received nothing for the item he/she may still have to pay CGT. The disposal will be treated as if the donor had received the market value for the item, and the recipient will be treated as if he/she had acquired the asset at the same market value.

If an individual gives away a 'business asset', the transaction can qualify for 'gift relief'. This has the effect of delaying the onset of the tax, and transferring the liability to the recipient of the gift.

The relief can only be claimed if both parties agree. It means that the donor has no CGT liability, but that the CGT liability of the recipient in the future could be greater – if the item is disposed of.

Gift relief works by reducing the base cost of the asset for the recipient by the amount of the deferred gain. This means that the base cost would now be the market value less the deferred gain, and any eventual gain would therefore be greater than if gift relief had not been claimed.

Gift relief applies to business assets, including:

■ assets used in the donor's business or in his/her personal trading company

■ shares in the donor's personal trading company

■ unquoted shares in other trading companies

Gift relief applies to some of the same business assets as entrepreneurs' relief. It is therefore possible that where an asset incorporating a gain deferred by gift relief is disposed of again, the gain could be subject to entrepreneurs' relief.

Case Study

JAN NICE: GIFT RELIEF

Jan Nice bought a shop in October 1998 for £100,000, and used it in her business until June 2007, when she gave it to her niece, Norah. The market value of the shop at that time was £180,000.

Norah ran the shop as a sole trader for a while, but decided to sell the shop in October 2019. She received £220,000 for the shop.

Jan and Norah claimed gift relief on the shop. Norah had no other disposals in 2019/20.

Norah is a higher rate Income Tax payer.

required

Calculate the Capital Gains Tax payable by Norah on her disposal of the shop:

(a) ignoring any entrepreneurs' relief

(b) assuming that Norah is entitled to entrepreneurs' relief

solution

(a) The gain deferred by Jan is (£180,000 – £100,000) = £80,000.

The disposal by Norah will have the following gain:

	£	£
Proceeds		220,000
Less Market value at acquisition	180,000	
less deferred gain	(80,000)	
		100,000
Gain		120,000
less annual exempt amount		(£12,000)
Amount subject to CGT		£108,000
Capital Gains Tax	£108,000 x 20% =	£21,600

(b) If entrepreneurs' relief is available the calculation would be identical up to the point where the amount subject to CGT is calculated. It will then be as follows:

Amount subject to CGT		108,000
Capital Gains Tax	£108,000 x 10% =	£10,800

SUMMARY OF RULES AND RELIEFS

In this book we have looked at both chargeable gains for companies (taxed through Corporation Tax) and individuals (taxed through Capital Gains Tax). This is an area of study where it is easy to get confused, so the following table is produced to summarise the various rules and reliefs that we have looked at and to whom they apply.

	Individuals (Capital Gains Tax)	Companies (Corporation Tax)
Annual Exempt Amount	✔	Not applicable
Indexation	Not applicable	✔ (To date of disposal or December 2017)
Links with capital allowances	✔	✔
Part Disposal Rules	✔	✔
Chattel Rules	✔	✔
Improvement Expenditure	✔	✔
Shares: matching rules/bonus/rights issues (but note rules are different)	✔ (Rules for individuals)	✔ (Rules for companies)
Gift Relief	✔	Not Applicable
Rollover Relief	✔	✔
Entrepreneurs' Relief	✔	Not applicable
Investors' Relief	✔	Not applicable

PAYMENT OF CAPITAL GAINS TAX

Capital Gains Tax is payable as one amount on the 31 January following the end of the tax year. This is the same date as the final submission date of the online tax return (the paper-based tax return would be due by the preceding 31 October). There is no requirement for payments on account of CGT.

KEEPING RECORDS

Since capital gains can arise when assets that have been held for a considerable time are disposed of, this has implications for record keeping. Taxpayers need to plan ahead, and retain records relating to the acquisition of assets that will be chargeable if disposed of.

Typical records that should be kept include:

- contracts, invoices or other purchase documentation relating to the acquisition of assets

- details of any valuations (eg valuations relating to part disposals)

- documentation relating to the sale of assets

Records for CGT purposes should be retained for the same period of time as those relating to Income Tax. For those in business this is five years after the date that the online return must be submitted (eg for 2019/20, records should be kept until 31/01/26). Where records will also relate to later disposals, for example gift relief claims, rollover relief claims, entrepreneurs' relief claims, and information relating to part disposals, they will need to be retained until all the relevant assets have been disposed of.

Chapter Summary	

- Capital Gains Tax applies to individuals (including sole traders and partners) who dispose of chargeable assets. In this unit we are concerned with the disposal of business assets. Although there is some common ground with the way that chargeable gains for companies are taxed under Corporation Tax, the computations for individuals exclude indexation allowances and include annual exempt amounts.

- The treatment of gains for individuals and companies include common areas such as capital allowances, part disposals, improvement expenditure, chattel rules and rollover relief.

- Where a whole business is disposed of, a separate computation is carried out for each chargeable asset that is included in the business. This includes goodwill, which is an intangible asset that may arise when the business is sold as a going concern. These gains may have entrepreneurs' relief available.

- Gift relief is available on the gift of business assets where both parties agree. It has the effect of deferring the gain, so that the donor is not subject to CGT, but the recipient may pay more tax if the asset is subsequently disposed of.

- CGT is payable on the 31 January following the tax year. Records must be kept for five years after that date, or longer if they relate to assets that are still owned or subject to deferral reliefs.

Key Terms	**capital gains tax (CGT)**	the tax that applies to individuals who dispose of chargeable personal or business assets
	disposal	a disposal for CGT purposes is the sale, gift, loss or destruction of an asset
	chargeable asset	assets whose disposal can result in a CGT liability. All assets are chargeable unless they are exempt
	exempt asset	an asset that is not chargeable to CGT. Exempt assets include the current assets of a business
	chattel	a tangible, movable asset
	annual exempt amount (or annual exemption)	the amount that is deductible from an individual's net gains in a tax year before CGT is payable
	capital loss	a capital loss results when the allowable costs of an asset exceed the sale proceeds (or market value). A loss is used by setting it against a gain in the same year, or if this is not possible, by carrying the loss forward to set against gains in the next available tax year
	part disposal	this occurs when part of an asset is disposed of, but the remainder is retained
	improvement expenditure	capital expenditure that enhances an asset. If the enhancement is still evident at disposal then the improvement expenditure is an allowable cost
	rollover relief	a deferral relief available to businesses (including sole traders). It has the effect of postponing a chargeable gain when the proceeds of disposal have been reinvested
	goodwill	goodwill is a chargeable asset. It is the amount of the proceeds on disposal of a business that does not relate to any individual assets, but is instead due to the intangible value of the business as a going concern

gift relief

a relief claimable jointly by the donor and the recipient of certain assets, including business assets. It allows the original gain by the donor to be deferred by increasing the possible future gain of the recipient

entrepreneurs' relief

this relief applies to individuals who dispose of all or part of a trading business and / or shares in a 'personal trading company'. The relief works by charging CGT at 10%. It is subject to a lifetime limit of £10m gains

investors' relief

this relief applies to individuals who dispose of ordinary shares that were acquired when they were issued and held for at least three years (with further conditions). The relief works by charging CGT at 10%, subject to a lifetime limit of £10m gains.

Activities

8.1 Analyse the following list of business assets into those that are chargeable to CGT and those that are exempt.

		Chargeable	Exempt
(a)	Moveable plant, sold at a gain for £5,000		
(b)	Trading inventory (stock)		
(c)	Shares in CIC plc		
(d)	An office block		
(e)	Goodwill		
(f)	Land		
(g)	A car		
(h)	Government securities		

8.2 Vikram is a sole trader. In January 1995 he bought a small shop for £40,000. In April 1998 he extended the shop at a cost of £20,000. He sold the shop for £140,000 in July 2019. This was his only disposal in the tax year. Vikram is a higher rate Income Tax payer.

Required:

Calculate the amount of Capital Gains Tax payable by Vikram for 2019/20, assuming that:

(a) Entrepreneurs' Relief does not apply.

(b) Vikram is entitled to Entrepreneurs' Relief.

8.3 Jane is a sole trader. In January 1999 she bought 1,000 unquoted shares at £10 each in a similar business to help her increase her market share. She sold 600 of the shares in July 2019 for a total of £23,000. This was her only disposal in the tax year. The company is not a 'Personal Trading Company'. Jane's taxable income in 2019/20 is £20,000.

Required:

Calculate the amount of Capital Gains Tax payable by Jane for 2019/20.

8.4 In January 1995 George bought an office building to use in his business. In December 2000 he gave the office building to his son, William, who used it in his business. The building was valued at £100,000 at that time, and they claimed gift relief on the transaction, deferring a gain of £33,160. William sold the building for £200,000 in July 2019. This was his only disposal in 2019/20. William is a higher rate Income Tax payer.

Required:

Calculate the amount of Capital Gains Tax payable by William for 2019/20, assuming that:

(a) Entrepreneurs' Relief does not apply.

(b) William is entitled to Entrepreneurs' Relief.

8.5 Josie started a business as a sole trader in January 1990. She ceased trading on 31/1/2020, and on that date sold her business as a going concern for a total of £900,000.

The summarised statement of financial position of the business on 31/1/2020 is as follows:

	£
Premises	400,000
Plant & Machinery	30,000
Net Current Assets	50,000
Total Net Assets	480,000

The premises were bought in January 1999. A gain of £60,000 on the previous premises was rolled over into these premises when the whole proceeds of the first premises were reinvested. The amount shown represents the actual cost in 1999 of the current premises.

The plant and machinery is shown at cost minus depreciation to date. Capital allowances had been claimed on all plant and machinery.

It was agreed with the purchaser of the business that the premises were to be valued at £700,000 in the sale. The plant and machinery is valued at £20,000 in the sale, and the net current assets are valued at the amounts shown in the statement of financial position.

Required:

Calculate the Capital Gains Tax liability arising on the sale of the business, assuming that Entrepreneurs' Relief **is available**.

8.6 Which of the following statements is correct?

(a) A capital loss made by an individual can be carried back against capital gains made in the preceding tax year	
(b) A capital loss made by an individual can be carried forward to the following tax year without offsetting it against the current year gains	
(c) When a capital loss made by an individual is offset against gains in the following tax year, it is only to the extent that it reduces those gains to the amount of the annual exemption	
(d) A capital loss made by an individual can only be carried forward for one tax year	

8.7 John made a disposal in August 2019 that qualified for entrepreneurs' relief. The proceeds were £6,000,000 and the gain was calculated as £3,000,000.

John is a higher rate Income Tax payer. This was John's only disposal in the tax year. He had claimed entrepreneurs' relief in the previous tax year on gains of £5,000,000.

How much Capital Gains Tax will John need to pay in 2019/20?

(a) None	
(b) £298,800	
(c) £300,000	
(d) £480,000	
(e) £597,600	
(f) £840,000	

8.8 Which of the following statements is correct? (select **one**.)

(a) Entrepreneurial relief is restricted to £10,000,000 for the lifetime of the taxpayer	
(b) Entrepreneurial relief is restricted to £10,000,000 for each capital disposal	
(c) Entrepreneurial relief has no restrictions	
(d) Entrepreneurial relief is restricted to £1,000,000 for the lifetime of the taxpayer	

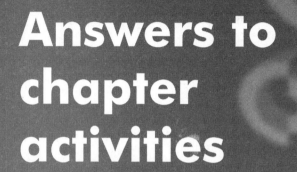

Answers to chapter activities

CHAPTER 1: INTRODUCTION TO BUSINESS TAXATION

1.1 The following statements are true: **(a)**, **(d)**, **(e)**.

The other statements are false as follows: (b) the Finance Act is not the only relevant law. (c) the return is completed for each CAP, not each financial year. (f) It is unethical to bend rules or omit items. (g) The self-employed do not pay Income Tax under PAYE.

1.2 **(a)** **Corporation Tax Computation for DonCom plc for year ended 31/3/2020**

	£
Trading Profits	1,300,000
Income from Property	100,000
Chargeable Gains	500,000
Taxable Total Profits (TTP)	1,900,000
Corporation Tax on TTP (£1,900,000 x 19%)	361,000

Note: Taxable Total Profits is also known as PCTCT.

(b)	Filing date for CT600 return	31/3/2021
	Final Payment date for Corporation Tax	1/1/2021

1.3 **(a)** **Income Tax Computation for 2019/20**

	£
Trading Income (Share of Partnership Profits)	16,000
Other Taxable Income	2,000
	18,000
Less personal allowance	12,500
Taxable Income	5,500
Tax payable at 20%	1,100

(b) A paper-based return must be submitted by 31/10/2020 whether or not HM Revenue & Customs are to calculate the tax.

Final payment date is 31/1/2021.

1.4 **John**

		£
Class 2	£3.00 x 52 weeks	156.00
Class 4	(£25,000 – £8,632) x 9%	1,473.12
		1,629.12

Class 2 and Class 4 is paid with the Income Tax liability.

1.5 The Walvern Water Company Limited will require a company tax return (form CT600). This will relate to the chargeable accounting period (CAP) 1/8/2018 to 31/7/2019. The form must be submitted online by 12 months after the end of the accounting period, ie 31/7/2020. The final Corporation Tax payment must be made by 1/5/2020 (nine months and one day after the end of the CAP).

Wally Weaver will need a tax return for the tax year 2019/20. The accounting period of 1/8/2018 to 31/7/2019 will form the basis period for this tax year. The main part of the form will need to be completed, along with the supplementary pages relating to self-employment. The online tax return must be submitted by 31/1/2021. The final Income Tax payment relating to 2019/20 will also need to be made by 31/1/2021.

1.6 **(1)** (d) An individual failing to keep appropriate records for the correct length of time is subject to a penalty of up to £3,000 for each tax year

(2) £70,000 − £50,000 = £20,000

(3) (£35,000 − £8,632) x 9% = £2,373.12

CHAPTER 2: CORPORATION TAX – TRADING PROFITS

2.1 1 no action (allowable)

2 add back (disallowable expense)

3 deduct (not trading income)

4 deduct (not taxable income)

5 no action (allowable)

6 deduct (not trading income – possible chargeable gain)

7 no action (taxable trading income)

8 add back (disallowable expense since tobacco)

9 add back (disallowable expense – not specific)

10 add back (disallowable expense – not trading)

11 no action (allowable)

12 add back (charge against whole TTP)

2.2

	£	£
Net Profit per accounts		130,300
Add Back:		
Expenditure that is shown in the accounts but is not allowable		
Depreciation		42,000
Loss on Sale of Non-current Assets		5,000
Gifts of Chocolates		4,900
Entertaining Customers		6,000
		188,200
Deduct:		
Income that is not taxable as Trading Income		
Interest Received	20,000	
Dividends Received	70,000	
Decrease in General Bad Debt Provision	5,000	
Capital Allowances	23,000	
		(118,000)
Trading Income Assessment		70,200

2.3

	£	£
Net Profit per accounts		276,600
Add Back:		
Expenditure that is shown in the accounts but is not allowable		
Depreciation		51,000
Directors' Speeding Fines		2,000
Gift Vouchers		5,000
Entertaining Customers		4,000
		338,600
Deduct:		
Income that is not taxable as Trading Income		
Interest Received	40,000	
Gains on Disposal of Non-current Assets	50,000	
Rental Income Received	60,000	
Capital Allowances	31,500	
		(181,500)
Trading Income Assessment		157,100

2.4

	£
Net Profit for 16-month period per accounts	4,070
Add back non-allowable expenditure:	
Depreciation etc	10,000
Entertaining customers	1,930
Adjusted profit before capital allowances	16,000

Time apportionment of adjusted profit:		
CAP 1/12/2018 to 30/11/2019	£16,000 x 12/16	= £12,000
CAP 1/12/2019 to 31/3/2020	£16,000 x 4/16	= £4,000

Deduction of Capital Allowances:	1/12/18 - 30/11/19	1/12/19 - 31/3/20
	£	£
Adjusted profit	12,000	4,000
Capital allowances	(8,000)	(2,500)
Trading Income assessment	4,000	1,500

2.5

	£	£
Profit before Tax		294,000
Add Back:		
Expenditure that is shown in the accounts but is not allowable		
Depreciation		20,000
Employee Loan Written Off		8,000
Increase in General Bad Debt Provision		7,700
Entertaining Customers		9,100
		338,800
Deduct:		
Income that is not taxable as Trading Income		
Rental Income	200,000	
Interest Received from Investments	30,000	
Profit on Sale of Non-current Assets	33,000	
Dividends Received	15,000	
Capital Allowances	153,000	
		(431,000)
Adjusted Trading Loss		(92,200)
Trading Income assessment = zero		

The trading loss of £92,200 could be relieved without carrying it forward (provided the profits are large enough) as follows:

- by offsetting against the taxable total profits (TTP) before deduction of Gift Aid payments in the CAP y/e 31/3/2020, and then if any loss remains
- by offsetting against the taxable total profits (TTP) before deduction of Gift Aid payments arising in the 12 months to 31/3/2019

2.6 The following statements is true: **(b)**

The other statements are false.

CHAPTER 3: CORPORATION TAX – CAPITAL ALLOWANCES

3.1

	Main pool	Capital allowances
	£	£
WDV bf	21,000	
add		
Acquisitions		
without FYA or AIA:		
Car (100 g/km)	16,000	
Acquisitions qualifying for AIA:		
Plant 993,000		
Van 10,000		
1,003,000		
AIA claimed (1,000,000)		1,000,000
	3,000	
less		
Proceeds of Disposals	(2,000)	
	38,000	
18% WDA	(6,840)	6,840
WDV cf	31,160	
Total Capital Allowances		1,006,840

3.2

	Main pool	S/L asset	Capital allowances
	£	£	£
WDV bf	60,000	10,000	
add			
Acquisitions			
without FYA or AIA:			
Car (95 g/km)	24,000		
Acquisitions qualifying for AIA:			
FL Truck 30,000			
Computer 5,000			
35,000			
AIA claimed (35,000)*			35,000
	0		
less			
Proceeds of Disposals:	(3,000)	(4,000)	
	81,000	6,000	
WDA 18%	(14,580)		14,580
Balancing Allowance		(6,000)	6,000
WDV cf	66,420	0	
Total Capital Allowances			55,580

*The maximum AIA limit for the CAP is: £1,000,000

Trading Income for CAP year ended 31/3/2020:

	£
Adjusted trading profits	154,000
Plant & Machinery Capital Allowances	(55,580)
Trading Income	98,420

3.3

	Main pool	Special rate pool	Capital allowances
	£	£	£
WDV bf	10,000	2,800	
Acquisitions qualifying for AIA:			
Plant 996,750			
Machinery 12,000			
1,008,750			
AIA claimed (1) (800,000)			800,000
	208,750		
less			
Proceeds of			
Disposals	(3,500)	———	
	215,250	2,800	
WDA at 18%	(38,745)		38,745
WDA at 7% (2)		(196)	196
WDV cf	176,505	2,604	
Total Capital Allowances			838,941

(1) AIA limit: (£200,000 x 3/12) + (£1,000,000 x 9/12) = £800,000

(2) Special Rate WDA: (6/12 x 8%) + (6/12 x 6%) = 7%

3.4   The CAPs will be:

1/4/2018 - 31/3/2019   (12 months)

1/4/2019 - 30/6/2019   (3 months)

CAP YEAR ENDED 31/3/2019			
	Main pool	Special rate pool	Capital allowances
	£	£	£
WDV bf	60,000	14,000	
add			
Acquisitions			
without FYA or AIA:			
Car (103 g/km)	16,000		
less			
Proceeds of			
Disposals:	(4,000)	———	
	72,000	14,000	
WDA 18% / 8%	(12,960)	(1,120)	14,080
WDV cf	59,040	12,880	
Total Capital Allowances			14,080

CAP 3 MONTHS ENDED 30/6/2019

		Main pool	Special rate pool	Capital allowances
	£	£	£	£
WDV bf		59,040	12,880	
Acquisitions qualifying for AIA:				
Plant	45,000			
AIA claimed*	(45,000)			45,000
		0		
		59,040	12,880	
WDA 18% x 3/12		(2,657)		2,657
WDA 6% x 3/12			(193)	193
WDV cf		56,383	12,687	
Total Capital Allowances				47,850

*AIA limit £1,000,000 x 3/12 = £250,000

Calculation of trading income assessments

Time apportionment of adjusted trade profits:
CAP 1/4/2018 to 31/3/2019   £480,000 x 12/15 = £384,000
CAP 1/4/2019 to 30/6/2019   £480,000 x 3/15 = £96,000

Capital allowances are then deducted from the adjusted profit for each CAP

	1/4/18 – 31/3/19	1/4/19 – 30/6/19
	£	£
Adjusted profit	384,000	96,000
Capital allowances:	(14,080)	(47,850)
Trading Income	369,920	48,150

3.5

PLANT & MACHINERY CAPITAL ALLOWANCES COMPUTATION:

	Main pool	Special rate pool	Capital allowances
	£	£	£
WDV bf	90,000	13,000	
Additions			
without FYA or AIA:			
BMW Car		27,000	
Low Emission Car 20,000			
100% FYA (20,000)	0		20,000
Additions qualifying for AIA:			
Plant 857,500			
AIA (833,333)			833,333
[limit of	24,167		
10/12 x £1,000,000			
= £833,333]			
Disposals			
Plant	(1,000)		
	113,167	40,000	
WDA 18% x 10/12	(16,975)		16,975
WDA 6% x 10/12		(2,000)	2,000
WDV cf	96,192	38,000	
Total Capital Allowances			872,308

	£
Adjusted trading profit for 10 month CAP to 31/1/2020	1,510,000
less capital allowances	(872,308)
Trading Income assessment	637,692

CHAPTER 4: CORPORATION TAX – CHARGEABLE GAINS

4.1 Chargeable Assets: **(a)**, **(b)**, **(c)**, **(d)**, **(f)**.

Exempt Assets: **(e** – chattel sold for a gain for under £6,000**)**, **(g)**, **(h)**, **(i)**.

4.2

	£
Proceeds	1,300,000
less Cost	(600,000)
Unindexed gain	700,000
less Indexation allowance £600,000 x 0.859	(515,400)
Chargeable Gain	184,600
less capital loss brought forward	(15,000)
Chargeable Gain to be brought into the taxable total profits	169,600

4.3

	£
Proceeds	145,000
less Cost	(50,000)
less Indexation £50,000 x 0.729	(36,450)
Chargeable Gain	58,550
less capital loss brought forward	(25,000)
Chargeable Gain to be brought into the taxable total profits	33,550

4.4 Chargeable Gains

Factory	£
Proceeds	500,000
less Cost	(300,000)
less Indexation £300,000 x 1.829 (restricted)	(200,000)
Chargeable Gain	nil

The indexation is restricted to avoid turning an unindexed gain into a loss.

Land	£
Proceeds	30,000
less apportioned cost:	
£50,000 x £30,000 / £150,000	(10,000)
less indexation allowance	
£10,000 x 1.051	(10,510)
Chargeable Gain	9,490

Total Chargeable Gain from two disposals	=	£9,490

4.5 Chargeable Gain on Shares

The disposal in January 2000 will be matched with the pool, and deducted from it before the current disposal is dealt with.

FA 1985 Pool Workings

	Number	Cost	Indexed cost
		£	£
1/1/1992 Purchase	3,000	9,000	9,000
Indexation to Jan 1995:			
£9,000 x 0.077			693
1/1/1995 Purchase	12,000	42,000	42,000
	15,000	51,000	51,693
Bonus Shares	3,000		
Indexation to January 2000:			
£51,693 x 0.141			7,289
Balance	18,000	51,000	58,982

1/1/2000 Disposal	(5,000)	(14,167)	(16,384)
Balance	13,000	36,833	42,598
Indexation to December 2017:			
£42,598 x 0.669			28,498
Balance	13,000	36,833	71,096
30/3/2019 Disposal	(10,000)	(28,333)	(54,689)
Balance	3,000	8,500	16,407

Share disposal March 2019:	£
Proceeds	60,000
less cost	(28,333)
less indexation (£54,689 – £28,333)	(26,356)
Chargeable Gain	5,311

Chargeable gain on machine

	£
Proceeds	6,900
less cost	(3,000)
less indexation allowance £3,000 x 0.669	(2,007)
Gain	1,893
But gain limited to 5/3 (£6,900 – £6,000) = £1,500.	1,500

The total Chargeable Gain from two disposals	=	£6,811

Capital allowances procedure regarding disposal of machine.

Since the machine is sold for more than the original cost, the original cost is deducted in the capital allowance computation instead of the disposal proceeds. There will be no balancing charge since the machine is in the main pool.

4.6 Vintage car = Exempt asset

Antique vase = Chargeable asset

Greyhound = Exempt asset

4.7

	£
Proceeds	12,000
Cost	4,000
Indexation allowance	2,524
Gain	5,476
Chattel restriction on gain	10,000

The chattel restriction will have no effect on the original gain.

4.8

	No. Shares	Cost £	Indexed cost £
Purchase October 2001	5,000	15,500	15,500
Indexation 0.114			1,767
Rights Issue	100	200	200
Subtotal	5,100	15,700	17,467
Indexation 0.534			9,327
Total	5,100	15,700	26,794
Disposal	(5,100)	(15,700)	(26,794)
Pool balance	0	0	0

Proceeds	£45,900
Indexed Cost	£26,794
Gain	£19,106

CHAPTER 5: CORPORATION TAX – CALCULATING THE TAX

5.1   Corporation Tax Computation

	£	£
Adjusted Trading Profits	1,120,000	
less capital allowances – P & M	(63,000)	
Trading Income		1,057,000
Property Income		23,000
Interest Receivable		60,000
Chargeable Gains		48,000
less Gift-Aid payment		(45,000)
Taxable total profits		1,143,000

	£
Taxable total profits at main rate: £1,143,000 x 19%	217,170

5.2   Corporation Tax Computation

	£	£
Adjusted Trading Profits	1,420,000	
less capital allowances – P & M	(205,000)	
Trading Income		1,215,000
Property Income		92,000
Interest Receivable		12,000
Chargeable Gains	88,000	
less capital loss bf	(18,000)	
Net Chargeable Gains		70,000
less Gift-Aid payment		(8,000)
Taxable total profits		1,381,000

	£
Taxable total profits at main rate: £1,381,000 x 19%	262,390

5.3   Corporation Tax Computation

	£	£
Trading Income		0
Property Income		35,000
Interest Receivable		40,000
Chargeable Gains	90,000	
less capital loss bf	(8,000)	
Net Chargeable Gains		82,000
		157,000
less trading loss		(120,000)
less rental loss bf		(13,000)
less Gift-Aid payment		(10,000)
Taxable total profits		14,000

Corporation Tax is £14,000 x 19% = £2,660

An alternative option would be to carry the loss forward against future taxable total profits.

5.4

	£	£
Net Profit per accounts		251,000
Add Back:		
Expenditure that is shown in the accounts but is not allowable		
Depreciation		41,000
Directors' Speeding Fines		1,000
Gifts of Food (Hampers)		10,000
Entertaining Customers		6,000
		309,000
Deduct:		
Income that is not taxable as trading income:		
Interest Receivable	50,000	
Profit on Disposal of Non-current Assets	50,000	
Rental Income Receivable	40,000	
Capital Allowances	11,000	
		(151,000)
Trading Income Assessment		158,000

Corporation Tax Computation

Trading Income	158,000
Property Income	40,000
Interest Receivable	50,000
Chargeable Gains	41,000
Taxable total profits	289,000
Corporation Tax at main rate: £289,000 x 19%	£54,910

The CT600 extract is shown on the next page.

Tax calculation
Turnover

		£	
145	Total turnover from trade		7 2 0 0 0 0 · 0 0

150	Banks, building societies, insurance companies and other financial concerns – put an 'X' in this box if you do not have a recognised turnover and have not made an entry in box 145	☐

Income

		£	
155	Trading profits		1 5 8 0 0 0 · 0 0
160	Trading losses brought forward set against trading profits		0 · 0 0
165	Net trading profits – box 155 minus box 160		1 5 8 0 0 0 · 0 0
170	Bank, building society or other interest, and profits from non-trading loan relationships		5 0 0 0 0 · 0 0

172	Put an 'X' in box 172 if the figure in box 170 is net of carrying back a deficit from a later accounting period	☐

		£	
175	Annual payments not otherwise charged to Corporation Tax and from which Income Tax has not been deducted		· 0 0
180	Non-exempt dividends or distributions from non–UK resident companies		· 0 0
185	Income from which Income Tax has been deducted		· 0 0
190	Income from a property business		4 0 0 0 0 · 0 0
195	Non-trading gains on intangible fixed assets		· 0 0
200	Tonnage Tax profits		· 0 0
205	Income not falling under any other heading		· 0 0

Chargeable gains

		£	
210	Gross chargeable gains		4 1 0 0 0 · 0 0
215	Allowable losses including losses brought forward		0 · 0 0
220	Net chargeable gains – box 210 minus box 215		4 1 0 0 0 · 0 0

Profits before deductions and reliefs

		£	
225	Losses brought forward against certain investment income		· 0 0
230	Non-trade deficits on loan relationships (including interest) and derivative contracts (financial instruments) brought forward set against non-trading profits		· 0 0
235	Profits before other deductions and reliefs – net sum of boxes 165 to 205 and 220 minus sum of boxes 225 and 230		2 8 9 0 0 0 · 0 0

5.5

	£
Net Profit for 16-month period per accounts	4,070
Add back non-allowable expenditure:	
Depreciation etc	10,000
Entertaining customers	1,930
Adjusted profit before capital allowances	16,000

Time apportionment of adjusted profit:

CAP 1/4/2018 to 31/3/2019 £16,000 x 12/16 = £12,000

CAP 1/4/2019 to 31/7/2019 £16,000 x 4/16 = £ 4,000

Deduction of Capital Allowances:

	1/4/2018 to 31/3/2019	1/4/2019 to 31/7/2019
	£	£
Adjusted profit	12,000	4,000
Capital allowances	(8,000)	(2,500)
Trading Income	4,000	1,500

Corporation Tax Computation – CAP 1/4/2018 to 31/3/2019

	£
Trading Income	4,000
Taxable total profits	4,000

Corporation Tax at Main Rate: £4,000 x 19%	£760

Corporation Tax Computation – CAP 1/4/2019 to 31/7/2019

	£
Trading Income	1,500
Chargeable Gains	45,000
Taxable total profits	46,500

Corporation Tax at main rate:	
£46,500 x 19%	£8,835

5.6 The following statements are true: **(a)**, **(c)**, **(d)**.

CHAPTER 6: INCOME TAX – TRADING PROFITS

6.1 **Profit motive**. Michelle seems to deliberately buy and sell at a profit. She buys property in need of renovation, and times the sale to obtain most profit. This indicates trading.

Subject matter. Michelle gets personal use from the properties that she buys, and this could indicate that she is not trading. She could argue that she is simply changing homes like most people.

Length of ownership. After renovating the buildings, Michelle only keeps them for a few months. Such a short time indicates trading.

Frequency of transactions. The buying and selling of property seems to be quite a regular activity, although with each transaction spaced nearly a year apart it could be argued that it is not particularly frequent.

Supplementary work. Renovating the properties counts as supplementary work, and this is clearly carried out with a view to a future sale.

Reason for acquisition and sale. Although the first property was bequeathed to her, she seems to have subsequently bought with the ultimate sale in mind. This indicates trading.

6.2

1	add back (disallowable expense)
2	add back (disallowable expense)
3	deduct (not trading income)
4	deduct (not trading income)
5	add back (disallowable expense)
6	deduct (not taxable income)
7	add back (disallowable expense)
8	add back (disallowable expense since food)
9	no action (taxable trading income)
10	add back (disallowable expense – part of drawings)
11	no action (allowable)
12	add back (disallowable expense)

6.3

	£	£
Net Profit per accounts		144,000
Add Back:		
Expenditure that is shown in the accounts but is not allowable		
Drawings		18,000
Depreciation		22,000
Loss on Sale of Non-current Assets		4,000
Gift Vouchers		3,000
Entertaining Customers		4,500
Owner's Pension Contribution		2,400
		197,900

	£	£
Deduct:		
Income that is not taxable as trading income		
Interest Received	12,000	
Rental Income	10,000	
Capital Allowances	23,000	
		(45,000)
Trading Income Assessment		152,900

6.4   The capital allowance computation is as follows:

The following acquisitions qualify for AIA:

Computer System	£2,000
Shop Counter	£3,000
Total	£5,000 (below AIA limit)

	£	Main pool £	Single asset pool car (40% private) £	Capital allowances £
WDV bf		25,000	10,000	
Additions with FYAs:				
Low emission car	26,000			
FYA (100%)	(26,000) x 60%			15,600
Acquisitions qualifying for AIA:				
Computer	2,000			
Shop Counter	3,000			
AIA claimed	(5,000)	0		5,000
Disposals:				
Private use car			(4,000)	
Food Processor		(200)		
Sub totals		24,800	6,000	
WDA 18%		(4,464)		4,464
Balancing Allowance			(6,000) x 60%	3,600
WDV cf		20,336	–	
Total Capital Allowances				28,664

Calculation of Adjusted Profit (Loss):

	£
Adjusted trading profits (before capital allowances)	12,000
Capital allowances (as above)	(28,664)
Loss	(16,664)

The trading income assessment for 2019/20 is nil.

The loss of £16,664 could be:

- carried forward against future trading profits
- set against the total income of John for 2019/20 and / or 2018/19
- total income claims could be extended to capital gains

6.5 There is no AIA claimable.

Plant & Machinery Capital Allowances Computation

	Main pool	Car 20% private BMW	Single Asset Pools S/L asset	Special rate 20% private Range Rover	Capital allowances
	£	£	£	£	£
WDV bf	66,300	16,000	2,000	–	
Additions without FYA or AIA:					
Range Rover (200 g/km)				28,000	
Ford Focus (105g/km)	19,000				
Disposals:					
BMW		(12,000)			
Vauxhall	(4,000)				
	81,300	4,000	2,000	28,000	
WDA 18%	(14,634)		(360)		14,994
WDA 6%				(1,680) x 80%	1,344
Balancing Allowance		(4,000) x 80%			3,200
WDV cf	66,666	–	1,640	26,320	
Total Capital Allowances					19,538

Adjustment of Trading Profits:

	£	£
Net Profit per accounts		110,000
Add Back:		
Expenditure that is shown in the accounts but is not allowable		
Drawings		45,000
Depreciation		38,000
Loss on Sale of BMW		3,000
Entertaining Customers		2,000
		198,000

Deduct:

Income that is not taxable as trading income

Reduction in general bad debt provision	4,000	
Gain on Sale of Vauxhall	1,000	
Capital Allowances – Plant & Machinery	19,538	
		(24,538)
Trading Income Assessment		173,462

6.6

Net loss		(3,785)
Add		
Depreciation	28,019	
Mr Chang's salary	30,000	
Gifts to customers	2,250	
Subscription to golf club	220	
Motor expenses for Mr Chang's car	5,700	
		66,189
		62,404
Less		
Capital allowances		9,878
Adjusted trading profits		52,526

CHAPTER 7: INCOME TAX – FURTHER ISSUES

7.1   The first three tax years for the business will be 2016/17, 2017/18 and 2018/19.

The assessments for these years are calculated as follows:

Tax year	Basis period	Trading income assessment	
2016/17	1/12/2016 - 5/4/2017	£48,000 x 4/12 =	£16,000
2017/18	1/12/2016 - 30/11/2017		£48,000
2018/19	1/12/2017 - 30/11/2018		£30,000

Overlap profits are £16,000, relating to the period 1/12/2016 - 5/4/2017.

7.2 The first three tax years for the business will be 2016/17, 2017/18 and 2018/19.

The assessments for these years are calculated as follows:

Tax year	Basis period	Trading income assessment	
2016/17	1/2/2017 - 5/4/2017	£33,000 x 2/11 =	£6,000
2017/18	1/2/2017 - 31/1/2018 (First 12 months)	£33,000 + (£48,000 x 1/12)	£37,000
2018/19	1/1/2018 - 31/12/2018		£48,000

Overlap profits total £10,000, relating to the periods 1/2/2017 - 5/4/2017 (£6,000) and 1/1/2018 - 31/1/2018 (£4,000).

7.3

Tax year	Basis period		Trading income assessment
2018/19	1/7/2017 - 30/6/2018		£36,000
2019/20	1/7/2018 - 31/5/2019	£20,000	
	less overlap profits bf	(£5,000)	
			£15,000

7.4

2019/20	Basis period 1/1/2019 – 28/2/2020		£56,000
	Less 2 months previous overlap (£6,000 x 2/3)		(£4,000)
Trading Income Assessment 2019/20			£52,000

The overlap profits to be carried forward are £2,000.

7.5

2019/20   Basis period 1/10/2018 – 30/9/2019

Trading Income Assessment 2019/20:

£36,000 + (3/12 x £60,000)   £51,000

The overlap profits to be carried forward are £6,000 + £15,000 = £21,000

7.6 The accounting year to 31/12/2019 profits of £96,000 will need to be time-apportioned before dividing them amongst the partners:

1/1/2019 - 30/9/2019	9/12 x £96,000 = £72,000
Alice (50%)	£36,000
Bob (50%)	£36,000

1/10/2019 - 31/12/2019	3/12 x £96,000 = £24,000
Alice (45%)	£10,800
Bob (40%)	£9,600
Colin (15%)	£3,600

The accounting year to 31/12/2020 profits of £108,000 are divided as follows:

Alice (45%)	£48,600
Bob (40%)	£43,200
Colin (15%)	£16,200

The basis periods for the partners and assessments are as follows:

Tax year	Basis period	Trading income assessments	
Alice			
2019/20	y/e 31/12/2019	£36,000+ £10,800	£46,800
2020/21	y/e 31/12/2020		£48,600
Bob			
2019/20	y/e 31/12/2019	£36,000+ £9,600	£45,600
2020/21	y/e 31/12/2020		£43,200
Colin			
2019/20	1/10/2019 - 5/4/2020	£3,600 + (3/12 x £16,200)	£7,650
2020/21	y/e 31/12/2020		£16,200

(Colin's overlap profits are £4,050)

7.7   Capital Allowances:

Plant & Machinery

	Main pool	Single asset pool car (30% private)	Capital allowances
	£	£	£
WDV bf	35,000	16,000	
Disposal:			
Car		(10,000)	
WDA 18%	(6,300)		6,300
Balancing Allowance		(6,000) x 70%	4,200
WDV cf	28,700	0	–
Total Capital Allowances			10,500

Adjustment of Profits

	£	£
Net Profit per accounts		71,000
Add Back:		
Expenditure that is shown in the accounts but is not allowable		
Depreciation		12,250
Private motor expenses		500
Increase in General Provision for Bad Debts		200
Gift Vouchers for customers		400
		84,350
Deduct:		
Allowable expenditure not shown in accounts		
Plant & Machinery Capital Allowances	10,500	
		(10,500)
Adjusted Profits for y/e 31/3/2020		73,850

Trading Income assessment for Olga for 2019/20

This is her last tax year for the business. The basis period is 1/4/2019 - 31/3/2020.

Her share of the adjusted profits is: £73,850 x 1/3 = £24,617

Trading Income assessment   £24,617

Class 4 National Insurance

This is calculated based on the trading income figure.

9% of (£24,617 – £8,632) = £1,438.65

Supplementary tax return page

This is shown on the next page. The 2018/19 version is used to illustrate the form.

Partnership Statement (short) for the year ended 5 April 2019

Please read these instructions before completing the Statement

Use these pages to allocate partnership income if the only income for the relevant
return period was trading and professional income or untaxed interest and alternative
finance receipts from UK banks and building societies. Otherwise you must download the
'Partnership Statement (Full)' pages to record details of the allocation of all the partnership
income. Go to www.gov.uk/taxreturnforms

Step 1   Fill in boxes 1 to 29 and boxes A and B as appropriate. Get the figures you need
from the relevant boxes in the Partnership Tax Return. Complete a separate
Statement for each accounting period covered by this Partnership Tax Return and
for each trade or profession carried on by the partnership.

Step 2   Then allocate the amounts in boxes 11 to 29 attributable to each partner using
the allocation columns on this page and page 7, read the Partnership Tax Return
Guide, go to www.gov.uk/taxreturnforms
If the partnership has more than 3 partners, please photocopy page 7.

Step 3   Each partner will need a copy of their allocation of income to fill in their personal
tax return.

PARTNERSHIP INFORMATION
If the partnership business includes a trade or
profession, enter here the accounting period
for which appropriate items in this statement
are returned.

Start	**1**	1 / 4 / 19
End	**2**	31 / 3 / 20

Nature of trade **3**

MIXED PARTNERSHIPS

Tick here if this Statement is drawn
up using Corporation Tax rules **4**

Tick here if this Statement is drawn up
using tax rules for non-residents **5**

Individual partner details

6 Name of partner   O L G A

Address

Postcode

Date appointed as a partner
(if during 2017–18 or 2018–19) Partner's Unique Taxpayer Reference (UTR)

7   /   /   **8**

Date ceased to be a partner
(if during 2017–18 or 2018–19) Partner's National Insurance number

9 31 / 3 / 20   **10**

Partnership's profits, losses, income and tax credits	Tick this box if the items entered in the box had foreign tax taken off ▼	Partner's share of profits, losses, income and tax credits Copy figures in boxes 11 to 29 to boxes in the individual's Partnership (short) pages as shown below	
for an accounting period ended in 2018 to 2019			
from box 3.83 Profit from a trade or profession **A**	**11** £ 7 3 8 5 0	Profit **11** £ 2 4 6 1 7	Copy this figure to box 8
from box 3.82 Adjustment on change of basis	**11A** £	**11A** £	Copy this figure to box 10
from box 3.84 Loss from a trade or profession **B**	**12** £	Loss **12** £	Copy this figure to box 8
from box 3.94 Disguised remuneration	**12A**	**12A**	Copy to box 15
for the period 6 April 2018 to 5 April 2019*			
from box 7.9A Income from untaxed UK savings	**13** £	**13** £	Copy this figure to box 28
from box 3.97 CIS deductions made by contractors on account of tax	**24** £	**24** £	Copy this figure to box 30
from box 3.98 Other tax taken off trading income	**24A** £	**24A** £	Copy this figure to box 31
from box 3.117 Partnership charges	**29** £	**29** £	Copy this figure to box 4, 'Other tax reliefs' section on page Ai 2 in your personal tax return

* If you're a 'CT Partnership' see the Partnership Tax Return Guide

7.8

Payment date	31 Jan 2018 £	31 July 2018 £	31 Jan 2019 £	31 July 2019 £	31 Jan 2020 £	31 July 2020 £
Tax year 2017/18	0	0	6,200	0	0	0
Tax year 2018/19	0	0	3,100	3,100	4,800	0
Tax year 2019/20	0	0	0	0	5,500	5,500
Totals due	0	0	9,300	3,100	10,300	5,500

7.9

	£	£
Net profit per accounts		21,500
add disallowable expenditure		
Private van running costs		1,260
Depreciation		2,800
Entertaining		1,000
Private telephone and postage		200
		26,760
less allowable expenditure		
Heating and lighting office	150	
Capital allowances	4,200	
		(4,350)
Adjusted profit		22,410
Less Trading Loss brought forward		(6,000)
Trading Income Assessment 2019/20		16,410

7.10 **(a)** 2017/18

(b) £12,000

(c) £72,750

(d) £81,000

(e) £18,750

(f) from the profits in the final year of trading, or on change of accounting date

7.11 Only **(c)** and **(f)** are true, the rest are false

CHAPTER 8: CAPITAL GAINS TAX FOR INDIVIDUALS

8.1 **(a)** Exempt, as a chattel

(b) Exempt

(c) Chargeable

(d) Chargeable

(e) Chargeable

(f) Chargeable

(g) Exempt

(h) Exempt

8.2

		£
(a)	Proceeds	140,000
	less cost	(40,000)
	extension	(20,000)
	Gain	80,000
	less annual exempt amount	(12,000)
	Amount subject to CGT	68,000
	Capital Gains Tax £68,000 x 20% =	13,600

		£
(b)	Gain	80,000
	less annual exempt amount	(12,000)
	Amount subject to CGT	68,000
	Capital Gains Tax £68,000 x 10% =	6,800

8.3

	£
Proceeds	23,000
less cost (600 x £10)	(6,000)
Gain	17,000
less annual exempt amount	(12,000)
Amount subject to CGT	5,000
Capital Gains Tax £5,000 x 10% =	500

All the gain is within the basic rate band limit of £37,500 when added to the taxable income.

8.4 **(a)** Amount of William's gain:

	£	£
Proceeds		200,000
less market value when received	100,000	
minus deferred gain	(33,160)	
		(66,840)
Gain		133,160
less annual exempt amount		(12,000)
Amount subject to CGT		121,160
Capital Gains Tax £121,160 x 20% =		24,232

(b)

	£
Gain	133,160
less annual exempt amount	(12,000)
Amount subject to CGT	121,160
Capital Gains Tax £121,160 x 10% =	12,116

8.5 The first step is to allocate the sale proceeds to the individual assets, and determine which assets are chargeable.

	£	
Premises	700,000	Chargeable
Plant & Machinery	20,000	Proceeds < Cost. Dealt with through capital allowance computation
Net Current Assets	50,000	Exempt
Goodwill	130,000	Chargeable
Total Proceeds	900,000	

The goodwill is calculated as the balancing figure, after accounting for the other assets.

The computations are then carried out individually on the chargeable assets.

	£	£
Premises		
Proceeds		700,000
less Cost	400,000	
minus deferred gain	(60,000)	
		(340,000)
Gain		360,000
Goodwill		
Proceeds		130,000
Less Cost		0
Gain		130,000

Summary	£
Gain on premises	360,000
Gain on goodwill	130,000
Total Gains	490,000
Less Annual Exempt Amount	(12,000)
Amount subject to CGT	478,000
CGT £478,000 x 10%	47,800

8.6 **(c)** When a capital loss made by an individual is offset against gains in the following tax year, it is only to the extent that it reduces those gains to the amount of the annual exemption

8.7 **(b)** Gain = £3,000,000
Less annual exempt amount £12,000 = £2,988,000
Taxed at 10% = £298,800.

8.8 **(a)** Entrepreneurial relief is restricted to £10,000,000 for the lifetime of the taxpayer

Photocopiable tax forms

These pages may be photocopied for student use.

It is recommended that they are enlarged to A4 size.

These pages are also available for download from the Products and Resources Section of www.osbornebooks.co.uk or from www.gov.uk

The tax forms include:

- company – tax return CT600   pages 10.0 - 10.10
- self-employed supplementary pages - short version   pages 10.11 - 10.12
- self-employed supplementary pages - full version   pages 10.13 - 10.18
- partnership tax return   pages 10.19 - 10.26

All these forms illustrated are those in use for 2018/19. The forms for 2019/20 were not available when this book was published.

HM Revenue & Customs

Company Tax Return

CT600 (2019) Version 3
for accounting periods starting on or after 1 April 2015

Your Company Tax Return

If we send the company a 'Notice' to deliver a Company Tax Return it has to comply by the filing date or we charge a penalty, even if there is no tax to pay.

A return includes a Company Tax Return form, any supplementary pages, accounts, computations and any relevant information. The CT600 Guide tells you how the return must be formatted and delivered. It contains general information you may need to deliver your return, links to more detailed advice and box-by-box guidance for this form and the supplementary pages.

The forms in the CT600 series set out the information we need and provide a standard format for calculations.

Company information

1	Company name	
2	Company registration number	
3	Tax reference	
4	Type of company	

Northern Ireland

Put an 'X' in the appropriate box(es) below

5	NI trading activity		6	SME	
7	NI employer		8	Special circumstances	

About this return

This is the above company's return for the period

30 from DD MM YYYY   **35** to DD MM YYYY

Put an 'X' in the appropriate box(es) below

40	A repayment is due for this return period	
45	Claim or relief affecting an earlier period	
50	Making more than one return for this company now	
55	This return contains estimated figures	
60	Company part of a group that is not small	
65	Notice of disclosable avoidance schemes	

Transfer Pricing

70	Compensating adjustment claimed	
75	Company qualifies for SME exemption	

About this return - continued

Accounts and computations

80 I attach accounts and computations for the period to which this return relates ☐

85 I attach accounts and computations for a different period ☐

90 If you are not attaching the accounts and computations, say why not

```
[                                                              ]
```

Supplementary pages enclosed

95 Loans and arrangements to participators by close companies – form CT600A ☐

100 Controlled foreign companies and foreign permanent establishment exemptions – form CT600B ☐

105 Group and consortium – form CT600C ☐

110 Insurance – form CT600D ☐

115 Charities and Community Amateur Sports Clubs (CASCs) – form CT600E ☐

120 Tonnage Tax – form CT600F ☐

125 Northern Ireland - form CT600G ☐

130 Cross-border Royalties – form CT600H ☐

135 Supplementary charge in respect of ring fence trades – form CT600I ☐

140 Disclosure of Tax Avoidance Schemes – form CT600J ☐

141 Restitution Tax – form CT600K ☐

Tax calculation

Turnover

145 Total turnover from trade £ [   ] · 0 0

150 Banks, building societies, insurance companies and other financial concerns – ☐
put an 'X' in this box if you do not have a recognised turnover and have not made an entry in box 145

Income

155 Trading profits £ [   ] · 0 0

160 Trading losses brought forward set against trading profits £ [   ] · 0 0

165 Net trading profits – box 155 minus box 160 £ [   ] · 0 0

170 Bank, building society or other interest, and profits from non-trading loan relationships £ [   ] · 0 0

172 Put an 'X' in box 172 if the figure in box 170 is net of carrying back a deficit from a later accounting period ☐

Income - continued

		£		· 0 0
175	Annual payments not otherwise charged to Corporation Tax and from which Income Tax has not been deducted			
180	Non-exempt dividends or distributions from non–UK resident companies			
185	Income from which Income Tax has been deducted			
190	Income from a property business			
195	Non-trading gains on intangible fixed assets			
200	Tonnage Tax profits			
205	Income not falling under any other heading			

Chargeable gains

210	Gross chargeable gains	£	· 0 0
215	Allowable losses including losses brought forward	£	· 0 0
220	Net chargeable gains - box 210 minus box 215	£	· 0 0

Profits before deductions and reliefs

225	Losses brought forward against certain investment income	£	· 0 0
230	Non-trade deficits on loan relationships (including interest) and derivative contracts (financial instruments) brought forward set against non-trading profits	£	· 0 0
235	Profits before other deductions and reliefs – net sum of boxes 165 to 205 and 220 minus sum of boxes 225 and 230	£	· 0 0

Deductions and reliefs

240	Losses on unquoted shares	£	· 0 0
245	Management expenses	£	· 0 0
250	UK property business losses for this or previous accounting period	£	· 0 0
255	Capital allowances for the purposes of management of the business	£	· 0 0
260	Non-trade deficits for this accounting period from loan relationships and derivative contracts (financial instruments)	£	· 0 0

Deductions and Reliefs - continued

263 Carried forward non-trade deficits from loan relationships and derivative contracts (financial instruments) £ [ ] · 0 0

265 Non-trading losses on intangible fixed assets £ [ ] · 0 0

275 Total trading losses of this or a later accounting period £ [ ] · 0 0

280 Put an 'X' in box 280 if amounts carried back from later accounting periods are included in box 275 [ ]

285 Trading losses carried forward and claimed against total profits £ [ ] · 0 0

290 Non-trade capital allowances £ [ ] · 0 0

295 Total of deductions and reliefs –
total of boxes 240 to 275, 285 and 290 £ [ ] · 0 0

300 Profits before qualifying donations and group relief –
box 235 minus box 295 £ [ ] · 0 0

305 Qualifying donations £ [ ] · 0 0

310 Group relief £ [ ] · 0 0

312 Group relief for carried forward losses £ [ ] · 0 0

315 Profits chargeable to Corporation Tax –
box 300 minus boxes 305, 310 and 312 £ [ ] · 0 0

320 Ring fence profits included £ [ ] · 0 0

325 Northern Ireland profits included £ [ ] · 0 0

Tax calculation

Enter how much profit has to be charged and at what rate

	Financial year (yyyy)		Amount of profit		Rate of tax %		Tax	
330		335	£	340		345	£	p
		350	£	355		360	£	p
		365	£	370		375	£	p
380		385	£	390		395	£	p
		400	£	405		410	£	p
		415	£	420		425	£	p

Corporation Tax total of boxes 345, 360, 375, 395, 410 and 425 **430** £ [ ] ·

Marginal relief for ring fence trades **435** £ [ ] ·

Corporation Tax chargeable box 430 minus box 435 **440** £ [ ] ·

Reliefs and deductions in terms of tax

445 Community investment relief £ ⬚.⬚

450 Double taxation relief £ ⬚.⬚

455 Put an 'X' in box 455 if box 450 includes an underlying Rate relief claim ⬚

460 Put an 'X' in box 460 if box 450 includes any amount carried back from a later period ⬚

465 Advance Corporation Tax £ ⬚.⬚

470 Total reliefs and deduction in terms of tax
- total of boxes 445, 450 and 465 £ ⬚.⬚

Calculation of tax outstanding or overpaid

475 Net Corporation Tax liability – box 440 minus box 470 £ ⬚.⬚

480 Tax payable on loans and arrangements to participators £ ⬚.⬚

485 Put an 'X' in box 485 if you completed box A70 in the supplementary pages CT600A ⬚

490 CFC tax payable £ ⬚.⬚

495 Bank levy payable £ ⬚.⬚

496 Bank surcharge payable £ ⬚.⬚

500 CFC tax, bank levy and bank surcharge payable
- total of boxes 490, 495 and 496 £ ⬚.⬚

505 Supplementary charge (ring fence trades) payable £ ⬚.⬚

510 Tax chargeable – total of boxes 475, 480, 500 and 505 £ ⬚.⬚

515 Income Tax deducted from gross income included in profits £ ⬚.⬚

520 Income Tax repayable to the company £ ⬚.⬚

525 Self-assessment of tax payable before restitution tax
- box 510 minus box 515 £ ⬚.⬚

527 Restitution tax £ ⬚.⬚

528 Self-assessment of tax payable - total of boxes 525 and 527 £ ⬚.⬚

Tax reconciliation

Box	Description	
530	Research and Development credit	£ [ ] . [ ]
535	(not currently used)	£ [ ] . [ ]
540	Creative tax credit	£ [ ] . [ ]
545	Total of Research and Development credit and creative tax credit – total box 530 to 540	£ [ ] . [ ]
550	Land remediation tax credit	£ [ ] . [ ]
555	Life assurance company tax credit	£ [ ] . [ ]
560	Total land remediation and life assurance company tax credit – total box 550 and 555	£ [ ] . [ ]
565	Capital allowances first-year tax credit	£ [ ] . [ ]
570	Surplus Research and Development credits or creative tax credit payable – box 545 minus box 525	£ [ ] . [ ]
575	Land remediation or life assurance company tax credit payable – total of boxes 545 and 560 minus boxes 525 and 570	£ [ ] . [ ]
580	Capital allowances first-year tax credit payable – boxes 545, 560 and 565 minus boxes 525, 570 and 575	£ [ ] . [ ]
585	Ring fence Corporation Tax included	£ [ ] . [ ]
586	NI Corporation Tax included	£ [ ] . [ ]
590	Ring fence supplementary charge included	£ [ ] . [ ]
595	Tax already paid (and not already repaid)	£ [ ] . [ ]
600	Tax outstanding – box 525 minus boxes 545, 560, 565 and 595	£ [ ] . [ ]
605	Tax overpaid including surplus or payable credits – total sum of boxes 545, 560, 565 and 595 minus 525	£ [ ] . [ ]
610	Group tax refunds surrendered to this company	£ [ ] . [ ]
615	Research and Development expenditure credits surrendered to this company	£ [ ] . [ ]

Indicators and information

620 Franked investment income/Exempt ABGH distributions £ ☐☐☐☐☐☐☐☐☐☐☐ · 0 0

625 Number of 51% group companies ☐

Put an 'X' in the relevant boxes, if in the period, the company:

630 should have made (whether it has or not) instalment payments as a large company under the Corporation Tax (Instalment Payments) Regulations ☐

631 should have made (whether it has or not) instalment payments as a very large company under the Corporation Tax (Instalment Payments) Regulations ☐

635 is within a group payments arrangement for the period ☐

640 has written down or sold intangible assets ☐

645 has made cross-border royalty payments ☐

Information about enhanced expenditure
Research and Development (R&D) or creative enhanced expenditure

650 Put an 'X' in box 650 if the claim is made by a small or medium-sized enterprise (SME), including a SME subcontractor to a large company ☐

655 Put an 'X' in box 655 if the claim is made by a large company ☐

660 R&D enhanced expenditure £ ☐☐☐☐☐☐☐☐☐☐☐ · 0 0

665 Creative enhanced expenditure £ ☐☐☐☐☐☐☐☐☐☐☐ · 0 0

670 R&D and creative enhanced expenditure total box 660 and 665 £ ☐☐☐☐☐☐☐☐☐☐☐ · 0 0

675 R&D enhanced expenditure of a SME on work subcontracted to it by a large company £ ☐☐☐☐☐☐☐☐☐☐☐ · 0 0

680 Vaccine research expenditure £ ☐☐☐☐☐☐☐☐☐☐☐ · 0 0

Land remediation enhanced expenditure

685 Enter the total enhanced expenditure £ ☐☐☐☐☐☐☐☐☐☐☐ · 0 0

Information about capital allowances and balancing charges
Allowances and charges in calculation of trading profits and losses

	Capital allowances	Balancing charges
Annual investment allowance	690 £	
Machinery and plant – special rate pool	695 £	700 £
Machinery and plant – main pool	705 £	710 £
Business premises renovation	715 £	720 £
Enterprise zones	721 £	722 £
Zero emissions goods vehicles	723 £	724 £
Other allowances and charges	725 £	730 £

Allowances and charges not included in calculation of trading profits and losses

	Capital allowances	Balancing charges
Annual investment allowance	735 £	
Business premises renovation	740 £	745 £
Enterprise zones	746 £	747 £
Zero emissions goods vehicles	748 £	749 £
Other allowances and charges	750 £	755 £

Qualifying expenditure

760 Machinery and plant on which first year allowance is claimed £ · 0 0

765 Designated environmentally friendly machinery and plant £ · 0 0

770 Machinery and plant on long-life assets and integral features £ · 0 0

775 Other machinery and plant £ · 0 0

Losses, deficits and excess amounts
Amount arising

	Amount		Maximum available for surrender as group relief	
Losses of trades carried on wholly or partly in the UK	780 £		785 £	
Losses of trades carried on wholly outside the UK	790 £			
Non-trade deficits on loan relationships and derivative contracts	795 £		800 £	
UK property business losses	805 £		810 £	
Overseas property business losses	815 £			
Losses from miscellaneous transactions	820 £			
Capital losses	825 £			
Non-trading losses on intangible fixed assets	830 £		835 £	

Excess amounts

	Amount		Maximum available for surrender as group relief	
Non-trade capital allowances			840 £	
Qualifying donations			845 £	
Management expenses	850 £		855 £	

Northern Ireland information

856 Amount of group relief claimed which relates to NI trading losses used against rest of UK/mainstream profits

£ [   ] · 0 0

857 Amount of group relief claimed which relates to NI trading losses used against NI trading profits

£ [   ] · 0 0

858 Amount of group relief claimed which relates to rest of UK/mainstream losses used against NI trading profits

£ [   ] · 0 0

Overpayments and repayments
Small repayments

860 Do not repay sums of £ [   ] · 0 0 or less.

Read the overpayments and repayments section of the Company Tax Return Guide for specific guidance on when and how to make an entry in this box.

Repayments for the period covered by this return

865 Repayment of Corporation Tax

£ [   ] · [ ]

870 Repayment of Income Tax

£ [   ] · [ ]

875 Payable Research and Development tax credit

£ [   ] · [ ]

880 Payable Research and Development expenditure credit

£ [   ] · [ ]

885 Payable creative tax credit

£ [   ] · [ ]

890 Payable land remediation or life assurance company tax credit

£ [   ] · [ ]

895 Payable capital allowances first-year tax credit

£ [   ] · [ ]

Surrender of tax refund within group

Including surrenders under the Instalment Payments Regulations.

900 The following amount is to be surrendered

£ [   ] · [ ]

Put an 'X' in the appropriate box(es) below

the joint Notice is attached **905** [ ]

or

will follow **910** [ ]

915 Please stop repayment of the following amount until we send you the Notice

£ [   ] · [ ]

Bank details (for person to whom a repayment is to be made)

920 Name of bank or building society

925 Branch sort code

930 Account number

935 Name of account

940 Building society reference

Payments to a person other than the company

945 Complete the authority below if you want the repayment to be made to a person other than the company

I, as (enter status - company secretary, treasurer, liquidator or authorised agent, etc)

950 of (enter company name)

955 authorise (enter name)

960 of address (enter address)

965 Nominee reference

to receive payment on company's behalf

970 Name

Declaration

Declaration

I declare that the information I have given on this Company Tax Return and any supplementary pages is correct and complete to the best of my knowledge and belief.

I understand that giving false information in the return, or concealing any part of the company's profits or tax payable, can lead to both the company and me being prosecuted.

975 Name

980 Date DD MM YYYY

985 Status

HM Revenue & Customs

Self-employment (short)

Tax year 6 April 2018 to 5 April 2019 (2018-19)

Please read the 'Self-employment (short) notes' to check if you should use this page or the 'Self-employment (full)' page.

For help filling in this form, go to www.gov.uk/taxreturnforms and read the notes and helpsheets.

Your name	Your Unique Taxpayer Reference (UTR)

Business details

1 Description of business

2 Postcode of your business address

3 If your business name, description, address or postcode have changed in the last 12 months, put 'X' in the box and give details in the 'Any other information' box of your tax return

4 If you are a foster carer or shared lives carer, put 'X' in the box

5 If your business started after 5 April 2018, enter the start date DD MM YYYY

6 If your business ceased before 6 April 2019, enter the final date of trading DD MM YYYY

7 Date your books or accounts are made up to

8 If you used cash basis, money actually received and paid out, to calculate your income and expenses put 'X' in the box

Business income – if your annual business turnover was below £85,000

9 Your turnover – the takings, fees, sales or money earned by your business
£ · 0 0

10 Any other business income not included in box 9
£ · 0 0

10.1 Trading income allowance - read the notes
£ · 0 0

Allowable business expenses

If your annual turnover was below £85,000 you may just put your total expenses in box 20, rather than filling in the whole section.

11 Costs of goods bought for resale or goods used
£ · 0 0

12 Car, van and travel expenses – after private use proportion
£ · 0 0

13 Wages, salaries and other staff costs
£ · 0 0

14 Rent, rates, power and insurance costs
£ · 0 0

15 Repairs and maintenance of property and equipment
£ · 0 0

16 Accountancy, legal and other professional fees
£ · 0 0

17 Interest and bank and credit card financial charges
£ · 0 0

18 Phone, fax, stationery and other office costs
£ · 0 0

19 Other allowable business expenses – client entertaining costs are not an allowable expense
£ · 0 0

20 Total allowable expenses – total of boxes 11 to 19
£ · 0 0

Net profit or loss

21   **Net profit** – if your business income is more than your expenses (if box 9 + box 10 minus box 20 is positive)

£ _____ · 0 0

22   **Or, net loss** – if your expenses exceed your business income (if box 20 minus (box 9 + box 10) is positive)

£ _____ · 0 0

Tax allowances for vehicles and equipment (capital allowances)

Do not include the cost of these in your business expenses.

23   **Annual Investment Allowance**

£ _____ · 0 0

25   **Other capital allowances**

£ _____ · 0 0

24   **Allowance for small balance of unrelieved expenditure**

£ _____ · 0 0

26   **Total balancing charges** - for example, where you have disposed of items for more than their tax value

£ _____ · 0 0

Calculating your taxable profits

Your taxable profit may not be the same as your net profit. Please read the 'Self-employment (short) notes' to see if you need to make any adjustments and fill in the boxes which apply to arrive at your taxable profit for the year.

27   **Goods and/or services for your own use**

£ _____ · 0 0

28   **Net business profit for tax purposes** (if box 21 + box 26 + box 27 minus (boxes 22 to 25) is positive). If you're claiming trading income allowance (box 21 + box 26 + box 27 minus box 10.1)

£ _____ · 0 0

29   **Loss brought forward from earlier years set off against this year's profits** – up to the amount in box 28

£ _____ · 0 0

30   **Any other business income not included in box 9 or box 10** – for example, non arm's length reverse premiums

£ _____ · 0 0

Total taxable profits or net business loss

If your total profits from all Self-employments and Partnerships for 2018–19 are less than £6,205, you do not have to pay Class 2 National Insurance contributions, but you may want to pay voluntarily (box 36) to protect your rights to certain benefits.

31   **Total taxable profits from this business** (if box 28 + box 30 minus box 29 is positive).

£ _____ · 0 0

32   **Net business loss for tax purposes** (if boxes 22 to 25 minus (box 21 + box 26 + box 27) is positive)

£ _____ · 0 0

Losses, Class 2 and Class 4 National Insurance contributions (NICs) and CIS deductions

If you've made a loss for tax purposes (box 32), read the 'Self-employment (short) notes' and fill in boxes 33 to 35 as appropriate.

33   **Loss from this tax year set off against other income for 2018–19**

£ _____ · 0 0

34   **Loss to be carried back to previous year(s) and set off against income (or capital gains)**

£ _____ · 0 0

35   **Total loss to carry forward after all other set-offs** - including unused losses brought forward

£ _____ · 0 0

36   **If your total profits for 2018–19 are less than £6,205 and you choose to pay Class 2 NICs voluntarily, put 'X' in the box**

☐

37   **If you're exempt from paying Class 4 NICs, put 'X' in the box**

☐

38   **Total Construction Industry Scheme (CIS) deductions taken from your payments by contractors** – CIS subcontractors only

£ _____ · 0 0

HM Revenue & Customs

Self-employment (full)

Tax year 6 April 2018 to 5 April 2019 (2018-19)

Please read the 'Self-employment (full) notes' to check if you should use this page or the 'Self-employment (short)' page.

For help filling in this form, go to www.gov.uk/taxreturnforms and read the notes and helpsheets.

Your name	Your Unique Taxpayer Reference (UTR)

Business details

1 Business name – unless it's in your own name

2 Description of business

3 First line of your business address – unless you work from home

4 Postcode of your business address

5 If the details in boxes 1, 2, 3 or 4 have changed in the last 12 months, put 'X' in the box and give details in the 'Any other information' box

6 If your business started after 5 April 2018, enter the start date DD MM YYYY

7 If your business ceased after 5 April 2018 but before 6 April 2019, enter the final date of trading

8 Date your books or accounts start – the beginning of your accounting period

9 Date your books or accounts are made up to or the end of your accounting period – read the notes if you have filled in box 6 or 7

10 If you used cash basis, money actually received and paid out, to calculate your income and expenses, put 'X' in the box

Other information

11 If your accounting date has changed permanently, put 'X' in the box

12 If your accounting date has changed more than once since 2013, put 'X' in the box

13 If special arrangements apply, put 'X' in the box

14 If you provided the information about your 2018-19 profit on last year's tax return, put 'X' in the box

Business income

15 Your turnover – the takings, fees, sales or money earned by your business

£ · 0 0

16 Any other business income not included in box 15

£ · 0 0

16.1 Trading income allowance – read the notes

£ · 0 0

10.14

Business expenses

Please read the 'Self-employment (full) notes' before filling in this section.

Total expenses

If your annual turnover was below £85,000, you may just put your total expenses in box 31

Disallowable expenses

Use this column if the figures in boxes 17 to 30 include disallowable amounts

17 **Cost of goods bought for resale or goods used**

£ · 0 0

32

£ · 0 0

18 **Construction industry – payments to subcontractors**

£ · 0 0

33

£ · 0 0

19 **Wages, salaries and other staff costs**

£ · 0 0

34

£ · 0 0

20 **Car, van and travel expenses**

£ · 0 0

35

£ · 0 0

21 **Rent, rates, power and insurance costs**

£ · 0 0

36

£ · 0 0

22 **Repairs and maintenance of property and equipment**

£ · 0 0

37

£ · 0 0

23 **Phone, fax, stationery and other office costs**

£ · 0 0

38

£ · 0 0

24 **Advertising and business entertainment costs**

£ · 0 0

39

£ · 0 0

25 **Interest on bank and other loans**

£ · 0 0

40

£ · 0 0

26 **Bank, credit card and other financial charges**

£ · 0 0

41

£ · 0 0

27 **Irrecoverable debts written off**

£ · 0 0

42

£ · 0 0

28 **Accountancy, legal and other professional fees**

£ · 0 0

43

£ · 0 0

29 **Depreciation and loss or profit on sale of assets**

£ · 0 0

44

£ · 0 0

30 **Other business expenses**

£ · 0 0

45

£ · 0 0

31 **Total expenses (total of boxes 17 to 30)**

£ · 0 0

46 **Total disallowable expenses (total of boxes 32 to 45)**

£ · 0 0

Net profit or loss

47 Net profit – if your business income is more than your expenses (if box 15 + box 16 minus box 31 is positive)

£ . 0 0

48 Or, net loss – if your expenses are more than your business income (if box 31 minus (box 15 + box 16) is positive)

£ . 0 0

Tax allowances for vehicles and equipment (capital allowances)

There are 'capital' tax allowances for vehicles, equipment and certain buildings used in your business (do not include the cost of these in your business expenses). Please read the 'Self-employment (full) notes' and use the examples to work out your capital allowances.

49 Annual Investment Allowance

£ . 0 0

50 Capital allowances at 18% on equipment, including cars with lower CO_2 emissions

£ . 0 0

51 Capital allowances at 8% on equipment, including cars with higher CO_2 emissions

£ . 0 0

52 Zero-emission goods vehicle allowance

£ . 0 0

Box 53 and 54 are not in use

55 100% and other enhanced capital allowances

£ . 0 0

56 Allowances on sale or cessation of business use (where you've disposed of assets for less than their tax value)

£ . 0 0

57 Total capital allowances (total of boxes (49 to 52) + 55 + 56)

£ . 0 0

Box 58 is not in use

59 Balancing charge on sales of assets or on the cessation of business use (including where Business Premises Renovation Allowance has been claimed) for example, where you've disposed of assets for more than their tax value

£ . 0 0

Calculating your taxable profit or loss

You may have to adjust your net profit or loss for disallowable expenses or capital allowances to arrive at your taxable profit or your loss for tax purposes. Please read the 'Self-employment (full) notes' and fill in the boxes below that apply.

60 Goods and services for your own use

£ . 0 0

61 Total additions to net profit or deductions from net loss (box 46 + box 59 + box 60)

£ . 0 0

62 Income, receipts and other profits included in business income or expenses but not taxable as business profits

£ . 0 0

63 Total deductions from net profit or additions to net loss (box 57 + box 62)

£ . 0 0

64 Net business profit for tax purposes (if box 47 + box 61 minus (box 48 + box 63) is positive)

£ . 0 0

65 Net business loss for tax purposes (if box 48 + box 63 minus (box 47 + box 61) is positive)

£ . 0 0

Calculating your taxable profit or loss (continued)

If you start or finish self-employment and your accounting period is not the same as your basis period (or there are overlaps or gaps in your basis periods) or in certain situations or trades or professions, you may need to make further tax adjustments - read the 'Self-employment (full) notes'. In all cases, please complete boxes 73 and 76, or box 77, as applicable.

If a disguised remuneration charge has arisen in this tax year, please complete box 75.1 - read the 'Self-employment (full) notes' for further details.

If your total profits from all Self-employments and Partnerships for 2018-19 are less than £6,205, you do not have to pay Class 2 National Insurance contributions, but you may want to pay voluntarily (box 100) to protect your rights to certain benefits. Read the notes.

66 Date your basis period began DD MM YYYY

67 Date your basis period ended

68 If your basis period is not the same as your accounting period, enter the adjustment needed to arrive at the profit or loss for the basis period - if the adjustment needs to be taken off the profit figure, put a minus sign (-) in the box

£ · 0 0

69 Overlap relief used this year

£ · 0 0

70 Overlap profit carried forward

£ · 0 0

71 Adjustment for change of accounting practice

£ · 0 0

72 Averaging adjustment (only for farmers, market gardeners and creators of literary or artistic works) - if the adjustment needs to be taken off the profit figure, put a minus sign (-) in the box

£ · 0 0

73 Adjusted profit for 2018-19 (see the working sheet in the notes) - if a loss, enter it in box 77

£ · 0 0

74 Loss brought forward from earlier years set off against this year's profits

£ · 0 0

75 Any other business income not included in boxes 15, 16 or 60 - for example, non arm's length reverse premiums

£ · 0 0

75.1 Disguised remuneration additions to profits - read the notes

£ · 0 0

76 Total taxable profits from this business (box 73 minus box 74 + box 75 + box 75.1) - or use the working sheet in the notes

£ · 0 0

Losses

If you have made a net loss for tax purposes (in box 65), or if you have losses from previous years, read the 'Self-employment (full) notes' and fill in boxes 77 to 80, as appropriate.

77 Adjusted loss for 2018-19 (see the working sheet in the notes)

£ · 0 0

78 Loss from this tax year set off against other income for 2018-19

£ · 0 0

79 Loss to be carried back to previous year(s) and set off against income (or capital gains)

£ · 0 0

80 Total loss to carry forward after all other set-offs - including unused losses brought forward

£ · 0 0

CIS deductions and tax taken off

81 Total Construction Industry Scheme (CIS) deductions taken from your payments by contractors - CIS subcontractors only

£ · 0 0

82 Other tax taken off trading income

£ · 0 0

Balance sheet

If your business accounts include a balance sheet showing the assets, liabilities and capital of the business, fill in the relevant boxes below. If you do not have a balance sheet, go to box 100. Read the 'Self-employment (full) notes' for more information.

Assets

83 Equipment, machinery and vehicles

£ [   ] · 0 0

84 Other fixed assets

£ [   ] · 0 0

85 Stock and work in progress

£ [   ] · 0 0

86 Trade debtors

£ [   ] · 0 0

87 Bank or building society balances

£ [   ] · 0 0

88 Cash in hand

£ [   ] · 0 0

89 Other current assets and prepayments

£ [   ] · 0 0

90 Total assets (total of boxes 83 to 89)

£ [   ] · 0 0

Liabilities

91 Trade creditors

£ [   ] · 0 0

92 Loans and overdrawn bank account balances

£ [   ] · 0 0

93 Other liabilities and accruals

£ [   ] · 0 0

Net business assets

94 Net business assets (box 90 minus (boxes 91 to 93))

£ [   ] · 0 0

Capital account

95 Balance at start of period

£ [   ] · 0 0

96 Net profit or loss (box 47 or box 48)

£ [   ] · 0 0

97 Capital introduced

£ [   ] · 0 0

98 Drawings

£ [   ] · 0 0

99 Balance at end of period

£ [   ] · 0 0

Class 2 and Class 4 National Insurance contributions (NICs)

100 If your total profits for 2018–19 are less than £6,205 and you choose to pay Class 2 NICs voluntarily, put 'X' in the box

[ ]

101 If you are exempt from paying Class 4 NICs, put 'X' in the box

[ ]

102 Adjustment to profits chargeable to Class 4 NICs

£ [   ] · 0 0

10.18

Any other information

103 **Please give any other information in this space**

HM Revenue & Customs

Partnership Tax Return 2019
for the year ended 5 April 2019 (2018-19)

Tax reference

Date

HM Revenue and Customs office address

Issue address

Telephone

For
Reference

This notice requires you by law to send us a tax return giving details of income and disposals of chargeable assets, and any documents we ask for, for the year 6 April 2018 to 5 April 2019. You can file the tax return using either:

- this form and any supplementary pages you need
- the internet (you'll need to buy commercial software). Most people file online. If you file online you'll receive an instant online acknowledgement telling you that we've received your tax return safely. To file online, go directly to our official website by typing www.gov.uk/file-your-self-assessment-tax-return into your internet browser address bar. Do not use a search website to find HMRC services online

Make sure that your tax return, and any documents asked for, reach us by:

- **31 October 2019** if you complete a paper tax return
- **31 January 2020** if you file online

Please see the Partnership Tax Return Guide for filing dates if this notice was given after 31 July 2019 or if the partnership includes a company as a partner.

Each partner who was a member of the partnership during the return period is liable to automatic penalties if the Partnership Tax Return does not reach us by the relevant filing date shown above. They'll have to pay interest and may have to pay a late payment penalty on any tax they pay late.

We check all tax returns and there are penalties for supplying false or incomplete information.

Who should send the Partnership Tax Return?
If this Partnership Tax Return has been issued in the name of the partnership, then the partner nominated by the other members of the partnership during the period covered by the tax return is required by law to complete it and send it back to us. If the partners are unable to nominate someone, they should ask us to nominate one of them.

If this Partnership Tax Return has been issued in the name of a particular partner, that partner is required by law to send it back to us.

The Partnership Tax Return – your responsibilities
We've sent you pages 1 to 8 of the tax return for the most common types of partnership income. You might need other supplementary pages, which we have not sent you, for other types of income and disposals.

You are responsible for making sure that you have the right pages. Answer the questions on page 2 of this form to find out if you have the right ones.

You should make sure that the information needed by individual partners to complete their personal tax returns is given to them as quickly as possible (some partners may want to send their own returns by 31 October 2019).

If you need help:

- refer to the Partnership Tax Return Guide, go to www.gov.uk/taxreturnforms
- phone the number above – we can answer most questions by phone
- when the office is closed, phone our helpline on 0300 200 3310 for general advice
- go to www.gov.uk/self-assessment-tax-returns

Partnership business and investment income for the year ended 5 April 2019

Answer Questions 1 to 6 on this page and Question 7 on page 8 to check that you have the pages you need to make a complete return of partnership income and related information for the year ended 5 April 2019. If you answer 'Yes', you must make sure that you have the right pages and then fill in the relevant boxes. If not, go to the next question.

To get the appropriate supplementary pages and notes that will help you fill in this form, go to www.gov.uk/taxreturnforms

Check to make sure that you have the right supplementary pages (including the Partnership Savings pages – see Question 7) and then tick the box below

Q1 Did the partnership receive any rent or other income from UK property (read the Partnership Tax Return Guide if you've furnished holiday lettings)?   YES ☐   UK PROPERTY ☐

Q2 Did the partnership have any foreign income?   YES ☐   FOREIGN ☐

Q3 Did the partnership business include a trade or profession at any time between 6 April 2018 and 5 April 2019?   YES ☐   **If yes**, complete boxes 3.1 to 3.117 on pages 2 to 5 as appropriate.

Q4 Did the partnership dispose of any chargeable assets?   YES ☐   CHARGEABLE ASSETS ☐

Q5 During the return period has the partnership included any member who is:

- a company   YES ☐
- not resident in the UK   YES ☐

If yes, read the Partnership Tax Return Guide about filling in the Partnership Statement, go to www.gov.uk/taxreturnforms

- a partner in a business controlled and managed abroad and who is not domiciled in the UK or is not ordinarily resident in the UK?   YES ☐

If yes, read the Partnership Tax Return Guide.

Q6 Are you completing this tax return on behalf of a European Economic Interest Grouping (EEIG)?   YES ☐

If yes, read the Partnership Tax Return Guide.

Trading and professional income for the year ended 5 April 2019

You have to fill in a set of boxes for each trade carried on by the partnership and you may have to fill in a separate set if partnership accounts were made up to more than one date in the year ended 5 April 2019. Check the rules in the **Partnership Tax Return Guide**.
Box numbers 3.3, 3.6, 3.18, 3.19, 3.74 to 3.81, 3.85 to 3.92, 3.95 and 3.96 are not used.

■ **Partnership details**

Name of business

3.1 ☐

Description of partnership trade or profession

3.2 ☐

Accounting period – read the Partnership Tax Return Guide, go to www.gov.uk/taxreturnforms

Start

3.4 / /

End

3.5 / /

- Date of commencement (if after 5 April 2018)   3.7 / /
- Date of cessation (if before 6 April 2019)   3.8 / /
- Tick box 3.9 if you used the 'cash basis', money actually received and paid out, to calculate your income and expenses – read the guide   3.9 ☐
- Tick box 3.10 if you do not need to complete boxes 3.14 to 3.93 and boxes 3.99 to 3.115   3.10 ☐

- Tick box 3.11 if the partnership's accounts do not cover the period from the last accounting date (explain why in the 'Additional information' box, box 3.116 on page 3)   3.11 ☐
- Tick box 3.12 if your accounting date has changed (only if this is a permanent change and you want it to count for tax)   3.12 ☐
- Tick box 3.13 if this is the second or further change (explain why you've not used the same date as last year in the 'Additional information' box, box 3.116 on page 3).   3.13 ☐

Trading and professional income for the year ended 5 April 2019 – continued

■ **Capital allowances – summary**

	Capital allowances	Balancing charges
● Annual Investment Allowance (include any balancing charges in box 3.17 below)	**3.13A** £	
● Zero-emission goods vehicle allowance	**3.14** £	**3.15** £
● Capital allowances at 18% on equipment, including cars with lower CO_2 emissions	**3.14A** £	**3.15A** £
● Capital allowances at 8% on equipment, including cars with higher CO_2 emissions	**3.16** £	**3.17** £

Boxes 3.18 and 3.19 are not used

	Capital allowances	Balancing charges
● 100% and other enhanced capital allowances claimed (you must make separate calculations).	**3.20** £	**3.21** £
Total capital allowances/balancing charges	total of column above **3.22** £	total of column above **3.23** £

■ **Income and expenses for this accounting period**

Read the **Partnership Tax Return Guide** before completing this section.

If your annual turnover was below £85,000 (or would have been if you had traded for the whole year) fill in boxes 3.24 to 3.26 instead of page 4.

If your annual turnover was between £85,000 and £15 million (or would have been if you had traded for a whole year) ignore boxes 3.24 to 3.26. Now fill in page 4.

If the combined annualised turnover from all of your activities was more than £15 million fill in boxes 3.24 to 3.26 and send in partnership accounts and computations as well.

In all cases, complete box 3.83 or box 3.84 on page 5, and the other boxes on page 5 if applicable.

● Turnover including other business receipts, and goods taken for personal use (and balancing charges from box 3.23)	**3.24** £
● Expenses allowable for tax (including capital allowances from box 3.22)	**3.25** £
Net profit for this accounting period (put figure in brackets if a loss)	box 3.24 minus box 3.25 **3.26** £

3.116 Additional information

Trading and professional income for the year ended 5 April 2019 – continued

■ **Income and expenses for this accounting period**

You must fill in this page if your annual turnover was between £85,000 and £15 million. If the combined annualised turnover from all your activities was more than £15 million, fill in boxes 3.24 to 3.26 on page 3 and send in the partnership accounts and computations as well. In all cases, complete box 3.83 or box 3.84 on page 5, and the other boxes on page 5 if applicable. Read the Partnership Tax Return Guide, go to **www.gov.uk/taxreturnforms**

If you were registered for VAT, do the figures in boxes 3.29 to 3.64 include VAT? **3.27** [ ] or exclude VAT? **3.28** [ ]

	Disallowable expenses included in boxes 3.46 to 3.63	Total expenses	Sales/business income (turnover)
			3.29 £
● Cost of sales	**3.30** £	**3.46** £	
● Construction industry subcontractor costs	**3.31** £	**3.47** £	
● Other direct costs	**3.32** £	**3.48** £	
Gross profit/(loss)			box 3.29 minus (boxes 3.46 + 3.47 + 3.48) **3.49** £
Other income/profits			**3.50** £
● Employee costs	**3.33** £	**3.51** £	
● Premises costs	**3.34** £	**3.52** £	
● Repairs	**3.35** £	**3.53** £	
● General administrative expenses	**3.36** £	**3.54** £	
● Motor expenses	**3.37** £	**3.55** £	
● Travel and subsistence	**3.38** £	**3.56** £	
● Advertising, promotion and entertainment	**3.39** £	**3.57** £	
● Legal and professional costs	**3.40** £	**3.58** £	
● Bad debts	**3.41** £	**3.59** £	
● Interest and alternative finance payments	**3.42** £	**3.60** £	
● Other finance charges	**3.43** £	**3.61** £	
● Depreciation and loss/(profit) on sale	**3.44** £	**3.62** £	
● Other expenses including partnership charges	**3.45** £	**3.63** £	
	Put the total of boxes 3.30 to 3.45 in box 3.66 below	Total expenses **3.64** £ boxes 3.51 to 3.63	
		Net profit/(loss) **3.65** £ boxes 3.49 + 3.50 minus 3.64	

■ **Tax adjustments to net profit or loss for this accounting period**

● Disallowable expenses	boxes 3.30 to 3.45 **3.66** £
● Goods taken for personal use and other adjustments (apart from disallowable expenses) that increase profits	**3.67** £
● Balancing charges (from box 3.23)	**3.68** £
Total additions to net profit (deduct from net loss)	boxes 3.66 + 3.67 + 3.68 **3.69** £
● Capital allowances (from box 3.22)	**3.70** £
● Deductions from net profit (add to net loss)	**3.71** £ — boxes 3.70 + 3.71 **3.72** £
Net business profit for tax purposes for this accounting period (put figure in brackets if a loss)	boxes 3.65 + 3.69 minus box 3.72 **3.73** £

Partnership business and investment income for the year ended 5 April 2019

■ **Taxable profit or loss for this accounting period**

- Adjustment on change of basis

3.82 £ _____
Copy this figure to box 11A in the **Partnership Statement**

Net profit for this accounting period (if loss, enter '0' here) from box 3.26 or box 3.73

3.83 £ _____
Copy this figure to box 11 in the Partnership Statement

Allowable loss for this accounting period (if profit, enter '0' here) from box 3.26 or box 3.73

3.84 £ _____
Copy this figure to box 12 in the Partnership Statement

Tick box 3.93 if the figure in box 3.83 or box 3.84 is provisional

3.93 ____

Tick box 3.94 if the figure in box 3.83 or box 3.84 includes any disguised remuneration income

3.94 ____
Copy to box 12A in the Partnership Statement

■ **Subcontractors in the construction industry**

- Deductions on payment and deduction statements from contractors – construction industry subcontractors only

3.97 £ _____
Copy this figure to box 24 in the Partnership Statement

■ **Tax taken off trading income**

- Tax taken off trading income (excluding deductions made by contractors on account of tax)

3.98 £ _____

Read the Partnership Tax Return Guide if you are a 'CT Partnership', go to www.gov.uk/taxreturnforms
Copy this figure to box 24A in the Partnership Statement

■ **Summary of balance sheet for this accounting period**

Leave these boxes blank if you do not have a balance sheet or your annual turnover was more than £15 million.

Assets
- Plant, machinery and motor vehicles — **3.99** £ _____
- Other fixed assets for example, premises or goodwill investments — **3.100** £ _____
- Stock and work in progress — **3.101** £ _____
- Debtors/prepayments/other current assets — **3.102** £ _____
- Bank/building society balances — **3.103** £ _____
- Cash in hand — **3.104** £ _____

boxes 3.99 to 3.104
3.105 £ _____

Liabilities
- Trade creditors/accruals — **3.106** £ _____
- Loans and overdrawn bank accounts — **3.107** £ _____
- Other liabilities — **3.108** £ _____

boxes 3.106 to 3.108
3.109 £ _____

box 3.105 minus box 3.109
3.110 £ _____

Net business assets (put the figure in brackets if you had net business liabilities)

Represented by partners' current and capital accounts

- Balance at start of period* — **3.111** £ _____
- Net profit/(loss)* — **3.112** £ _____
- Capital introduced — **3.113** £ _____
- Drawings — **3.114** £ _____

boxes 3.111 to 3.113 minus box 3.114
3.115 £ _____

- Balance at end of period*

* If the capital account is overdrawn, or the business made a net loss, show the figure in brackets.

Box 3.116 'Additional information' is on page 3.

■ **Partnership trade charges**

- Net partnership charges paid in the period 6 April 2018 to 5 April 2019 (**not** the accounting period)

3.117 £ _____

Partnership Statement (short) for the year ended 5 April 2019

Please read these instructions before completing the Statement

Use these pages to allocate partnership income if the only income for the relevant return period was trading and professional income or untaxed interest and alternative finance receipts from UK banks and building societies. Otherwise you must download the 'Partnership Statement (Full)' pages to record details of the allocation of all the partnership income. Go to www.gov.uk/taxreturnforms

Step 1   Fill in boxes 1 to 29 and boxes A and B as appropriate. Get the figures you need from the relevant boxes in the Partnership Tax Return. Complete a separate Statement for each accounting period covered by this Partnership Tax Return and for each trade or profession carried on by the partnership.

Step 2   Then allocate the amounts in boxes 11 to 29 attributable to each partner using the allocation columns on this page and page 7, read the Partnership Tax Return Guide, go to www.gov.uk/taxreturnforms
If the partnership has more than 3 partners, please photocopy page 7.

Step 3   Each partner will need a copy of their allocation of income to fill in their personal tax return.

PARTNERSHIP INFORMATION

If the partnership business includes a trade or profession, enter here the accounting period for which appropriate items in this statement are returned.

Start **1** / /

End **2** / /

Nature of trade **3**

MIXED PARTNERSHIPS

Tick here if this Statement is drawn up using Corporation Tax rules **4**

Tick here if this Statement is drawn up using tax rules for non-residents **5**

Individual partner details

6 Name of partner

Address

Postcode

Date appointed as a partner
(if during 2017–18 or 2018–19)

7 / /

Partner's Unique Taxpayer Reference (UTR)

8

Date ceased to be a partner
(if during 2017–18 or 2018–19)

9 / /

Partner's National Insurance number

10

Partnership's profits, losses, income and tax credits

Tick this box if the items entered in the box had foreign tax taken off ▼

- for an accounting period ended in 2018 to 2019

Partner's share of profits, losses, income and tax credits

Copy figures in boxes 11 to 29 to boxes in the individual's Partnership (short) pages as shown below

from box 3.83	Profit from a trade or profession	**A**	**11** £	Profit **11** £		Copy this figure to box 8
from box 3.82	Adjustment on change of basis		**11A** £	**11A** £		Copy this figure to box 10
from box 3.84	Loss from a trade or profession	**B**	**12** £	Loss **12** £		Copy this figure to box 8
from box 3.94	Disguised remuneration		**12A**	**12A**		Copy to box 15

- for the period 6 April 2018 to 5 April 2019*

from box 7.9A	Income from untaxed UK savings	**13** £	**13** £		Copy this figure to box 28
from box 3.97	CIS deductions made by contractors on account of tax	**24** £	**24** £		Copy this figure to box 30
from box 3.98	Other tax taken off trading income	**24A** £	**24A** £		Copy this figure to box 31
from box 3.117	Partnership charges	**29** £	**29** £		Copy this figure to box 4, 'Other tax reliefs' section on page Ai 2 in your personal tax return

* If you're a 'CT Partnership' see the Partnership Tax Return Guide

Partnership Statement (short) for the year ended 5 April 2019 – continued

Individual partner details

6 Name of partner

Address

Postcode

Date appointed as a partner
(if during 2017–18 or 2018–19)

7 / /

8 Partner's Unique Taxpayer Reference (UTR)

Date ceased to be a partner
(if during 2017–18 or 2018–19)

9 / /

10 Partner's National Insurance number

Partner's share of profits, losses, income and tax credits

Copy figures in boxes 11 to 29 to boxes in the individual's Partnership (short) pages as shown below

Profit **11** £ — Copy this figure to box 8

11A £ — Copy this figure to box 10

Loss **12** £ — Copy this figure to box 8

12A — Copy to box 15

13 £ — Copy this figure to box 28

24 £ — Copy this figure to box 30

24A £ — Copy this figure to box 31

29 £ — Copy this figure to box 4, 'Other tax reliefs' section on page Ai 2 in your personal tax return

---

Individual partner details

6 Name of partner

Address

Postcode

Date appointed as a partner
(if during 2017–18 or 2018–19)

7 / /

8 Partner's Unique Taxpayer Reference (UTR)

Date ceased to be a partner
(if during 2017–18 or 2018–19)

9 / /

10 Partner's National Insurance number

Partner's share of profits, losses, income and tax credits

Copy figures in boxes 11 to 29 to boxes in the individual's Partnership (short) pages as shown below

Profit **11** £ — Copy this figure to box 8

11A £ — Copy this figure to box 10

Loss **12** £ — Copy this figure to box 8

12A — Copy to box 15

13 £ — Copy this figure to box 28

24 £ — Copy this figure to box 30

24A £ — Copy this figure to box 31

29 £ — Copy this figure to box 4, 'Other tax reliefs' section on page Ai 2 in your personal tax return

Other information for the year ended 5 April 2019

Q7 **Did the partnership receive any other income which you've not already included elsewhere in the Partnership Tax Return?**
Make sure that you fill in the pages for Questions 1 to 4 before answering Question 7

YES ☐   If Yes, read the guidance below

If you ticked the 'Yes' box and the only income was untaxed interest, or alternative finance receipts, from UK banks and building societies, fill in box 7.9A below. Otherwise download the Partnership Savings pages, go to www.gov.uk/taxreturnforms and leave box 7.9A blank. If you have more than one account, enter totals in the box.

Untaxed interest and alternative finance receipts from UK banks and building societies

Taxable amount

7.9A £ ☐

Copy this figure to box 13 in the Partnership Statement (short)

Q8 **Are the details on the front of the Partnership Tax Return wrong?**

YES ☐   If yes, make any corrections on the front of the form

---

Q9 **Please give a daytime phone number (including the area code) in boxes 9.1 and 9.2**
It's often simpler to phone if we need to ask you about your tax return.

Your phone number

9.1 ☐

or, if you prefer, your adviser's phone number

9.2 ☐

Your adviser's name and address

9.3 ☐

Postcode

Q10 **Other information**

Please tick box 10.1 if this Partnership Tax Return contains figures that are provisional because you do not yet have final figures. The Partnership Tax Return Guide explains the circumstances in which provisional figures may be used and asks you to provide some additional information in box 3.116 on page 3.

10.1 ☐

Disclosure of tax avoidance schemes – read the notes about boxes 10.2 and 10.3 in the Partnership Tax Return Guide.

Scheme reference number or promoter reference number

10.2 ☐

Tax year in which the expected advantage to the partners arises – year ended 5 April

10.3 ☐

Q11 **Declaration** – I have filled in and am sending back to you the following:

1 TO 5 OF THIS FORM ☐	PARTNERSHIP FOREIGN ☐
6 AND 7 PARTNERSHIP STATEMENT (SHORT) ☐	PARTNERSHIP TRADING ☐
6 AND 7 PARTNERSHIP STATEMENT (FULL) ☐	PARTNERSHIP DISPOSAL OF CHARGEABLE ASSETS ☐
PARTNERSHIP UK PROPERTY ☐	PARTNERSHIP SAVINGS ☐

I attach **11.1** ☐ additional copies of page 7. There were **11.2** ☐ partners in this partnership for that period.

Before you send the completed tax return back to your current HM Revenue and Customs office, you must sign the statement below. If you give false information or conceal any part of the partnership's income or details of the disposal of chargeable assets, you may be liable to financial penalties and/or we may prosecute you.

11.3 **I the nominated partner,** declare that the information I have given on this Partnership Tax Return is correct and complete to the best of my knowledge and belief.

Nominated Partner Signature   Date

Print name in full here

If you have signed for someone else, please also:
- state the capacity in which you are signing (for example, as executor or receiver)
- give the name of the person you are signing for and **your** name and address in the 'Additional information' box, box 3.116, on page 3.

11.4 ☐

Reference Material

for AAT Assessment of Business Tax

Finance Act 2019

For assessments from 1 January – 31 December 2020

Note: this reference material is accessible by candidates during their live computer based assessment for Business Tax.

This material was current at the time this book was published, but may be subject to change. Readers are advised to check the AAT website or Osborne Books website for any updates.

Reference material for AAT assessment of Business Tax

Introduction

This document comprises data that you may need to consult during your Business Tax computer-based assessment. The material can be consulted during the practice and live assessments through pop-up windows. It is made available here, so you can familiarise yourself with the content before the test.

Do not take a print of this document into the exam room with you. Unless you need a printed version as part of reasonable adjustments for particular needs, in which case you must discuss this with your tutor at least six weeks before the assessment date.

This document may be changed to reflect periodical updates in the computer-based assessment, so please check you have the most recent version while studying. This version is based on Finance Act 2019 and is for use in AAT assessments from January 2020.

Note: Page numbers are those of the original AAT Reference Document

Contents

1.   Taxation tables for business tax – 2019/20

1.1.   Capital allowances

Annual investment allowance
  Prior to 1 January 2019   £200,000
  From 1 January 2019   £1,000,000

Plant and machinery writing down allowance
  Long life assets and integral features
    Prior to 1 April 2019 (Companies)/6 April 2019 (Individuals)   8%
    From 1 April 2019 (Companies)/6 April 2019 (Individuals)   6%
  Other assets   18%

Motor cars
  CO_2 emissions up to 50 g/km   100%
  CO_2 emissions between 51 and 110 g/km   18%
  CO_2 emissions over 110 g/km -Prior to 1 April 2019/6 April 2019   8%
  CO_2 emissions over 110 g/km -From 1 April 2019/6 April 2019   6%

Energy efficient and water saving plant
  First year allowance   100%

1.2.   Capital gains

Annual exempt amount   £12,000

Standard rate   10%
Higher rate   20%
Entrepreneurs' relief rate   10%
Investors' relief rate   10%

Entrepreneurs' relief limit   £10,000,000
Investors' relief limit   £10,000,000

1.3.   National Insurance rates

Class 2 contributions: £3.00 per week
Small profits threshold   £6,365p.a.

Class 4 contributions:
Main rate   9%
Additional rate   2%
Lower earnings limit   £8,632
Upper earnings limit   £50,000

1.4.   Trading allowance

This allowance is available to individuals only.   £1,000

1.5. Corporation tax

Financial year	**2019**	**2018**
All profits and gains	19%	19%

2. Introduction to business tax

2.1. Administration

- Taxation administered by HM Revenue & Customs (HMRC).
- Rules covering tax are contained in statute (law) which is passed every year (Finance Act).
- Decisions reached by the courts interpreting the law are known as case law.
- HMRC also issue guidance – Extra Statutory Concessions and Statements of Practice.

2.2. Taxes

- Corporation Tax – paid by companies on both income and chargeable gains.
- Income Tax – paid by individuals on their income.
- Capital Gains Tax – paid by individuals on their capital gains.

2.3. Tax avoidance and tax evasion

- Tax evasion: any action taken to evade tax by illegal means; this carries a risk of criminal prosecution. Examples of tax evasion include failing to declare income and claiming false expenses.
- Tax avoidance: use of legitimate means to minimise taxpayer's tax liability, for example by investing in a tax-free ISA (Individual Savings Account).

3. Adjustment of profits – sole traders, partnerships and companies

3.1. Pro forma for adjustment of profits

	£	£
Net profit as per accounts		X
Add: Expenses charged in the accounts that are not allowable as trading expenses	X	
		X
		X
Less: Income included in the accounts which is not assessable as trading income	X	
		(X)
Adjusted profit/(loss)		X

3.2. Disallowed expenses

- Expenses that fail the remoteness test so not "wholly and exclusively" for trading purposes.
- Fines on the business or fraud by directors/owners.
- Donations to charity are generally disallowed in calculating trading profits (however qualifying charitable donations are deductible in the corporation tax computation).
- Political donations are never allowable.
- Capital expenditure e.g. purchase of equipment included in profit and loss account.
- Depreciation. Capital allowances granted instead.
- Costs of bringing newly acquired second-hand assets to useable condition.
- Legal and professional expenses relating to capital items or breaking the law.
- Customer entertaining. Staff entertaining can be allowable.
- Customer gifts, unless gift incorporates business advertising, cost is less than £50 per annum per customer, and gift is not food, drink, tobacco or cash vouchers.

3.3. Non-assessable income

- Income taxed in any other way, e.g. interest or property income for individuals.
- Profits on sale of fixed assets.

4. Unincorporated businesses – trading income

4.1. Trading income calculated for each period of account:

	£
Adjusted accounting profit	X
Less: Capital allowances:	(X)
Less: Balancing allowances	(X)
Plus: Balancing charges	X
Trading income for the period of account	X

4.2. Expenses charged in the accounts which are not allowable as trading expenses

- See adjustment of profits – sole traders, partnerships and companies.
- Transactions with the owner of the business. For example:
  - Add back salary paid to owner. Salaries paid to family members do not need to be added back.
  - Private expenditure included in accounts.
  - Class 2 and Class 4 National Insurance contributions.
  - Goods taken for own use.

5. Sole traders – basis periods

Tax year – 2019/20 tax year runs from 6 April 2019 to 5 April 2020

5.1. Basis period rules

- First year – runs from start date of trading to the next 5 April.
- Second year and third year:

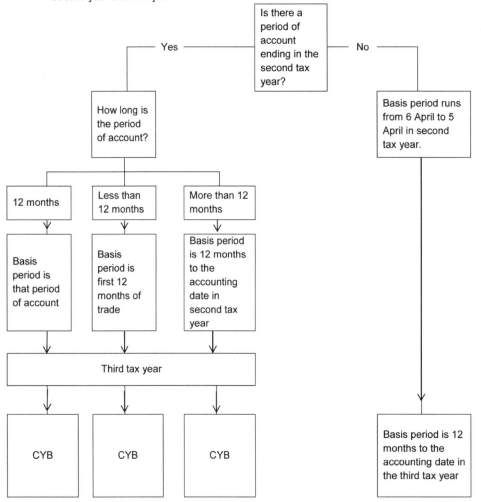

Later years – basis period is the period of account ending in the tax year = Current Year basis (CYB).

Final year – basis period is the period from the end of the basis period for the previous tax year to cessation date.

Overlap profits - opening year rules may lead to profits being taxed twice. Relief is given on cessation of the business.

6.   Sole traders – change of accounting date

For an accounting date change to be recognised for tax purposes the following conditions must be satisfied:

- The first accounts ending on the new date must not exceed 18 months in length.
- The sole trader or partnership must give notice of the change in the tax return by the filing date of the tax return.
- The change will not be permitted if there has been a change of accounting date in the previous 5 years unless there are genuine commercial reasons for the change.

Steps:

Step 1: Identify the year of change. This is the first year when current year basis is not possible.

Step 2: For all years before the year of change, the basis period is the 12 months to the old year end date.

Step 3: For all years after the year of change, the basis period is the 12 months to the new year end date.

Step 4: In the year of change, identify the 'relevant period'. The relevant period is the time to the new accounting date from the end of the previous basis period (example: all profits which have not been assessed as a result of steps 2 and 3)

- If the relevant period > 12 months, tax the profits of the relevant period but deduct overlap profits from commencement such that 12 months in total are taxed. The basis period is the same as the relevant period.
- If the relevant period is < 12 months, tax the 12 month period to the end of the relevant period (this will mean taxing some profits from the previous period twice, creating additional overlap profits). The basis period is the 12 months to the end of the relevant period.

6.1.   Example 1 – relevant period is less than 12 months

Jasmin changes her accounting date as follows:

Accounts	Year	Period
Year to 31 December 2018	2018/19	1/1/18 to 31/12/18
9 months to 30 September 2019	2019/20	1/10/18 to 30/9/19
Year to 30 September 2020	2020/21	1/10/19 to 30/9/20

Year of change – 2019/20
Relevant period – 9 months to 30 September 2019
Basis period for 19/20 – 12 months to 30 September 2019

6.2. Example 2 – relevant period is greater than 12 months

Vaughan changes his accounting date as follows:

Accounts	Year	Period
Year to 31 December 2018	2018/19	1/1/18 to 31/12/18
15 months to 31 March 2020	2019/20	1/1/19 to 31/3/20
Year to 31 March 2021	2020/21	1/4/20 to 31/3/21

Year of change – 2019/20
Relevant period – 15 months to 31 March 2020
Basis period for 19/20 – 15 months to 31 March 2020

7. Capital allowances on plant and machinery

7.1. Layout of capital allowances on plant and machinery computation

(see taxation tables for rates)

	First Year Allowance (FYA)	Annual Investment Allowance (AIA)	General pool	Special rate pool	Short Life Asset	Total allowances
	£	£	£	£	£	£
WDV b/f			X	X	X	
Additions	X	X	X			
Disposals			(X)		(X)	
	X	X	X	X	X	
Balancing allowance/balancing charge (BA/BC)					X/(X)	X/(X)
					Nil	
AIA/FYA	(X)	(X)				X
Writing down allowance@ 18% pa			(X)			X
Writing down allowance@ X% pa				(X)		X
WDV c/f	Nil ===	Nil ===	X ===	X ===		
Total allowances						X ===

- Plant – defined by 'function/setting' distinction and case law.
- AIA – 100% allowance for expenditure (other than cars) in 12 month period (pro rata). Expenditure in excess of AIA qualifies for writing down allowance (WDA). If the accounting period straddles 1 January 2019, the AIA must be pro-rated but the maximum allowance in the part of the period prior to 31 December 2018 cannot exceed £200,000.

- Full WDA for the period is given regardless of date of purchase of item. WDA is scaled for periods other than 12 months.
- The WDA % on the special rate pool is calculated as: ((8 x number of months before 1 April) + (6 x number of months after 1 April))/number of months in the chargeable period. This % should be rounded to 2 decimal places.
- FYA – 100% allowance given on purchase of environmentally friendly cars and certain energy and water saving equipment. FYA is not scaled for short accounting periods.
- If the written down value (WDV) on the general pool (= WDV b/f + additions-disposals) is £1,000 or less then an election can be made to write off the pool balance, known as a 'small pools allowance'.
- Short life assets (SLA) – de-pool asset if life expected to be less than 8 years. Not available for cars.

7.2. Unincorporated Businesses - Private use assets

- Private use assets have separate column in Capital Allowance computation.
- Disallow private use % of WDA/AIA/FYA.

7.3. Capital allowances – business cessation

- In the cessation period of account, no WDA/AIA/FYA.
- Include additions and disposals as normal. Any asset taken over by owner, treat as a disposal at market value. Balancing adjustment made (balancing charge or balancing allowance).

8. Partnerships

- Each partner is taxed like a sole trader on their share of the partnership profits

- First step is to share accounting profits between partners:
  - Allocate the correct salaries and interest on capital for the period to each partner.
  - Divide the remaining profit for each set of accounts between the partners based upon the profit sharing arrangement.
  - You may need to split the period if there is a change such as a partner joining or leaving.

- Opening year and cessation rules apply to partners individually when they join or leave the partnership.

- Allocate the profit for each partner to the correct tax year using usual basis period rules.

- Basis periods for continuing partners are unaffected by joiners or leavers.

- Each partner enters their share of profits for a tax year in the partnership pages of their own tax return.

9. Trading losses for sole traders and partners

9.1. Trading losses for sole traders and partners

- A loss is computed in the same way as a profit, making the same adjustments to the net profit as per the accounts and deducting capital allowances.

9.2. Set off of trading loss against total income

- Set off loss against total income of the preceding tax year and/or the tax year of loss, e.g. loss in 2019/20 set off against total income in 2018/19 and/or 2019/20.
- Cannot restrict loss to preserve use of personal allowance so personal allowance may be wasted.
- For 2019/20 loss claim needed by 31 January 2022.

9.3. Carry forward of trading losses

- If any loss remains unrelieved after current year and carry back claim has been made, or no such claims are made, then carry forward the loss against first available profits of the same trade.

9.4. Choice of loss relief – consider the following:

- Utilise loss in the tax year in which income is taxed at a higher rate.
- Possible wastage of personal allowance.
- Review the projected future profits to ensure the loss can be utilised.
- If cash flow is important, a loss carry back claim may result in a tax refund being paid to the business.

10. Payment and administration – sole traders and partners

10.1. The return must be filed by:

- 31 October following the end of the tax year if filing a paper return.

- 31 January following the end of the tax year if filing online.

10.2. Penalties for late filing and payment

Late filing	Late payment	Penalty
Miss filing deadline		£100
	30 days late	5% of tax outstanding at that date
3 months late		Daily penalty £10 per day for up to 90 days (max £900)
6 months late		5% of tax due or £300, if greater
	6 months late	5% of tax outstanding at that date
12 months late		5% of tax due or £300, if greater
	12 months late	5% of tax outstanding at that date
12 months and information deliberately withheld		Based on behaviour: • deliberate and concealed withholding 100% of tax due, or £300 if greater. • deliberate but not concealed 70% of tax due, or £300 if greater. Reductions apply for prompted and unprompted disclosures and for cooperation with investigation.

10.3. Disclosure and errors

- Taxpayer must notify HMRC by 5 October following end of the tax year if a tax return is needed.
- Taxpayer can amend a tax return within 12 months of filing date or make a claim for overpayment relief within 4 years of the end of the tax year.

10.4. Payments on account (POA)

- Due 31 January (in tax year) and 31 July (after tax year end). Each instalment is 50% of the previous year's tax and Class 4 National Insurance contribution (NIC) liability after taking into account any tax deducted at source.
- Balancing payment made 31 January after tax year end.
- No POA due if:
    - last year's tax and Class 4 NIC liability is less than £1,000 or
    - if greater than 80% of last year's liability was deducted at source.
- Can reduce this year's POA if this year's liability expected to be less than last year's. Penalties and interest will be charged if a deliberate incorrect claim is made.
- Capital gains tax (CGT) liability and Class 2 National Insurance is paid 31 January following the tax year end. No POA needed for CGT and Class 2 National Insurance.

10.5. Interest on tax paid late/overpaid tax

- Interest charged daily on late payment.

11. Enquiries and other penalties

- HMRC must notify individual of enquiry within 12 months of submission of return.
- Basis of enquiry – random or HMRC believe income/expenses misstated.
- Penalty for failure to produce enquiry documents = £300 + £60 per day.
- Penalty for failure to keep proper records is up to £3,000. Records must be kept for 5 years after the filing date for the relevant tax year.
- Penalties for incorrect returns are detailed in the table below:

Type of behaviour	Maximum	Unprompted (minimum)	Prompted (minimum)
Genuine mistake: despite taking reasonable care	0%	0%	0%
Careless error and inaccuracy are due to failure to take reasonable care	30%	0%	15%
Deliberate error but not concealed	70%	20%	35%
Deliberate error and concealed	100%	30%	50%

12. National Insurance contributions

- Self-employed individuals pay Class 2 and Class 4 contributions.
- Class 4 contributions are at 9% on profits between the lower and upper limits, then 2% on profits above the upper limit.
- Percentages and limits are provided in the Taxation Tables.

13. An outline of corporation tax

- Companies pay corporation tax on their profits for each accounting period.
- There is one rate of corporation tax set each financial year.
- Profits = Income + Gains – Qualifying charitable donations
- Accounting periods are usually 12 months long but can be shorter.
- If a company's accounts are longer than 12 months, the first 12 months will be one accounting period and the remainder a second accounting period.
- All UK property income is pooled as a single source of income and taxed on an accruals basis.
- Borrowing or lending money by a company is a loan relationship.
- Trading loan relationships are part of trading income.
- Non-trading loan relationships (NTL-R) are pooled to give NTL-R credits or deficits.
- Donations to national charities are qualifying charitable donations.
- Company A is a related 51% group company of company B if:
  - A is a 51% subsidiary of B, or
  - B is a 51% subsidiary of A, or
  - A and B are both 51% subsidiaries of the same company.

'A' is a 51% subsidiary of 'B' if more than 50% of its ordinary share capital is beneficially owned (directly or indirectly) by 'B'.

14. The calculation of total profits and corporation tax payable

ABC Ltd

Corporation tax computation for the year/period ended DD/MM/20XX

	£
Trading income – accruals basis	X
Interest income (NTL-R) – accrual basis	X
Property income – accruals basis	X
Chargeable gains	X
	X
Less Qualifying charitable donations	(X)
Total taxable profits	X
Corporation tax payable – Total taxable profits × Corporation tax rate	X

14.1. Key points

- Trading income is adjusted from net profit per company accounts less capital allowances.
- Companies receive interest gross.
- Virtually all interest receivable is taxed as interest income (NTL-R).
- Dividends payable by a company are not an allowable expense.
- UK dividends receivable by a company are not taxable.
- Net-off current year capital losses against current year capital gains. If there is a net capital loss carry it forward.
- See taxation tables for corporation tax rates.

14.2. Long periods of account

- Will consist of two accounting periods = first 12 months and remainder of period.
- Split profits as follows:
    - Adjusted trading profit and property income – time apportion.
    - Capital allowances – separate computations for each accounting period.
    - Interest income (NTL-R) – accruals basis.
    - Chargeable gains – according to date of disposal.
    - Qualifying charitable donations– according to date paid.

15. Corporation tax – trade losses

- Can elect to set trading losses against current accounting period 'total profits'. Qualifying charitable donations will remain unrelieved.

- If the above election is made, can also carry back trading loss to set against 'total profits' within the previous 12 months.

- Trading losses incurred before 1 April 2017 are carried forward to set against profits of the 'same trade' if not utilised by the above two claims

- Trading losses incurred from 1 April 2017 are more flexible. These are automatically carried forward and can be set against total profits.

- If there is a choice of loss relief, firstly consider when the loss was incurred, the rate of loss relief and then the timing of relief.

- Set out the use of the losses in a loss memorandum.

16. Corporation tax – payment and administration

16.1. Payment dates

- Small companies (annual profits less than £1.5 million): 9 months + 1 day after end of the accounting period (AP).
- Large companies (annual profits greater than £1.5 million) must estimate year's tax liability and pay 25% of the year's liability:
    - 6 months and 14 days after start of AP
    - 9 months and 14 days after start of AP
    - 14 days after end of AP
    - 3 months and 14 days after end of AP
- Estimate must be revised for each quarter. Penalties may be charged if company deliberately fails to pay sufficient instalments.
- No instalments due for first year company is large unless profits are greater than £10 million.
- 51% group companies share the annual profit limit of £1.5 million equally.

16.2. Interest on late payments

- Interest charged daily on late payment. Overpayment of tax receives interest from HMRC. Interest is taxable/tax allowable as interest income.

16.3. Filing the return

- Filed on the later of 12 months after end of AP or 3 months after the notice to deliver a tax return has been issued.
- Late filing penalties are: less than 3 months late: £100; greater than 3 months late: £200; greater than 6 months late: 10% of tax due per return; greater than 12 months late: 20% of tax due per return.
- Company must notify HMRC it is within scope of corporation tax within 3 months of starting to trade.
- Company can amend return within 12 months of the filing date.

16.4. Enquiries and other penalties

- HMRC must notify company of enquiry within 12 months of submission of return.
- Basis of enquiry – random or HMRC believe income/expenses misstated.
- Penalty for failure to produce enquiry documents: £300 + £60 per day.
- Penalty for failure to keep proper records is up to £3,000. Records must be retained for six years after the end of the relevant accounting period.
- Penalties for incorrect returns are the same as for sole traders and partners – see sole traders and partners link.

17. Current tax reliefs and other tax issues

17.1. Research and Development (R&D) Tax Credits for Small and Medium Sized Companies

A small or medium sized enterprise (SME) is a company with less than 500 employees with either:
- an annual turnover under €100 million, or
- a balance sheet under €86 million.

17.2. The SME tax relief scheme

From 1 April 2015, the tax relief on allowable R&D costs is 230%.

17.3. R&D tax credits

If a company makes a loss, it can choose to receive R&D tax credits instead of carrying forward a loss.

17.4. Costs that qualify for R&D tax relief

To qualify as R&D, any activity must contribute directly to seeking an advance in science or technology or must be a qualifying indirect activity. The costs must relate to the company's trade - either an existing one, or one that they intend to start up based on the results of the R&D.

17.5. Intermediaries (IR35) legislation

IR35 legislation prevents personal service companies ("PSC") being used to disguise permanent employment.

The rules apply where the relationship between the worker and the client, would be considered to be an employment relationship if the existence of the PSC was ignored.

If the rules apply, a **deemed employment income tax charge** is charged on the PSC.

The **deemed employment income tax charge** is calculated based upon the actual payments made to the PSC by the client.

18. Introduction to capital / chargeable gains

- Individual pays Capital Gains Tax (CGT) on net chargeable gains in a tax year.
- For companies, chargeable gains are included as income in calculating total profits.
- Individuals receive an annual exempt amount from CGT – for 2019/20 this is £12,000.
- Gains/losses arise when a chargeable person makes a chargeable disposal of a chargeable asset.
- Chargeable person – individual or company.
- Chargeable disposal – sale, gift or loss/destruction of the whole or part of an asset.
  Exempt disposals – on death and gifts to approved charities.
- Chargeable asset – all assets unless exempt. Exempt assets are motor cars and some chattels.

18.1. Calculation of capital gains tax

Net chargeable gains – total gains in the tax year after netting off any current year or brought forward losses and the annual exempt amount.

18.2. Annual exempt amount (AE)

- For individuals only.
- AE cannot be carried forward or carried back.
- Current year losses must be netted off against current year gains before AE. This means AE can be wasted.
- Brought forward capital losses are set off against current year gains after AE so AE is not wasted.

19. Calculation of gains and losses for individuals

19.1. Pro forma computation

	£	£
Consideration received		X
Less Incidental costs of sale		(X)
Net sale proceeds		NSP
Less Allowable expenditure		
- Acquisition cost	X	
- Incidental costs of acquisition	X	
- Enhancement expenditure	X	
		(Cost)
Gain/(Loss)		X/(X)

- Consideration received is usually sales proceeds, but market value will be used instead of actual consideration where the transaction is a gift or between connected persons.
- An individual is connected with their spouse, relatives (and their spouses) and spouse's relatives (and their spouses). Relative means brother, sister, lineal ancestor or lineal descendent.
- Husband and wife/civil partner transfers – nil gain nil loss.

Part disposals – the cost allocated to the disposal = Cost × (A/(A+B))

A = consideration received on part disposal   B = market value of the remainder of the asset

Chattels - tangible moveable object. Two types:

- Wasting – expected life of 50 years or less (e.g. racehorse or boat). CGT exempt.
  Non-wasting – expected life greater than 50 years (e.g. antiques or jewellery).

19.2. CGT, £6,000 rule

Buy Sell	£6,000 or less	More than £6,000
Less than £6,000	Exempt	Allowable loss but proceeds are deemed = £6,000
More than £6,000	Normal calculation of the gain, then compare with 5/3(gross proceeds - £6,000) - Take the lower gain	Chargeable in full

20. Shares and securities – disposals by individuals

20.1. CGT on shares and securities

Disposal of shares and securities are subject to CGT except for listed government securities (gilt-edged securities or 'gilts'), qualifying corporate bonds (e.g. company loan notes/debentures) and shares held in an Individual Savings Account (ISA).

20.2. The identification rules

Used to determine which shares have been sold and so what acquisition cost can be deducted from the sale proceeds (e.g. match the disposal and acquisition).

Disposals are matched:

- Firstly, with acquisitions on the same day as the day of disposal.
- Secondly, with acquisitions made in the 30 days following the date of disposal (FIFO basis).
- Thirdly, with shares from the share pool.

20.3. The Share Pool

- The share pool contains all shares acquired prior to the disposal date.
- Each acquisition is not kept separately, but is 'pooled' together with other acquisitions and a running total kept of the number of shares and the cost of those shares.
- When a disposal from the pool is made, the appropriate number of shares are taken from the pool along with the average cost of those shares.
- The gain on disposal is then calculated.

20.4. Bonus issues and rights issues

- Bonus issue – no adjustment to cost needed.
- Rights issue – adjustment to cost needed.

21. Chargeable gains – reliefs available to individuals

Replacement of business assets (Rollover) relief – when a qualifying business asset is sold at a gain, taxpayer can defer gain by reinvesting proceeds in a qualifying replacement asset.

- Deferred gain is deducted from the cost of the replacement asset so gain crystallises when the replacement asset is sold.
- Qualifying assets (original and replacement) – must be used in a trade by the vendor and be land and buildings, fixed plant and machinery or goodwill.
- Qualifying time period – replacement asset must be purchased between 1 year before and 3 years after the sale of the original asset.
- Partial reinvestment – only some of the sales proceeds reinvested then the gain taxable is the lower of the full gain and the proceeds not reinvested.

Gift relief (holdover relief) – donee takes over asset at donor's base cost i.e. the gain is given away along with the asset.
- Qualifying assets – trade assets of donor or shares in any unquoted trading company or personal trading company (donor owns at least 5% of company).

Entrepreneurs' relief – gain taxable at 10% capital gains tax rate.

- The £10 million limit is a lifetime limit which is reduced each time a claim for the relief is made.
- For 2019/20 a claim must be made by 31 January 2022.
- Qualifying business disposals (assets must be owned for at least 24 months prior to sale)

    - The whole or part of a business carried on by the individual (alone or in partnership).
    - Assets of the individual's or partnership's trading business that has now ceased.
    - Shares in the individual's 'personal trading company' where they have at least 5% of shares, voting rights, entitlement to distributable profits and entitlement to net assets. Individual must have owned the shares and been an employee of the company for 24 months prior to sale.

Investors relief – gain taxable at 10% capital gains tax rate

- The £10 million limit is a lifetime limit which is reduced each time a claim for the relief is made.
- For 19/20 a claim must be made by 31 January 2022
- the individual subscribes for shares which are issued on or after 17 March 2016;
- the shares are ordinary shares;
- the issuing company is a trading company or holding company of a trading group;
- the shares are not listed on a recognised stock exchange;
- the individual has not been an officer or employee of the issuing company at any point during the ownership period; and
- the shares are held continuously for three years from the date of issue or from 6 April 2016 where the shares are issued between 17 March and 5 April 2016.

22. Calculation of gains and losses for companies

22.1. Pro forma computation

	£	£
Consideration received		X
Less Incidental costs of sale		(X)
Net sale proceeds		NSP
Less Allowable expenditure		
Acquisition cost + incidental costs of acquisition	X	
Indexation allowance [indexation factor × expenditure]	X	
Enhancement expenditure	X	
Indexation allowance	X	
		(Cost)
Chargeable gain		Gain

- Companies are entitled to an indexation allowance, based on the changes in the retail price index (RPI) from the date when expenditure was incurred to the date of disposal (or deemed disposal).
- Indexation allowance is frozen at 1 January 2018.
- Disposals taking place from 1 January 2018 will use the RPI at 31 December 2017 for indexation allowance purposes.
- Indexation allowance is not available where there is an unindexed loss; nor can it turn an unindexed gain into an indexed loss.
- Note that companies do not get an annual exempt amount.
- Losses relieved in order – current year first followed by losses brought forward.

22.2. Only relief available to companies is rollover relief:

- Rollover relief is a deferral relief – see Chargeable gains – reliefs available to individuals for main rollover relief rules.
- Key differences applying for companies:
    - Indexation is given on disposal of the original asset.
    - Goodwill is not a qualifying asset for companies.
    - Gain deferred is the indexed gain.
    - On disposal of the replacement asset, indexation is calculated on the 'base cost' not actual cost.

23. Shares and securities – disposals by companies

The identification rules - a disposal of shares is matched:

- firstly, with same-day transactions
- secondly, with transactions in the previous 9 days (FIFO). No indexation allowance is available.
- thirdly, with shares from the 1985 pool (shares bought from 1 April 1982 onwards).

1985 pool – pro forma working	No.	Cost £	Indexed cost £
Purchase	X	X	X
Index to next operative event			X
			___
			X
Operative event (purchase)	X	X	X
	___	___	___
	X	X	X
Index to next operative event			X
			___
			X
Operative event (sale)	(X)	(X)	(X)A
Pool carried forward	X	X	X
	===	===	===

Operative event = purchase, sale, rights issue. Bonus issue is not an operative event.

Computation

	£
Proceeds	X
Less indexed cost (A from pool)	(X)
Indexed gain	X

24. The badges of trade

24.1. 6 Badges of Trade

- Subject matter
- Ownership
- Frequency of transactions
- Improvement expenditure
- Reason for sale
- Motive for profit

25. Duties and responsibilities of a tax advisor

- Maintain client confidentiality at all times.
- AAT members must adopt an ethical approach and maintain an objective outlook.
- Give timely and constructive advice to clients.
- Honest and professional conduct with HMRC.
- A tax advisor is liable to a penalty if they assist in making an incorrect return.

Index

for your notes

for your notes

for your notes

for your notes

for your notes

for your notes

for your notes